Hard As
the Rock
Itself

SERIES EDITORS

Duane A. Smith
Robert A. Trennert
Liping Zhu

HARD AS THE ROCK ITSELF

PLACE AND IDENTITY IN
THE AMERICAN MINING TOWN

David Robertson

UNIVERSITY PRESS OF COLORADO

Published by the University Press of Colorado
5589 Arapahoe Avenue, Suite 206C
Boulder, Colorado 80303

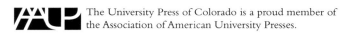 The University Press of Colorado is a proud member of
the Association of American University Presses.

The University Press of Colorado is a cooperative publishing enterprise supported, in part, by Adams
State College, Colorado State University, Fort Lewis College, Mesa State College, Metropolitan State
College of Denver, University of Colorado, University of Northern Colorado, and Western State
College of Colorado.

∞ The paper used in this publication meets the minimum requirements of the American National Standard for Information Sciences—Permanence of Paper for Printed Library Materials. ANSI
Z39.48-1992

Library of Congress Cataloging-in-Publication Data

Robertson, David, 1966–
    Hard as the rock itself : place and identity in the American mining town / David Robertson.
        p. cm.
    Includes bibliographical references and index.
    ISBN-13: 978-0-87081-850-9 (hardcover : alk. paper) — ISBN 978-1-60732-076-0 (pbk. : alk.
paper)
    ISBN-10: 0-87081-850-3 (hardcover : alk. paper) 1. Coal mines and mining—Illinois—Toluca—History. 2. Coal mines and mining—Colorado—Cokedale—History. 3. Mines and mineral
resources—Oklahoma—Picher—History. 4. Cities and towns—United States—Social conditions.
5. Group identity—United States—Case studies. I. Title.
    HD9548.T65R63 2006
    307.76'60973—dc22

                                                                                          2006015016

Design by Daniel Pratt

For Dana, Victoria, Isabella, and Finn

Contents

Illustrations

MAPS

FIGURES

Preface

I T CAN BE DIFFICULT TO PINPOINT PRECISELY THE ORIGINS OF A LARGE RESEARCH project, especially one that has evolved over a lengthy period of time. That is not the case with this book, however, which is the end-product of an encounter I had as a first-year geography graduate student. When I arrived at the University of Oklahoma more than a decade ago, I was planning to study environmental impacts and land reclamation in one of the region's historic oil fields. When the opportunity arose to study a partially reclaimed strip mine near Henryetta, Oklahoma, however, my attention shifted to mining, and as I later recognized, not only was my topical focus altered by this research experience, so was the broader direction of my academic career. I entered the Henryetta coal mine in the summer of 1993, having just completed coursework in physical geography, quantitative methods, and environmental impact assessment. I had come to the field equipped with a pH meter, water and soil sampling equipment, and a multi-variable matrix for assessing environmental quality. Needless to say, I found what I was looking for: acid mine drainage, acidic soils, and erosion and sedimentation problems. What most captured my attention, however, were qualities of the environment that would have eluded me had the property's owner not offered to show me around the mine site. Although I had anticipated finding environmental problems, I had not expected to discover that this landscape also had a significant functional and emotional value.

The landowner told me that he had lived close to the mine site for most of his life and that he had purchased the property in the mid-1980s. Although portions of the mine land lay barren and were unproductive, other areas were suitable for cattle grazing, including the wooded washboard-like ridges of spoil that bordered his property. As we strolled along a pathway winding through the Crosstimber forest that had recolonized the mine waste, the landowner showed me a spot where he was sowing grasses in order to enhance deer habitat. The area provided good hunting, he said, but he regretted that the property's pit ponds, a picturesque chain of translucent lakes rimmed by cattails and overhung by willow trees, were barren of fish. Before the water had turned acidic there had been good fishing here. In fact, when he was young, his grandparents had operated a summer concession stand on one of the lakes, which had served as a popular swimming area and fishing hole. "I ran all over this place, I know every inch of it," he told me as he pulled back a clump of bushes to reveal the foundations of his grandparents' onetime business, and as he continued to recount the history of the site and to tell me of his connection to it and as we talked about his future plans for the area, I was struck by the fact that there was a story to be told about this environment that I was unequipped to explore. My environmental assessment matrix contained no cells in which I could record the land's history or meaning, values that make up the mining landscape's character as a place, the most intimate—and in ways most indispensable—aspect of environmental quality.

In the popular imagination, mining environments are forsaken places, but my experience at Henryetta challenged this preconception and instilled in me a desire to learn more about the role mining landscapes play in the lives of those who inhabit them. I adopted a new research focus aimed at acquiring a better understanding of mining's physical and social legacies, a topic that drew me into the domains of cultural and historical geography, mining history, industrial preservation, and other literatures. I initially struggled, however, to find a way to transform this interest into a cohesive dissertation. Fortunately, Richard Francaviglia gave me the guidance I needed at this critical juncture. He encouraged me to follow the geographer's instinct for exploration: to leave my desk and to get out and explore as many historic mining districts as I could manage. Francaviglia's advice eventually led me to Picher, Oklahoma, and Cokedale, Colorado. The other case study presented in this work—Toluca, Illinois—was brought to my attention by fellow graduate student and always-reliable confidant, Blake Gumprecht. I remain indebted to both these individuals for directing me to these study sites, which came to serve as the focal point of my doctoral dissertation in geography, filed at the University of Oklahoma in 2001. This book is an outgrowth of that study.

Many others also deserve acknowledgment for helping me carry out this research. University of Oklahoma professors Gary Thompson, Neil Salisbury, and Mark Meo provided guidance in my early years of graduate school. Naturally, the members of my doctoral committee had essential roles in overseeing the research on which this work is based. Gavin Bridge educated me in the political and economic institutions of mining and its environmental effects; Deborah Dalton showed me how to look at mined land from the landscape architect and artist's perspective; Richard Nostrand taught me how to conduct historical research; Robert Rundstrom kept my research grounded in theory and matters of social identity; and, by example and exacting proofreader's pen, Bret Wallach showed me how to write. These individuals invested significant time and energy in my education, and each served as a vigilant and professional academic mentor. In this regard, additional recognition is due Robert Rundstrom, my doctoral committee chairperson and friend. Bob showed an unwavering commitment to this research. He gave me the freedom to explore my own interests but continually pushed me down unconsidered avenues of thought. His faith in this work was constant and his criticism was always constructive.

I recognize, too, others who provided assistance and advice during later development of this research. My colleagues in the Department of Geography at the State University of New York College at Geneseo, particularly chairperson Ren Vasiliev, deserve credit. Their support during the time it took to complete my dissertation, and to then write this book, was essential to the completion of both projects. Eleanor Bussell, Richard Gerardo, Jim Gregg, Bill Honker, Rebecca Jim, Robert Lynch, Robert Nairn, Lee Scamehorn, Jane Spear, and Vernon Williams provided important comments at various stages of manuscript preparation or in other ways helped me to complete this research. Special thanks as well to George F. Thompson and Randall B. Jones of the Center for American Places for assisting in the development of this project, and to Sandy Crooms, Laura Furney, Darrin Pratt, Daniel Pratt, and Ann Wendland at the University Press of Colorado for their commitment to seeing this study published. Portions of this work have previously appeared in print. In 2000, the *Journal of Illinois History* published my overview of Toluca and the Longwall Mining District. A chapter on preservation issues in Cokedale appeared in the edited volume *Preserving Western History* in 2005. I thank the editors of these publications for their support.

I also owe immeasurable debt to those who helped me at various libraries and archives, including staff at the University of Illinois Library and Illinois Historical Survey; Illinois State Historical Library; Marshall County Historical Society; Toluca Library; Chicago Sun Times Library; the Colorado Historical Society's Stephen H. Hart Library; Denver Public Library and Western History Collection; the Carnegie Public Library in Trinidad, Colorado; the Samuel Freudenthal Memorial Library at Trinidad State Junior College; the Miami Public Library in Oklahoma; Oklahoma Historical Society Library; the University of Oklahoma's Bizzell

Memorial Library, Laurence S. Youngblood Energy Library and Western Histories Collection; and Milne Library at the State University of New York College at Geneseo.

I would also like to express my gratitude to those who opened their lives to me in Toluca, Cokedale, and Picher, and especially to those who granted me permission to reproduce their words in this book. Lacking their participation, this research would be bereft of the voices of those who know the mining landscape best. In Toluca, thanks go to Marion Brandt, Barney DeRubeis, Gilbert Flynn, Jack Gerardo, Mayor Larry Harber, Pastor Michael S. Jones, William McCall, Elton Pearson, Anna Mae Johnson Terrell, and Pete Venturi. In Cokedale, I recognize Bette Arguello, Richard Bell, Doug Holdread, Joyce Holdread, Mayor Pat Huhn, John Johnson, and Pat Schorr. In Picher, Grace Beauchamp, Earl Hatley, John Mott, and Orval and Steven Ray deserve thanks. I sincerely hope that I have accurately conveyed the experiences of these individuals, as well as others who have lived and worked in Toluca, Cokedale, and Picher. Any errors or shortcomings in interpretation remain mine alone.

Finally, but above all, I thank my family for their role in sustaining me during the years taken to write and revise this study. The support of my mother and father, Valerie and Gordon Robertson, has been unconditional and their generosity unending. Moreover, they instilled in me an enthusiasm for learning and a curiosity for exploration and discovery that are central to my capabilities as a teacher and researcher. Their influence is embedded in every page of this publication and so, too, is the support of my wife, Dana, and children, Victoria, Isabella, and Finn. Without complaint, they endured my too-frequent absences from home and the emotional ups and downs that accompany book writing, a process made bearable, and far less lonely, by the nourishment of their love. I could not have accomplished this work without them.

Hard As the Rock Itself

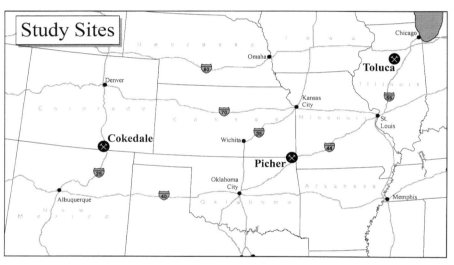

Map 1.1 Study site locations. Cartography by Brian Tomaszewski

Introduction

"**E**VERY MATURE NATION HAS ITS SYMBOLIC LANDSCAPES," WRITES GEOGRAPHER D. W. Meinig, idealized places that evoke commonly understood meaning. He cites the New England Village, the Main Street of Middle America, and the California Suburb as examples of symbolic landscapes that have come to represent idyllic spaces for American family life. But, as Meinig also observes, although the favorable imagery of these iconic places is familiar, their physical and social character is poorly understood. "Perhaps," he cautions, "we have been deluded by the very power of the symbols. When we attempt to penetrate the familiar generalizations and clichés . . . we may be startled at how narrow and uneven are the foundations upon which these stereotypes rest."[1]

Myth often obscures the complex realities of place, and this observation holds equally true for locales occupying unfavored perceptual territory. For example, symbols of difficult and unwholesome living, impoverished central cities, and isolated rural boondocks are also burdened by misperception. Negative stereotypes dominate these environments, and although not wholly inaccurate in terms of conventional economic and aesthetic measures, such generalizations obscure the internal value they hold as lived-in places. Mining has created a symbolic landscape similarly stigmatized. In the popular imagination, mining landscapes—mineral extraction and processing areas and the adjacent settlements for mine workers—have become icons of dereliction and decay. For those who live in these places, however, these landscapes may function as meaningful communities and homes.

Mining has played a vital role in U.S. economic development. The quest for mineral wealth was a dominant motive in early European colonization of the New World. Although not as driven as their Spanish counterparts by a desire to exploit the continent's mineral riches, the colonists of British North America wasted little time developing mines once ores were discovered. The first American ironworks were established at Jamestown, Virginia, in the 1620s. By the 1700s, the Atlantic colonies were trading significant quantities of iron and smaller amounts of copper and gold. As the nation grew, mineral prospecting followed, and frequently drove, advancement of the settlement frontier. Mining provided an impetus for settlement in numerous western states. By the early 1800s, lead was being produced by American settlers in the Mississippi River valley of Missouri, Illinois, and Wisconsin. By mid-century, copper was being extracted from Michigan and iron from Minnesota, and intensive mining of coal—a fuel that fired the furnaces of the American Industrial Revolution—in Appalachia was underway. By the mid-nineteenth century, manufacturers in the nation's economic core—the American Manufacturing Belt—had come to depend on a steady flow of metals and fuels from an ever-expanding and resource-rich periphery. Growing demand for minerals in the manufacturing belt, the extension of the national railroad network, and a succession of precious metal "fevers" produced dramatic growth in American mining. Bituminous coalfields of the Midwest were developed. Later, mountain and plains deposits came into production. Gold came to dominate the mineral economy of California after the Gold Rush of 1848–1849, and the metal, along with silver, copper, lead, and other mineral commodities, created distinctive mining districts across the American West.[2]

As a result of more than two centuries of mining activity, the United States has numerous historic mining districts. Although each is distinctive, they tend to share a common economic history. Mining is the quintessential "boom and bust" industry. Individual mining operations may differ in terms of mineral commodities, richness of deposits, and operating lifespans, but the finite nature of mineral deposits almost always results in the demise of mining-dependent economies.[3]

Typically, once the likely existence of a profitable prospect was discovered, America's historic mining districts would experience periods of rapid growth. These boom years were characterized by substantial capital investment in mine workings, transportation systems, and settlement infrastructure. Hastily developed, many mining communities sprung into existence seemingly overnight, and as a result of their isolation, they were often occupied by imported labor. North America's historic mining districts, particularly those originating in the late nineteenth and early twentieth centuries, served as foci for European immigration.[4]

Inexorably, the quality and accessibility of mineral deposits declines and mines typically become less profitable over time. Beginning in the late nineteenth century, worker organization often placed a further strain on the profitability of mining operations as workers began to claim a larger share of the return from the mines' output.[5] Although technological innovations in mining and mineral processing and increases in commodity prices may extend their lifespans, all mines eventually cease to be profitable. As mines close, deindustrialization of the mining region begins. This sustained decline in mineral production and employment is sometimes accompanied by a rise in alternate industries. In the majority of historic mining areas, however, remote locations and poorly diversified economies have ensured economic stagnation and decline following mine closure.

As single-industry communities dependent on the extraction of nonrenewable resources, mining towns often fail to survive deindustrialization. The backcountry of the American West is dotted with onetime mining settlements that have succumbed to wholesale abandonment and ruination. These mining ghost towns are particularly common in districts that contained company-owned settlements where operators salvaged and raised company towns in an attempt to recoup investments in community infrastructure. It is important to recognize, however, that community annihilation is not an inevitable outcome of mining's demise. Mining communities often outlast their industrial usefulness. It is a phenomenon that has not been quantified, but the survival of large numbers of American mining towns suggests that many persist in the midst of decay.[6] For these settlements, a mine's closure is followed by a period of economic decline characterized by falling income levels and high rates of unemployment. Significant population loss involving out-migration of younger, working-age residents may also occur. Economic decline and depopulation erode the local tax base, resulting in the loss of public services and a decline in the quality of community infrastructure. Residents of onetime mining towns are typically older and poorer than their rural counterparts, and more often than not their settlements have a worn-out appearance.[7]

Mining has also created some of the country's most environmentally troubled landscapes. Few industries have such a profound and visible impact on the environment. As early as the sixteenth century, mining was recognized as a destructive force in Europe; and environmental problems created by mining began to concern the U.S. public in the 1880s. Indeed, mining was among the nation's first industries to be regulated on the basis of environmental concerns, and as the industry's footprint spread into the nation's diminishing wild lands so did awareness that mining severely impaired the quality of land, water, and air.[8]

Mining's most visible impact involves land disturbance. Mining and mineral processing produce two categories of surface alterations: features associated with mineral extraction and those associated with deposits of mining, milling, and refining wastes. The former include shafts, pits, quarries, and subsidence depressions; the latter, piles of overburden and milling waste and deposits of slag and tailings. These land disturbances can produce radical changes in local topography, drainage systems, and vegetation regimes, and both aquatic and terrestrial habitats may suffer long-term harm. Mining also generates a variety of pollutants. Among the most problematic are those derived from the large volume of solid waste material that mining and mineral processing typically produce. Mining waste may contain reactive sulfides, minerals that when oxidized generate acid mine drainage and are the leading cause of diminished surface and groundwater quality in mining areas. In addition to emissions produced from mineral refining and metallurgical processing, mining wastes may also release toxic metals, stream-clogging sediments, and harmful particulates into the environment.[9]

THE MINING IMAGINARY

Historical geographer Richard Francaviglia has described mining regions as "hard places," areas whose residents are burdened by amply documented economic, social, and environmental problems. Less often recognized, however, is that those who call these difficult places home bear the additional burden of living in regions with pronounced image problems. There exists a long tradition of scholarly and literary description equating mining landscapes with dereliction and decay. Lewis Mumford's commentary in *Technics and Civilization,* a classic critique of industrial society in which mining plays a prominent role, attests to this fact. "Taking mining regions as a whole," he writes, "they are the very image of backwardness, isolation, raw animosities and lethal struggles. From the Rand to the Klondike, from the coal mines of South Wales to those of West Virginia, from the modern iron mines of Minnesota to the ancient silver mines of Greece, barbarism colors the entire picture."[10]

Mumford was the first scholar to seriously consider the links between mining and modernity, but he has hardly stood alone in condemning the industry's physical and social influences.[11] Prior to examining these critical appraisals, however, it is worth noting that as recently as the early twentieth century, mining's transformational effects were often viewed as symbols of progress, particularly in frontier mining districts and during the boom years of industrial development. Early mining activity in America was frequently celebrated for its ability to transform wilderness into economically useful space. As historian Duane Smith has described, frontier-era mining environments inspired admiration: "The land existed then solely to yield its bountiful mineral blessings to onrushing Americans who had the grit and determination (and, one might add, luck) to find them."[12]

Favorable opinions of the industry's influence began to wane as mining economies matured in the twentieth century and positive descriptions of industrial progress were replaced by a powerful set of negative stereotypes. Modern accounts of mining regions recurrently evoke images of landscape dereliction. The following excerpt from a 1962 Department of the Interior study on mining and its environmental effects provides a vivid example: "Our derelict acreage [abandoned mine land] is made up of tens of thousands of separate patches. In some regions they are often close together. Where one acre in ten is laid waste, the whole landscape is disfigured. The face of the earth is riddled with abandoned mineral workings packed with subsidence, gashed with quarries, littered with disused plant structures and piled high with dross and debris, and spoil and slag. . . . [The mining landscape] debases as well as disgraces our civilization." Indeed, the use of a common set of adjectives to describe the appearance of mining areas— "ugly," "ruined," and "wasted" are among the most prevalent—shows that these places are associated with misuse and failure. As Francaviglia properly observes, "[W]hen compared with the rolling farmland or wilderness so prevalent in our imagery of scenery, mining country does not fare well. . . . [O]bservers are likely to characterize mining country as a ruined, hellish wasteland."[13]

Geographer Gavin Bridge more precisely details the origins of unfavorable opinion. Bridge explores what he calls "the mining imaginary," popular idealizations of mining and its landscape effects. Reflecting the industry's visible impacts on environments and communities, like Francaviglia, Bridge suggests that objections to mining mirror societal misgivings to the visual intrusion of industrial activities into rural spaces. "Portrayed as an irreverent intrusion or a jarring juxtaposition symbolic of modernization," he writes, "mines are frequently described (in art, literature, and travelers' accounts) as either disrupting the natural sublime or terminating a pastoral idyll." Bridge reveals, however, that negative perceptions are also rooted in a belief that mining's physical assaults affect the morality of mining societies. The existence of a morally disruptive "culture of massive disturbance" has been observed by mining scholars, who are apt to contrast the moral landscape of mining to that of an imagined space of preindustrial integrity and harmony. "In many accounts," Bridge explains, "the technologies and rationalities of mining intrude to produce a 'dis-spirit of place' . . . mental changes that are interpreted as a fall from grace." In fact, in many historic mining regions, conditions of blight, lawlessness, depression, and fatalism have been explained in the context of a "derelict land mentality," a psychological insensibility alleged to be the product of daily interaction with a deranged and corrupting environment.[14]

Although images of dereliction often surface in descriptions of mining areas where the industry remains active, as a regional characterization dereliction tends to emerge most strongly in historic mining areas where deindustrialization has amplified and left bare an array of social, economic, and environmental problems. Deprived of their founding industry—their reason for being—and appearing idle, disordered, and environmentally abused, historic mining regions carry a particularly unfavorable aesthetic. Collectively, depictions of mining along with the environments and communities it produces have served to create a symbolic landscape. In the societal imagination, historic mining towns are emblems of decay and debasing moral influence. This portrayal is so prevalent that many historic mining regions—Appalachia is perhaps the best example—have become synonymous with failure and decay.[15]

PLACE, IDENTITY, AND THE MINING LANDSCAPE

Not all mining landscapes have become symbols of dereliction, and every mining settlement does not evoke repulse. Sometimes, historic mining towns stand as curious relics of a romanticized frontier age. Preserved in a state of arrested decay, the ghost town of Bodie, California, is now a state historic park, attracting some 200,000 visitors each year. Other historic mining towns have avoided dereliction or rebounded from its effects. Communities like Cripple Creek and Aspen, Colorado, where mining-based heritage tourism and outdoor recreation have produced opportunities for rejuvenation, show that dereliction is not an inevitable fate. Likewise, the unique settings of some historic mining towns, such as Bisbee, Arizona, have facilitated their evolution into artists' colonies or retreats for alternative life-stylers. On the whole, however, these are exceptional cases. Unlike Bodie, most historic mining towns that have succumbed to ghost-town status have perished without notice. Unlike Cripple Creek, Aspen, or Bisbee, those that survive mine closure mostly struggle to survive. Unfortunately, the unfavorable opinions of mining environments are often warranted. Yet, as is common of symbolic landscapes, these presumptions obscure important aspects of life and landscape in mining regions and, in some cases, have perpetuated outright falsehoods.

A case in point is the belief that mining settlements are impermanent. True, like the mineral deposits their economies relied on, many mining settlements experienced finite life-spans. The fact that a portion of a mining town's workforce was often transitory—bachelor miners in particular were highly mobile—has also reinforced their image as temporary settlements. This condition of impermanence is one of the mining community's most domineering images. It is also, however, an overgeneralization that has had a detrimental influence on our understanding of mining areas. As a result of their assumed impermanence, the persistence of historic mining towns, a phenomenon discussed earlier in this chapter, has not been given adequate attention. Nowhere is this better exemplified than in regional mining histories, the majority of which ignore the post-mining years or at best treat them in epilogue fashion.[16] The end of mining usually signals an end to the historical narratives of these "temporary" locales; and readers are left with the false impression that mining communities have rich pasts but inconsequential futures.

Moreover, as the comments of classics scholar James D. Muhly show, the belief that mining towns are impermanent also reinforces a myth that the ties binding their residents to place are weak or nonexistent. Historic mining towns, he alleges, "are most likely to be ephemeral affairs, created by individuals who always saw their residence at the site as temporary." Muhly erroneously concludes, "[M]ining provides a community of occupation, not a community of place," a falsehood that those residing in onetime mining towns would quickly have refuted had care been taken to consider their views. Alarmingly, however, Muhly's oversight is common in mining-related literature, little of which has attempted to refine the myths of the mining imaginary through direct engagement with the inhabitants of mining regions.[17] This book attempts to remedy that oversight.

To date, few studies of historic mining areas have attempted to convey their inner qualities as lived-in places. As a result, the persistence of historic mining towns and, more importantly, their internal value as communities and homes remain largely unrecognized. In truth, mining communities are rarely viewed as decayed and debasing locales by their inhabitants. Indeed, that the views of residents might lie in opposition to dominant societal perceptions should come as no surprise. As long recognized by cultural geographers, notions of dereliction, like all judgments made of landscapes, are highly subjective.[18] This point is raised not to deny the troubles and hardships that exist in mining areas but to show that there are other stories to be told about mining environments, which despite their shortcomings, may have a positive influence on their residents. In fact, mining's physical and social legacies are often central to a community's "sense of place" and may serve as a foundation on which local identity is structured and maintained.

These qualities of the mining landscape are the central focus of this work. This book interprets the historic mining town's meaning as *place,* a term that refers to the landscape's function as a center of meaning. All inhabited landscapes hold cultural meaning, emotional significance that is a product of interaction with the land over time. These less observable facets of landscape include its atmosphere and sentimental value. The phrase "sense of place" is also used to describe these meanings. Commonly, sense of place refers to the positive attachments people hold for the environments in which they live, those intangible qualities, built up over time, that make landscapes "special and worth defending."[19]

Attachments to place are an essential part of the human experience. "I do not think that one can survive as a human creature," writes geographer Peirce Lewis, "without special attachments to special places." A part of what makes places special is their capacity to provide inhabitants with a sense of rootedness, described by anthropologist Keith Basso as "an enduring affinity with known localities and the ways of life they sponsor."[20] Moreover, this sense of belonging may also provide a foundation on which local identities are structured. A rich area of contemporary landscape scholarship is the study of these people-place connections, whereby landscapes are recognized to be visible entities that both reflect and constitute individual and social-group identities.[21] In short, landscapes reinforce a sense of who we are. Kent C. Ryden explains:

> Part of the sentiment which people feel for places derives from the feelings of identification that they form with those places. We commonly and casually identify ourselves in terms of geographical labels, as being Midwesterners or New Yorkers; more important, if we feel that our present selves are inextricably bound to our pasts—that our lives have historical continuity, that we are the products of our past experiences—and if we tie memory to the landscape, then in contemplating place we contemplate ourselves. . . . This sense of identity may be one of the strongest of the feelings with which we regard places. . . . [T]his feeling of identity helps give order, structure, and value to the geographical world.[22]

The meanings ascribed to place are difficult to uniformly define as they often vary across places over time.[23] Place perceptions may differ across generations. They may also be influenced by aspects of social identity, such as gender, age, ethnicity, and class. In addition, place meanings may be multiple and conflicting, and they may be contested by individuals or groups living within the same region. Internal debates may exist over the meaning of place. So, too, debates over place values commonly occur across perspectival divides. That is, landscapes often hold different meaning for insiders (the residents of place) and outsiders (visitors or observers). This divide holds especially true for visually unpleasing and seemingly derelict places like historic mining towns. By and large, the mining imaginary, that popular body of images that defines society's view of mining landscapes, represents the external view of place. As I show in this book, however, these popular perceptions are incomplete.

Mining landscapes hold different meanings for residents and outsiders. In his 1987 article "Continuity and Decline in the Anthracite Towns of Pennsylvania," for example, geographer Ben Marsh expertly interprets the paradoxical nature of place perception in defunct mining towns. With a focus on onetime coal mining communities in eastern Pennsylvania, Marsh's work remains the definitive study on place and the mining landscape. "By conventional economic or demographic measures, and by the normal standards of landscape esthetics, this is the least attractive part of Pennsylvania," he writes. In terms of their local value, however, Marsh notes that these communities are considered fine and distinctive places to live. Arrays of economic, social, and environmental problems exist in these communities, but residents maintain a strong commitment to place. "The residents of the anthracite towns of Pennsylvania show a considerable loyalty to a landscape that provides them with little of material value," Marsh explains. "This should remind the observer that any broad concept of place must address two different aspects of a landscape: the physical support it provides (*means*) and the intangible rewards it offers (*meaning*)."[24]

Marsh calls this phenomena the "duality of place," explaining that "place is partly the *means* an area provides for its own continuation, but also the *meaning* derived from its past for its continuation."[25] In the mining imaginary, a popular image of the historic mining region has been constructed that is based almost exclusively on observations of the land's limited *means*. Yet, although mining landscapes may offer little in the way of material reward, as Marsh has shown they often hold emotional significance. Expanding on Marsh's pioneering work, I aim to dispel the perception that mining landscapes are necessarily derelict and morally debasing locales, an abstract external viewpoint that not only fails to recognize the internal value of historic mining regions but adds additional obstacles to addressing their myriad problems.

In the chapters that follow, the experiential qualities of place are explored in three historic mining towns from the mineral discovery phase through mine closure and deindustrialization. A broad range of place perceptions held by residents and outsiders is interpreted and compared to capture the varied and often conflicting meanings these areas hold as they cycle through the boom and bust stages of a mineral-dependent economy. Through this study, a new story of the historic mining town is presented, one that draws attention to its inner value as a community and home and emphasizes the roles mining landscapes play in maintaining and reinforcing local identities.

The study of place and identity in historic mining regions is not uncharted territory, but it is a subject lacking explicit focus. A fragmented body of research by historians, geographers, planners, sociologists, and others provides indirect insight into people–place relationships by way of investigation into related avenues of study. Regional mining histories, for example, usually focus on the social and economic evolution of specific mining communities, and many provide excellent insight into the lives of ordinary people. Consequently, regional histories can serve as resources for the study of place, the meaning of which is rooted in local history and resident experiences. Direct interpretation of place, however, or of the mining landscape's social significance rarely occurs in regional mining histories or in other mining literature. Even when it does, analysis is often limited to the landscape's role as a material symbol of defunct technologies and industrial systems.[26] Mining environments, however, hold broader and more far-reaching local meaning that most social research has left unexplored. As anthropologist Kathleen Stewart has observed in the coal camps of West Virginia, "[T]he detritus of history piled high on the local landscape has become central to a sense of place."[27]

As already noted, regional mining histories tend to overlook the place-based attachments that exist in mining communities that have survived mine closure, and a similar oversight exists in other mining-related research. As Douglas Porteous observes in his review of social research on single-industry communities, including mining towns, scholars have paid far more attention to the rise of industry and community than to their decline. "Clearly the boom end of the boom and bust cycle," he writes, "has been deemed more exciting and lucrative." Of particular concern, Porteous maintains, is the lack of research on the reactions of impacted populations in these failing places.[28]

Notable exceptions, however, do exist. A handful of scholars have explored the perceptual qualities of mining landscapes and their work provides a foundation on which this book builds. Despite the myriad problems that exist in historic mining areas, residents often retain positive visions of place. Marsh has observed this phenomenon in the anthracite valley of Pennsylvania. So, too, has social historian Thomas Dublin. Similar observations have been made by geographers William Wyckoff and Christopher Davies in historic mining districts in Montana and Wales, respectively; by American studies scholar Kent Ryden in Idaho; and by anthropologists Kathleen Stewart and Leslie Robertson in West Virginia and British Columbia, respectively. Notable as well is the multidisciplinary work *Coping with Closure: An International Comparison of Mine Town Experiences,* in which several case studies show "that it would be a mistake to underestimate the attachment of local residents to mining communities."[29]

Collectively, this small but important body of research shows that mining can create cohesive communities whose residents exhibit a deep and lasting commitment to place. In historic mining towns, attachment to place is rooted in mining-era experiences. The physical toil and danger of mining, historically among the most strenuous and hazardous of all occupations, created common hardships that brought miners and their families together. The meager and unpredictable wages also created a shared need for support. Day-to-day survival required cooperation, and labor organizations and ethnic groups provided networks for resident bonding that strengthened a sense of belonging to a community.

Products of the mining past, these qualities often continue to shape life in mining towns long after the industry's local demise. Community continuity, memories of the mining past, and the stories residents share of the mining way of life become a folklore passed down from one generation to the next and ensure that these aspects of place are not forgotten. The mining landscape also reminds residents of their mining heritage. Built structures and environments—miners' houses, neighborhoods, and commercial districts—as well as the remnants of mineral extraction and processing—industrial structures, mine sites, and waste piles—are reminders of the town's reason for being. They may also function as distinctive icons of home. A venue for the expression of common experiences, the mining landscape plays an important role in maintaining a collective sense of place. It provides a context for local existence, an attribute that can be especially powerful for immigrant miners and their relatives for whom mining represents the beginning of their lives in America. The labor and sacrifice of friends and family who toiled in the mines may also be embodied in the mining landscape. Frequently, mining's physical legacies come to memorialize those who died in the mines, particularly in communities where no formal miners' memorial has been constructed.

The mining landscape also reinforces individual and social-group identities. Mining communities identify with the rugged severity of a landscape and a life that has always been rich but difficult. In many ways, the land's tough, unpretentious, and toil-worn appearance mirror qualities of self-worth. Mining landscapes remind them that they are members of strong, hardworking, and persevering communities. In fact, the physical and economic challenges of mining life often produce communities with a marked ability to endure. The inhabitants of historic mining towns "get by," Marsh writes, "because they are so good at getting by. That skill is their heritage." This will to survive helps explain why, when given even marginal opportunity and resources to survive mine closure, mining communities frequently persist.[30]

As past scholarly research suggests, mining landscapes are perceptually complex. Through a focused, comparative analysis of place and identity in three separate mining towns, this book advances our understanding of the value they hold as enduring communities and homes. It is important to note, however, that such insight is of more than academic relevance. Traditionally, place research has been used to further our understanding of regions and to provide insight into the lives of geographical "others."[31] Increasingly, this research also is being recognized to have pragmatic relevance. By detailing the different perceptions residents and outsiders hold of historic mining regions and by considering the ways these meanings have shaped responses to problems in these regions, this book shows that an understanding of place has material applications that reach beyond historic mining towns.

On a continent where economic development has been fueled in large part by the exploitation of a seemingly limitless natural resource base and in a continually urbanizing, restructuring, and globalizing economy, derelict landscapes are numerous. North America contains failing rural communities and urban zones of numberless variety, including onetime oil boomtowns, logging and fishing villages, factory and mill towns, agricultural communities, and inner-city neighborhoods. Like historic mining towns, life struggles on in these locales. Despite their disadvantages, however, multitudes of "derelict" communities remain rich with personal meaning.[32] Attachments to place exhibited in mining towns serve to remind us, Ryden writes, "that the marginal can (and should) be seen as meaningful—that the obscure backwater that the outsider may view in a negative light can be a positive, nurturing place for the people who live there."[33]

Unfortunately, although the industrial past may leave positive imprints on local culture—solidifying societies, giving meaning to place, and reinforcing local identity—its negative legacies—economic decline and environmental degradation—also threaten the very survival of mining communities.[34] Place analysis reveals this predicament and provides specific insight into how such problems might be mediated.

Place meaning often guides individual and collective actions. Place is a powerful social influence in natural resource politics, where decisions regarding the management of environmental resources can transform place meanings around which individuals and group identities may be structured. By unearthing these less-tangible environmental values, place-based perspectives can provide more nuanced data than are typically available to environmental decision-makers. It can also transform the decision-making processes themselves by "redistributing power to voices and meanings that may not otherwise be expressed."[35] Place is recognized as a "humane and responsible way by which to approach larger questions of environmental prudence."[36] In historic mining regions, for example, questions surrounding the social benefits and costs of renewed mining activity may exist that place analysis can at least partially address. Likewise, as is shown in the case studies presented in this book, abandoned mine land remediation policy can be informed by place analysis. Locally acceptable reclamation and restoration programs require an understanding of the emotional value mining landscapes hold for their inhabitants.

Place meanings influence planning and cultural resource management politics as well. Planner Kevin Lynch said it best: "[T]he human experience of a landscape is as fundamental as any other factor and should be considered from the first."[37] Considerable planning challenges exist in onetime mining towns and development decisions can influence their future viability as habitable settlements. Depopulation, economic decline, and decaying infrastructure are critical issues whose address requires consideration of the needs and desires of those who still live and work in these communities.[38] Again, the case studies that follow highlight this fact. They also confirm that effective planning recognizes the need to maintain locally meaningful elements of the landscape.

Stewardship of historic resources also requires an understanding of place. Because the mining past plays an important role in maintaining a sense of place and reinforcing self and social-group identities, local support often exists for retaining mining's physical legacies. Preservation of mining landscapes, however, is a challenging task often complicated by the fact that the objects of historical and emotional significance may be hazardous to the environment and public health. From the outsider's perspective, they may also appear visually blighting. Balancing historic preservation objectives with environmental quality concerns, and overcoming negative outside biases inhibiting recognition that the mining landscape may contain something worthy of preserving, are problems faced by each community in this book.

Noted landscape scholar J. B. Jackson wrote often of the importance of abandoning the spectator stance when evaluating the worth of landscapes, whatever their form. Every planner, landscape architect, and conservationist, he believed, has an obligation to rethink what a landscape is worth to the people who inhabit it. The human landscape, Jackson wrote, is the "product of much sweat and hardship and earnest thought; we should never look at it without remembering that, and we should never tinker with the landscape without thinking of those who live in the midst of it—whether in a trailer in an oil field or in a city tenement."[39] Jackson's heartfelt plea also applies to historic mining towns, where widely held perceptions of dereliction cast an unsympathetic shadow. The mining imaginary obscures the value that these former mining towns hold as centers of human experience. This oversight is not a trivial matter as conflict between an inhospitable environment and a commitment to place is creating a difficult future for the residents of many historic mining regions.

By and large, the historic mining towns presented in this book represent unexamined places whose regional histories, the foundations on which past and present place perceptions are grounded, have not been carefully interpreted. The chapters that follow tell the story of evolving place meaning in Toluca, Illinois; Cokedale, Colorado; and Picher, Oklahoma (Map 1.1). A brief concluding chapter compares experiences in the case studies and presents closing observations.

Rural communities with populations in 2000 of approximately 1,300 (Toluca), 140 (Cokedale), and 1,700 (Picher), these mining towns have experienced the boom-and-bust cycle of a mineral-dependent economy. As early twentieth-century mining settlements, they endured significant economic decline and population loss following mine closure. Despite these and other commonalities, however, it would be unwise to suggest that Toluca, Cokedale, and Picher represent the experiences of every American mining town. They do, however, represent many.

Each mining town occupies a different physical and cultural region of the central United States: Toluca is located in the Central Lowlands of the Midwest; Cokedale, in the Southern Rocky Mountains; and Picher, on the border of the Ozark Plateau of the Upland South. Their industrial and social histories also differ. Toluca and Cokedale were coal mining towns; Picher was a hard-rock mining settlement producing lead and zinc. Many first-generation European immigrants settled Toluca and Cokedale, whereas Picher contained a predominantly Anglo-American workforce. Cokedale is the only study site that was a company town and it was owned and operated by a single mining firm. Mining's operational lifespans also varied in each of these communities. Toluca is the oldest; its mine closed in 1924 after thirty-one years of operation. Cokedale's mines lasted forty-one years, closing in 1947. Picher is the youngest of the three communities. Productive for more than fifty years, the last of Picher's mines closed in the late 1960s. The study sites also show different outcomes of deindustrialization. From a socioeconomic standpoint, Toluca's economy is faring relatively well, but Cokedale is only now beginning to recover from the shock of deindustrialization. Its economy is showing modest signs of rejuvenation and its population has stabilized. Picher, however, is a community still struggling to survive. Out-migration continues and Picher's economy remains severely depressed.

The mining landscapes of each community are also unique and mining's physical legacies have created different challenges. These include planning problems, and historic preservation and environmental remediation concerns. Although light manufacturing and agriculture now dominate the economy and landscape of Toluca, its residents have not forgotten their mining past. The most significant features remaining from the mining era are two mounds of coal mining waste that residents have affectionately named "the Jumbos." Beginning in the 1980s, conflicts arose over the future of these landmarks, spurring the community to rally for their protection. These efforts were successful and in the late 1990s a reclamation plan was initiated that protected the environment and preserved the Jumbos. In contrast to Toluca's residents, the residents of Cokedale and Picher occupy landscapes that are thoroughly dominated by visual reminders of the mining past. Cokedale was given National Register Historic District status in 1981 and is one of the country's best-preserved company coal mining towns. Although local identity in Cokedale is closely bound to the mining landscape, the complex issues of heritage interpretation and preservation planning remain unresolved. In Picher, industrial ruins and mining waste litter the local landscape and its citizens are plagued by a host of mining-related environmental problems that threaten Picher's very existence. The town was designated an EPA Superfund site in the early 1980s, yet many retain a deep attachment to the land. As all of the study sites show, a sense of place and identity remains intimately tied to the mining landscape. Residents share mining histories that continue to give meaning to land and life.

NOTES

1. D. W. Meinig, "Symbolic Landscapes: Some Idealizations of American Communities," in *The Interpretation of Ordinary Landscapes* (New York: Oxford University Press, 1979), 164, 172–173.

2. Early American mining and ironmaking are discussed by Otis E. Young and Robert Lenon, *Western Mining; An Informal Account of Precious-Metals Prospecting, Placering, Lode Mining, and Milling on the American Frontier, from Spanish Times to 1893* (Norman: University of Oklahoma Press, 1970). For the history of Western mining, see William Greever, *Bonanza West: The Story of the Western Mining Rushes, 1848–1880* (Norman: University of Oklahoma Press, 1963); Duane A. Smith, *Rocky Mountain Mining Camps: The Urban Frontier* (Lincoln: University of Nebraska Press, 1967); Clark Spence, *Mining Engineers and the American West: The Lace-Boot Brigade, 1849–1933* (New Haven: Yale University Press, 1970); and Mark Wyman, *Hard Rock Epic: Western Miners and the Industrial Revolution* (Berkeley: University of California Press, 1979).

3. Homer Aschmann, "The Natural History of a Mine," *Economic Geography* 46:2 (1970): 171–190.

4. For readings on mining and ethnicity, see A. L. Rowse, *The Cousin Jacks: The Cornish in America* (New York: Scribner, 1969); David Emmons, *The Butte Irish: Class and Ethnicity in an American Mining Town, 1875–1925* (Urbana: University of Illinois Press,

1989); and Susan L. Johnson, *Roaring Camp: The Social World of the California Gold Rush* (New York: W. W. Norton, 2000).

5. Notable works in mining labor history include Vernon H. Jenson, *Heritage of Conflict: Labor Relations in the Non-Ferrous Metals Industry up to 1930* (Ithaca: Cornell University Press, 1950); Richard Lingenfelter, *Hard Rock Miners: A History of the Mining Labor Movement in the American West* (Berkeley: University of California Press, 1974); and Priscilla Long, *Where the Sun Never Shines: A History of America's Bloody Coal Industry* (New York: Paragon House, 1989).

6. Douglas Porteous makes this claim in *Planned to Death: The Annihilation of a Place Called Howdendyke* (Toronto: University of Toronto Press, 1989), 229.

7. For readings on the economic and social impact of deindustrialization in single-industry communities, see Art Gallaher and Harland Padfield, eds., *The Dying Community* (Albuquerque: University of New Mexico Press, 1980); Roy Tyler Bowles, *Little Communities and Big Industries* (Toronto: Butterworths, 1982); and Porteous, *Planned to Death*. Mine closure is analyzed in Cecily Neil, Markku Tykklainen, and John Bradbury, eds., *Coping with Closure: An International Comparison of Mine Town Experiences* (New York: Routledge, 1992).

8. Richard V. Francaviglia, *Hard Places: Reading the Landscape of America's Historic Mining Districts* (Iowa City: University of Iowa Press, 1991), 214. Clarence Glacken describes Georgius Agricola's defense of sixteenth-century European mining in *Traces on the Rhodian Shore: Nature and Culture in Western Thought from Ancient Times to the End of the Eighteenth Century* (Berkeley: University of California Press, 1967), 468–469. The historical impact of mining in the United States and awareness of the industry's environmental harm are detailed by Duane A. Smith in *Mining America: The Industry and the Environment, 1800–1980* (Lawrence: University Press of Kansas, 1987).

9. Earle A. Ripley, Robert E. Redmann, and Adele A. Crowder, *Environmental Effects of Mining* (Delray Beach, FL: St. Lucie Press, 1996).

10. Francaviglia, *Hard Places*, 9; Kenneth L. Wallwork, *Derelict Land: Origins and Prospects of a Land-Use Problem* (London: David & Charles, 1974), 19; Lewis Mumford, *Technics and Civilization* (New York: Harcourt, Brace & World, 1962), 73.

11. Mumford's analysis of mining and its societal affects is discussed by Gavin Bridge in "Contested Terrain: Mining and the Environment," *Annual Review of Environment and Resources* 29 (2004): 245. In addition, a large body of research in the physical sciences details mining's environmental impacts. Social scientists and historians have also considered a broad range of mining-related topics, but a focus on the social and economic maladies of mining areas links much of this research. Likewise, the works of novelists and journalists exhibit similar themes and many of the most enduring depictions of mining landscapes exist in popular literature. Upton Sinclair's *King Coal*, Emile Zola's *Germinal*, Richard Llewellyn's *How Green Was My Valley*, and Henry Caudill's *Night Comes to the Cumberlands*, for example, provide powerful accounts of industrial exploitation, social and economic hardship, and environmental abuse. These and other widely read "place-defining" works have assigned powerful meaning to mining locales. See Upton Sinclair, *King Coal* (New York: Macmillan, 1917); Emile Zola, *Germinal* (New York: A. A. Knopf, 1937); Richard Llewellyn, *How Green Was My Valley* (New York: Macmillan, 1940); Harry M. Caudill, *Night Comes to the Cumberlands: A Biography of a Depressed Area* (Boston: Little Brown and Company, 1962). Place-defining literature is

discussed by James R. Shortridge, "The Concept of the Place-Defining Novel in American Popular Culture," *Professional Geographer* 43:3 (1991): 280–291.

12. Smith, *Mining America,* 5.

13. According to John Jakle and David Wilson, derelict landscapes are dominated by visual symbols of disinvestment, vacancy, and degradation. See *Derelict Landscapes: The Wasting of America's Built Environment* (Savage, MD: Rowman & Littlefield, 1992), 9; U.S. Department of the Interior, *Surface Mining and Our Environment* (Washington, DC: GPO, 1962), 51–52, quoted in John W. Simpson, "The Emotional Landscape and Public Law 95-87," *Landscape Architecture* 75:3 (1985): 60–63, 108–109, 112–113; Francaviglia, *Hard Places,* 9.

14. Bridge, "Contested Terrain," 243–244; U.S. Department of the Interior, *Surface Mining and Our Environment,* 51–52, quoted in Simpson, "The Emotional Landscape," 60. Discussion of a "derelict land mentality" is also included in Jakle and Wilson, *Derelict Landscapes,* 9; David H. Loof, "Growing Up in a Dying Community," *The Dying Community,* ed. A. Gallaher and H. Padfield (Albuquerque: University of New Mexico Press, 1980), 225; and Wallwork, *Derelict Land,* 294.

15. For example, Simpson writes: "Each of us has vivid mental images of ravaged Appalachian mountains, orange-colored streams clogged with mud, and the abject poverty hidden in the back hollows of the region." See Simpson, "The Emotional Landscape," 60. See also Loof, "Growing Up in a Dying Community," 224.

16. Two notable exceptions are Peter Goin and C. Elizabeth Raymond's *Changing Mines in America* (Santa Fe: The Center for American Places, 2004) and Eric L. Clements's *After the Boom in Tombstone and Jerome, Arizona: Decline in Western Resource Towns* (Reno: University of Nevada Press, 2003).

17. James D. Muhly, "Foreword," in *Social Approaches to an Industrial Past: The Archaeology and Anthropology of Mining,* ed. A. Bernard Knapp, Vincent C. Pigott, and Eugenia W. Herbert (New York: Routledge, 1998), xv.

18. See Jakle and Wilson, *Derelict Landscapes,* 9; David Lowenthal, "Not Every Prospect Pleases," in *Changing Rural Landscapes,* ed. E. H. Zube and M. J. Zube (Amherst: University of Massachusetts Press, 1977), 129–139; and D.W. Meinig, ed., "The Beholding Eye: Ten Versions of the Same Scene," in *The Interpretation of Ordinary Landscapes,* ed. D. W. Meinig (New York: Oxford University Press, 1979), 33–48.

19. James Duncan, "Place," in *The Dictionary of Human Geography,* ed. R. J. Johnston, D. Gregory, and D. M. Smith (Oxford: Blackwell, 1994), 442–443; Yi-Fu Tuan, *Space and Place: The Perspective of Experience* (Minneapolis: University of Minnesota Press, 1977), 138; David Seamon, "Phenomenology and Environment-Behavior Research," in *Advances in Environment, Behavior, and Design,* ed. G. T. Moore and E. Zube (New York: Plenum, 1987), 10; Peirce Lewis, "Defining a Sense of Place," *The Southern Quarterly* 17:3 (1979): 29.

20. Lewis, "Defining a Sense of Place," 29; Keith H. Basso, "Wisdom Sits in Places," in *Senses of Place,* ed. S. Feld and K. H. Basso, eds. (Santa Fe: School of American Research Press, 1996), 83.

21. Richard H. Schein, "The Place of Landscape: A Conceptual Framework for Interpreting an American Scene," *Annals of the Association of American Geographers* 87:4 (1997): 660.

22. Kent C. Ryden, *Mapping the Invisible Landscape: Folklore, Writing, and the Sense of Place* (Iowa City: University of Iowa Press, 1993), 39–40.

23. Antony S. Cheng, Linda E. Kruger, and Steven E. Daniels, "'Place' as an Integrating Concept in Natural Resource Politics: Propositions for a Social Science Research Agenda," *Society and Natural Resources* 16 (2003): 88.

24. Ben Marsh, "Continuity and Decline in the Anthracite Towns of Pennsylvania," *Annals of the Association of American Geographers* 77:3 (1987): 337.

25. Ibid., 338. Marsh sites Shotter for the conceptualization of place duality. See John Shotter, "'Duality of structure' and 'Intentionality' in an Ecological Psychology," *Journal for the Theory of Social Behavior* 13 (1983): 19–43.

26. Mining-related research in industrial preservation and archaeology has tended to focus on these aspects of the mining landscape's significance. See Robert L.S. Spude, David A. Poirier, and Ronald M. Greenberg, eds., *America's Mining Heritage* (Washington, DC: National Parks Service, 1998); and Arnold R. Alanen, "Considering the Ordinary: Vernacular Landscapes in Small Towns and Rural Areas," in *Preserving Cultural Landscapes in America,* ed. A. R. Alanen and R. Z. Melnick (Baltimore: Johns Hopkins University Press, 2000), 112–142.

27. Kathleen Stewart, "An Occupied Place," in *Senses of Place,* ed. S. Feld and K. H. Basso (Santa Fe: School of American Research Press, 1996), 137.

28. Porteous, *Planned to Death,* 227–230. Randall Rohe makes a similar claim in "The Geography and Material Culture of the Western Mining Town," *Material Culture* 16 (1984): 115.

29. Marsh, "Continuity and Decline"; Thomas Dublin, *When the Mines Closed: Stories of Struggles in Hard Times* (Ithaca: Cornell University Press, 1998); William Wyckoff, "Postindustrial Butte," *The Geographical Review* 85:4 (1995): 478–496; Christopher S. Davies, "Wales: Industrial Fallibility and Spirit of Place," *Journal of Cultural Geography* 4:1 (1983): 72–86; Ryden, *Mapping the Invisible Landscape*; Kathleen Stewart, *A Space on the Side of the Road: Cultural Poetics in an "Other" America* (Princeton: Princeton University Press, 1996); Leslie A. Robertson, *Imagining Difference: Legend, Curse, and Spectacle in a Canadian Mining Town* (Vancouver: University of British Columbia Press, 2005); Cecily Neil and Markku Tykklainen, "Introduction," in *Coping with Closure,* 19.

30. Ryden, *Mapping the Invisible Landscape,* 152; Marsh, "Continuity and Decline," 350.

31. Cary W. de Wit, "Field Methods for Investigating Sense of Place," *North American Geographer* 5:1–2 (2003): 5–30.

32. Marsh makes this claim in "Continuity and Decline," 351.

33. Ryden, *Mapping the Invisible Landscape,* 103.

34. See Marsh, "Continuity and Decline," 337–339.

35. Cheng, Kruger, and Daniels, "'Place' As an Integrating Concept," 89, 98, 100.

36. Jonathan M. Smith, Andrew Light, and David Roberts, "Introduction: Philosophies and Geographies of Place," in *Philosophies of Place,* ed. A. Light and J. M. Smith (New York: Rowman & Littlefield, 1998), 6.

37. Kevin Lynch, *Managing the Sense of a Region* (Cambridge: MIT Press, 1976), 3–4.

38. For a critical discussion of place attachment and planning policy in derelict environments, see John A. Agnew, "Devaluing Place: 'People Prosperity Versus Place Prosperity' and Regional Planning," *Environment and Planning D: Society and Space* 1 (1984): 35–45.

39. John Brinckerhoff Jackson, "Goodbye to Evolution," *Landscape* 13:1 (1963): 2.

2.1 Toluca, Illinois, 1999.
Courtesy U.S. Geological Survey—National Center, EROS

CHAPTER TWO

Toluca

IN JANUARY 1997 A NEWS STORY APPEARED ON CABLE NEWS NETWORK (CNN) describing a small Illinois community's fight to save two piles of mining waste—relics of a moribund coal mining industry—from being removed by city bulldozers. "Some people in an Illinois town are going to bat for slag," stated the report. "It looks like a mound of dirt . . . but some say the slag is a national treasure and they want to preserve it." The town was Toluca, a historic coal mining community located 120 miles southwest of Chicago. The television feature described how residents had organized to protect their two landmarks, locally known as "the Jumbos."[1]

Tolucans were grateful for the attention their cause received, but this momentary exposure in the media spotlight provided only a superficial glimpse into a much richer story. The CNN report was typical of mass media items used to round out coverage of the day's "hard" news: a vignette illustrating the seemingly eccentric behavior of folk in a far-off corner of the countryside. By portraying residents' reverence for the Jumbos as strange, CNN trivialized their fight to protect Toluca's industrial heritage.

2.2 The Jumbos. The north Jumbo, at left, rises to a height of approximately 110 feet. Photograph by the author, 1998

The significance of the Jumbos was only partly revealed when CNN stated that the mountains of mining waste represent "heaps of history." The Jumbos, and dozens of similar mounds of mining waste scattered across northern Illinois's historic Longwall Mining District, are the most notable landscape features remaining from a mining era that began more than a century ago (Figure 2.2). The piles, however, are more than just relics of a defunct industry: they are landmarks of complex local value. Resident attachment to the Jumbos is embedded in a past that has seen the community cohere through difficult periods of boom, bust, and economic recovery. They stand as emblems of endurance and serve as memorials to those who built Toluca, particularly those who toiled and died in its mine. The Jumbos are reminders of a past way of life, but they also reinforce Toluca's present value as a community and home. Mining became central to local identity, and although eight decades have passed since the last loads of coal were hauled from the Toluca mine, the industry's physical and social legacies remain central to a local sense of place.

The CNN report failed to accurately interpret mining's role in Toluca, which is consistent with most outside accounts of the town produced since mining began. Toluca's meaning as a lived-in place has been poorly communicated. As is true of many historic mining towns, life was hard in Toluca and the town developed a reputation, partly deserved, as a bawdy and unattractive industrial place. Nevertheless, many residents were satisfied with the lives they led and took pride in their work. They celebrated Toluca's achievements and cherished its spirit of community. Indeed, Toluca survived mine closure largely as a result of the attachments residents cultivated to this tightly knit mining town.

Although outsiders have long viewed Toluca's industrial imprint disparagingly, residents regarded mining's social and physical legacies in more favorable and meaningful ways. In this context, Toluca's struggle to defend the Jumbos takes on greater significance, an effort that culminated in the late 1990s when an innovative reclamation plan was put into action, designed to stabilize these mounds while preserving their historical integrity. At stake was the very meaning Toluca held as place.

THE LONGWALL MINING DISTRICT

Toluca was a part of the Longwall Mining District, which was the site of several notable developments in both the United States and Illinois coal industries. This district was one of the first large-scale commercial coal mining fields to be developed in Illinois and its product facilitated early industrialization of the state. It was also the only coalfield in the United States to rely almost exclusively on the longwall method of mining (described later in this chapter). Despite its significance, however, the Longwall Mining District has received relatively little scholarly attention and the need for a more comprehensive history of the area has been recognized.[2] Such historical background provides a foundation on which to build an understanding of the region's mining culture and the importance of the physical and social legacies the industry has left behind.

Two centuries of nonnative settlement have transformed the central lowlands of northern Illinois, once a poorly drained expanse of tallgrass prairie, into a bountiful agricultural landscape. In many ways, the area now adheres to the idealized images associated with Midwestern landscapes. It is a region of small towns platted along railroads, farming trade centers built around train depots and grain elevators. Fenceless fields of soybean and corn connect horizons, and isolated farmsteads with weathered barns and corncribs dot the countryside. Such pastoral representations, however, only tell part of the story. Although grain farming remains the dominant land use, this is also an industrial landscape. Less common than the grain silos—but no less part of the rural landscape—are the smokestacks, factories, and warehouses of power plants and food processing facilities, and the power lines, railroads, and interstate highways that connect this rural industry to urban markets. The relics of nineteenth-century coal mining operations are also an important part of the local landscape. In more than thirty northern Illinois towns, mounds of mining waste stand in testimony to the fact that industry has been a part of the regional economy for nearly as long as the frontier farm (Map 2.1).[3]

The first recorded discovery of coal in North America occurred in 1673 not far from the future site of Toluca. Discovered in outcrops along the upper Illinois

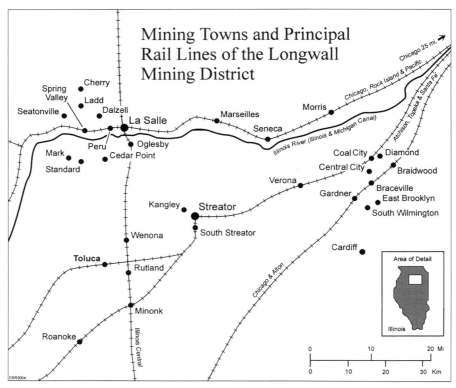

Map 2.1 The Longwall Mining District encompasses parts of nine northern Illinois counties. Shown are the primary coal mining settlements and railroad routes in the district, circa 1910.

River by French explorers Louis Jolliet and Jacques Marquette, this coal deposit would be among the state's first to be exploited when European American settlement pushed into northern Illinois in the 1800s. Early operations were limited to small-scale drift mining in the Illinois River bluffs. During the pre-railroad era, coal was used by blacksmiths and for local domestic purposes, but without a means to transport the bulky resource, growth of the fledgling coal industry stalled. Several developments occurred in northern Illinois in the 1850s, however, that facilitated the development of the coal mining industry. The growth of Chicago increased the demand for coal. The completion of the Illinois and Michigan Canal (1848) and the Chicago & Rock Island Railroad (1854) provided operators with a way to transport coal to that market. The first large-scale commercial coal mining operations in the region developed in 1856 near La Salle. The mines proved profitable, and the industry grew. By 1860, La Salle was the third largest coal-producing county in the state.[4]

La Salle County had become a significant coal-producing area, but the real boom for the northern Illinois district began in 1865 when coal was discovered in the Braidwood region of Will and Grundy Counties, fifty miles southwest of Chicago. Coal was shipped from this area to Chicago over the Chicago & Alton Railroad. Although the coal mining districts of central and southern Illinois are better known, it was the northern field that led in state coal production in the later decades of the nineteenth century. By 1870 the focus of Illinois coal production had shifted north, with Will, Grundy, and La Salle Counties ranked as the second, third, and fourth leading coal producers in the state. From 1875 to 1887 the northern district led all others in total coal production.[5]

Chicago had received coal primarily via water routes from Pennsylvania and Ohio, but with the development of the northern field the city began receiving coal from its hinterland. Northern Illinois coal helped power the early expansion of Chicago industry, and the proximity of the coalfield to that market gave it an economic significance once described as second to none in the state. More importantly, however, the northern coalfield became a supplier of fuel for Illinois railroads, whose operations were central to Chicago's development as a manufacturing and distribution center. The primary mine operators in the northern coalfield were railroad companies. The rapid expansion of the railroads in the 1850s and 1860s brought increased agricultural settlement to the uplands of northern Illinois, and as the discovery of coal in Braidwood revealed, the coal measure outcropping along the Illinois River stretched south into these newly settled regions. Aware that a vast fuel supply lay below their trunk lines, the railroads began developing collieries at points along their routes. Independent mining companies, which also served as fuel agents for the railroads, often operated the mines. Soon, coal mines began to appear farther south and west of established mining areas in La Salle and Braidwood, along the growing network of trunk lines radiating from Chicago. All of the major rail companies running lines west of Chicago developed coal mines in northern Illinois.[6]

As railroad and mining operations spread, the full extent of the coalfield, occupying 1,700 square miles, was realized. The bituminous coal measures underlie portions of nine counties. The most productive vein was the Wilmington Coal. In the Braidwood area, the Wilmington seam was relatively shallow, in places only sixty feet below the surface. In western portions of the field, the coal lay at depths from 350 to 550 feet. Unlike southern Illinois coal, which lay in thick seams averaging 84 to 108 inches, the Wilmington seam had an average thickness of only 38 inches. In terms of quality, the northern coal ranked relatively low with a heating capacity that was sixth among coals in the state. The northern Illinois coalfield, designated by the Illinois State Geological Survey as District One, was also known as the Longwall District.[7]

The relatively even distribution of the Wilmington Coal allowed mines in the Longwall District to be developed near preexisting trunk lines and railroad towns.

That colliery locations were determined by established settlement patterns instead of dictated strictly by geology is a unique characteristic of the Longwall District. Thus, many of the district's mining communities, especially those in southern portions of the field, began as farming villages.

The opening of coal mines quickly transformed these agricultural centers. Mining brought rapid population growth and an influx of European immigrants. Census data reveal that the population of mining settlements in the Longwall District nearly doubled every decade from the 1850s through the 1880s. By 1890 more than 49,000 people lived in the district's mining towns. In 1910 the population peaked at more than 75,000.[8] The district's pioneer miners were mostly of American, Scottish, Irish, and Welsh decent. As the field expanded at the turn of the century, however, labor needs stimulated an influx of immigrants from southern and eastern Europe, including Austro-Hungarians, French, Italians, Poles, Lithuanians, and Russians, of which Italians were the most numerous. The Italian presence was especially strong in the Braidwood and Spring Valley areas and in communities in southern portions of the field, such as Toluca. Many of these Italian immigrants left collieries in Italy to join family and friends already working in the area.[9]

Longwall settlements differed in appearance from mining towns found elsewhere in Illinois. A statement released by the Northern Illinois Coal Operators Association in 1923 reads: "Cities and villages in which the mines are located contain the best of advantages: paved streets, grade and high schools, water works; and living conditions are consequently second to none and must not be confused with the so-called mining camps [of southern Illinois] . . . the homes are owned by the employees, and company houses are practically a thing of the past." Other accounts of Longwall District communities confirm their favorable standing. According to a 1920 state investigation of living conditions in Illinois mining centers, Longwall towns were more "attractive" than the "raw" mining camps that had sprung into existence in southern Illinois. The fact that many of the area's mining towns evolved from agricultural villages largely explains this difference. Unlike southern Illinois mining settlements, public infrastructure and services were well established in these northern towns prior to the mining boom.[10]

Nonetheless, mining transformed Longwall's agricultural communities in ways consistent with traditional mining towns of the era. The industry brought a boom in construction of new businesses and residential areas. European immigration led to the development of an array of ethnically based churches, social organizations, and eateries. The saloon, billiard parlor, and union hall became commonplace. If there was any doubt that coal had not displaced corn as the Longwall mining towns' key commodity, it was soon dispelled by the impressive headframes, powerhouses, and coal chutes of the mining operations and by the growing piles of mine spoil that rose above the prairie landscape.

The Longwall District reached its peak productivity in the first decade of the twentieth century. The period of growth for most mining towns was short-lived, however, with the median lifespan of mines in the district being only fourteen years.[11] The demise of area mines had numerous causes, many of which were related to the longwall method of mining that was employed in the region. Unlike conventional room-and-pillar systems used elsewhere, in longwall mining the entire coal seam was removed, and mining progressed along an extended working face. The layout of longwall mines may be likened to a wheel, the hub representing the shaft pillar, a block of coal left in place to preserve hoisting and ventilation shafts, and the rim representing the constantly enlarging working face of the coal seam. In the longwall system, miners placed waste rock (gob) into the mined-out areas between the working face and the shaft pillar. After the removal of coal, the roof of the mine was allowed to settle onto the carefully stowed gob, which was relied on to preserve working spaces.[12]

The longwall system removed a greater portion of coal from a given seam than conventional room-and-pillar methods, a necessity in the Longwall District, providing a means to profitably exploit the area's thin coal bed. Unfortunately, the longwall method also had disadvantages that limited the competitiveness of district collieries. Longwall mines took a longer time and larger capital investment to bring into production. After a shaft reached coal-bearing strata, no coal could be produced until a stable shaft pillar and working face were cut into place, a process that took seven to ten months. Once under production, longwall mines were more expensive to run because miners spent a good deal of their time packing gob and brushing roofs—"dead work"—time that was more productively spent removing coal in room-and-pillar operations. In 1912 the average underground coal miner in Illinois produced 4.9 tons of coal per day, but miners in the Longwall District produced only 2.4 tons.[13]

Also contributing to the high cost of longwall mining was its relatively high rate of accidents. Longwall mines experienced fewer fatalities than other mining methods but ranked high in the number of non-fatal accidents, the majority of which were caused by falling rock. In 1912, for example, the Longwall District averaged one fatal accident per 1,000 employees, whereas the state average for all mining districts was 2.6 deaths. Still, the district averaged 16.8 nonfatal accidents per 1,000 employees, more than any other district (the state average in 1912 was 10.6). The high accident rate can be attributed to the hazards of longwall mining. The reduced number of fatalities was the result of the lower concentration of explosive gases in the northern coal bed as underground explosions tended to result in greater losses of life than other types of mishaps. Longwall mines, however, were not immune to catastrophe. One of the worst mining disasters in U.S. history occurred in 1909 in the Longwall town of Cherry, where 259 miners were killed in an underground fire. Although the human costs of such disasters and of the hundreds of debilitating accidents that occurred in the district are incalculable, such mishaps had a direct economic impact on operators as they represented lost time and labor. Because of its low coal output per employee and its high accident rate, the Longwall District produced the fewest tons of coal per accident in the state. In 1912 the Longwall District averaged 24,194 tons of coal produced per accident (the state average for all coal districts was 66,866 tons), a statistic that reveals the high human and economic cost of producing Longwall coal.[14]

Operators also faced external constraints that limited the viability of their collieries. Writing on the depressed economic condition of the Longwall District in 1915, geologist Gilbert Cady described how despite apparently ideal transportation facilities and market location, area operators paid higher freight rates than southern coal producers paid. A statement released in 1923 by the Northern Illinois Coal Operators Association described how Longwall coal was "practically barred" from the Chicago market because of the high freight costs. Although located close to the largest coal market in the Midwest, virtually the entire product that the field produced was being shipped westward. With higher transportation rates, lower quality, and less efficiently mined coal, the Longwall District's advantage of nearness to markets disappeared, and the center of Illinois coal production shifted south. The year of peak production in the Longwall District was 1907, when 6.4 million tons of coal was mined. After 1907, production steadily declined, and by 1913, only 4.2 million tons were produced. The decreasing number of Longwall mines operating after 1900 also demonstrates the field's decline: forty-three mines operated in the district between 1900 and 1910; twenty-eight in the 1920s; sixteen in the 1930s; and seven in the 1940s.[15]

With the advent of strip mining, those areas of the field containing shallow coal deposits continued production through the 1940s and 1950s, but the era of underground mining was over. As quickly as collieries opened, stimulating growth and prosperity in area mining towns, the mines closed, triggering out-migration and economic decline. The unemployed miner and his family faced great hardship, and most mining towns experienced significant population loss as miners moved to the southern Illinois coalfields or elsewhere in search of work. Colliery closure had less impact on the area's larger communities, where economies were more diversified and miners were more easily absorbed into other industries. Hard hit, however, were the district's smaller settlements. Of thirty-two Longwall mining towns, twenty experienced at least a 25 percent reduction in population in the decade following mine closure. Eleven of these lost more than 50 percent of their populations. For these centers, the social and economic impact of mine closure was severe, but few of even the hardest hit towns completely disappeared. Workers who chose to stay found new employment in agricultural, manufacturing, and service industries. Although many would never again see populations as large as those of the mining era, almost all of the Longwall District's mining communities endured. Toluca is one such town.

THE INITIAL SITE OF TOLUCA WAS PLATTED ON THE SOUTH SIDE OF THE SANTA FE'S Chicago–to–Kansas City main line in 1889, on land owned by local farmer William

Twist. Recognizing the need for a stop along this section of the railroad—an uninterrupted fifty-mile run between Streator and Chillicothe—Twist petitioned the Santa Fe for the establishment of a depot, and by 1890 the site was made a train stop. Located in Marshall County, the settlement was named Toluca, a toponym with uncertain origins. Allegedly, Mexican railroad laborers were responsible for naming the town after an industrial city in their homeland. According to folklore, a packing case displaying the address of the Mexican city fell from a train. The amused workers nailed a board from the case, which displayed the foreign address, to a shack in the switchyard and the name stuck.[16]

Toluca had humble beginnings. Servicing farmers within a twenty-mile radius, the town initially functioned as an agricultural trade center. Two years after its platting, the village comprised a small residential neighborhood nestled around a post office, a passenger train depot, lumber- and stockyards, and a grain elevator. Toluca's transformation into a mining town began in 1892 when Charles J. Devlin, a fuel agent for the Santa Fe Railroad, prospected the townsite for coal. Three veins of ore were discovered and the Devlin Coal Company purchased the coal rights underlying the village. Soon, more than 150 men were at work preparing the mines. Two mine shafts were sunk just west of the village. The lower vein of coal was reached on September 1, 1893. A third shaft was started one-half mile to the south but was abandoned when its walls caved in. Twist, Devlin, and the Santa Fe Railroad also organized a land company. Housing and business additions bearing their names were platted on the north side of the tracks. The Santa Fe built 200 company-owned homes and a number of rooming houses to accommodate the expected influx of miners.[17]

The first carloads of coal were removed from the mine in 1894 and Toluca soon grew into a bustling mining center. The Toluca mine was opened at a time when others in the district were closing and many who came to the community were unemployed miners from the Braidwood and La Salle areas. Some have estimated the town's population to have been as high as 6,000 in the late 1890s. Although it is possible that such totals were achieved, the 1900 census, the first conducted in Toluca, lists its population at 2,629, which is the highest population listed for Toluca in the census records.[18]

Population growth was directly tied to the fortunes of the colliery. Officially known as Devlin Coal Company Number One, the Toluca mine was reported to be one of the most productive and best equipped in the Longwall District (Figure 2.3). Two shafts penetrated the coal seam lying 512 feet below the surface and averaging a thickness of thirty-four inches. Both shafts accessed the same mine workings. The north (Number One) mine shaft, served as the primary hauling shaft for coal and waste rock. A tall wooden tower, later replaced by a steel headframe, was erected above the mouth of the shaft and was where loaded pit cars were drawn and weighed. Coal was graded and emptied into coal bins to await shipping, and waste rock was moved via an elevated tramway to a large spoil dump—

2.3 The Toluca coal mine, circa 1900. Used with permission, Jack Gerardo private collection

Toluca's north Jumbo. The south (Number Two) mine shaft housed a similar operation, but as the better coal was found in the northeast workings of the mine,
Number Two served primarily as a hauling shaft for men and equipment. Less
rock was removed via the Number Two shaft, resulting in the formation of a
smaller spoil dump where the south Jumbo stands.[19]

Coal production and employment at the Toluca mine dipped in 1897 and
1898 but grew every other year during the first ten years of its operation. Toluca
was the only coal stop for Santa Fe locomotives traveling on the main line between Chicago and Fort Madison, Iowa. Producing more than 1,000 tons of coal
a day, the mine reached both peak production (379,000 tons of coal) and peak
employment (a total of 771 workers, 664 underground) in 1905 (Figure 2.4).[20]

Paid on a piecework basis, miners were paid for each ton of coal they dug.
The mine operators and the United Mine Workers of America (UMWA) negotiated wage scales. In 1907 the Toluca colliery ran two shifts, and the average price
paid to the miners was seventy-five cents per ton. By the 1920s wages had increased to $1.10 per ton, however, eight cents was deducted by the company to
cover operating expenses of the mining machines that were introduced during
the later years of operation. Miners working in the Longwall District generally
earned less than their counterparts in southern Illinois and labor disputes over
wages were common. The wage was especially low considering the strenuous
nature and danger of the work. According to state statistics, 20 men died in the
Toluca mine, and 441 were injured during its operation (1894–1924).[21]

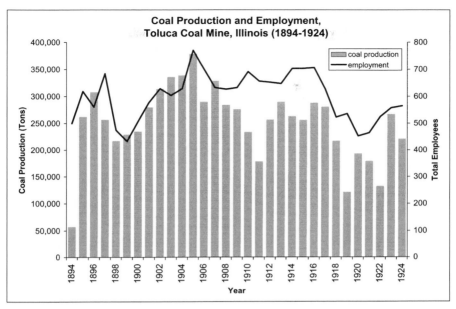

2.4 *Coal production and employment peaked at the Toluca mine in 1905. Over the thirty-one years of its operation, the mine produced an average of 250,000 tons of coal per year and employed 600 workers. The mine closed in 1924. Data from Illinois Bureau of Labor Statistics,* Annual Report . . . Coal in Illinois, *for the years 1894–1898; Illinois Bureau of Labor Statistics,* Annual Coal Report, *for the years 1899–1910; Illinois State Mining Board,* Annual Coal Report, *for the years 1911–1916; Illinois Department of Mines and Minerals,* Annual Coal Report, *for the years 1917–1924*

Some of the first laborers to work the Toluca colliery were African Americans. Little is known of their history in Toluca except that they and their families were not well received by the community. When a Toluca man was lynched near Lacon in 1896, the African American population reportedly moved on and were replaced by European immigrants. By 1900, 39 percent of Toluca's population was foreign-born, haling from places such as Scotland, Ireland, Lithuania, Poland, Russia, Serbia, Austria, and Italy. The majority of the foreign-born miners were Italian, and coal mining was the primary occupation for most male Italians in the area. A number of Italians, however, also established themselves in service enterprises as grocery owners, store clerks, and saloonkeepers. The Anglo majority often marginalized Italian immigrants, but class mobility was possible and several Italians held positions of prominence in the community, even serving as the town's city marshall, fire chief, tax collector, and mayor at times.

Social mobility, however, was not available for the majority of women living in Toluca, who were generally discouraged from working outside the home. Yet, as always, women's labor played an important role in the local economy. In addition to cooking, cleaning, laundering, and childrearing, most women also tended vegetable gardens and livestock. Many women also boarded workers in their homes or operated boardinghouses, an exhaustive, low-paying, and yet necessary service in a mining town.[22]

The types of social institutions and businesses Toluca developed reflects its ethnic diversity. The town contained Italian grocery stores and eateries but its cosmopolitan nature is best reflected in its churches. Anglo American and northern European residents established St John's Lutheran Church (1891–), the Toluca Methodist Episcopal Church (1891–1913), and the Antioch Christian Church (1892–). The First Baptist Church, established to serve Toluca's African American community, existed from 1893–1896. Two Catholic churches were also built; St. Joachim's Parish and schoolhouse (1900–1921) served the Italian community, and St. Ann's Parish (1893–) served the Irish.

The Toluca mine varied in productivity from year to year, but the general trend after 1905, the year of peak coal production and employment, was one of decline. A variety of factors caused fluctuations in production. Low output around 1911 was caused by a change in mine ownership following the bankruptcy of Devlin. Trustees sold the properties in Toluca to the Jackson-Walker Coal & Material Company of Wichita, Kansas, in 1909 for $500,000. The mines were reorganized as the Toluca Coal Company. Other events, such as the statewide strike called by the UMWA in 1910 and the destruction of the Number One shaft tower by fire in the summer of 1914, also diminished production and employment. Compared to other operations in the Longwall District, however, the Toluca colliery had a long lifespan. During the thirty-one years of its operation, the mine produced an average of 250,000 tons of coal per year and employed 600 workers. The colliery closed on May 8, 1924, following a general decline in the price of coal in the years following World War I.[23]

A "RIP-ROARING" TOWN

Written accounts of life in Toluca during the mining era are hard to come by, as its mine closed more than eighty years ago and relatively few documents from the period have been preserved. Nonetheless, information on Toluca's early character can be pieced together from archived newspaper clippings, town and county histories, and, most significantly, reminiscences of residents.

The earliest published accounts of Toluca are promotional in nature. Eager to attract workers to the area, developers began promoting the town prior to the opening of the colliery. "What has Toluca?" asked the first issue of the *Toluca Star,* published in 1893: "[T]he finest coal fields in the great commonwealth of Illinois; the finest farm land in the world and a climate superb. Its water is the purest that Mother Earth contains and its people are prosperous and happy . . . when the shafts have been sunk to coal. That will be the dawning of a new era of prosperity for Toluca. All hail the time!" Toluca was hailed as a soon-to-be "coal and manufacturing metropolis," but in typical fashion, many of the claims made by boosters were gross exaggerations. Described as having "the richest coalfields in the state," one promoter predicted in 1893 that the town would have a population of more than 10,000 inside of a year. Included as "certainties" of the future in an 1895 special Christmas edition of the newspaper was a population of 15,000 and three mines employing 2,000 men. None of these predictions would come true.[24]

Promoters depicted Toluca as a community with a bright future. Coal "is the rock on which Toluca is building, a rock as solid as the Rock of Ages," the *Toluca Star* exclaimed, deliberately ignoring the finite nature of the resource. Some promotional literature, however, did confront the negative aspects of mineral development. The lead article in the 1895 special edition of the *Toluca Star* reads: "The West has seen many towns spring up, as if by magic, during the last few decades. Many of these towns, some of them now important commercial centers, stand today as monuments to American push and enterprise; others with nothing to hold and employ the thousands attracted to them, have fallen to decay and unimportance. There has been so many of these wildcat towns, whose alluring prospects only existed in the heads of designing real estate speculators, that, as a people, we have become very wary, of real estate booms and 'boom-towns.'" The newspaper went on to claim, rather disingenuously, that only actual and existing facts about Toluca would be communicated, "any other course would be foolish and wrong."[25]

The existence of such qualifying statements in promotional material, however insincere, shows that the target audience was aware of the pitfalls of the mining way of life. Many workers were coming from onetime boomtowns elsewhere in the Longwall District; thus, they had experienced mine closure and knew that Toluca's future was uncertain. For the suffering unemployed miner and his family, however, the lure of work was strong and the notion put forth by promoters that Toluca *might* be a different kind of place was likely more than was needed to assuage the apprehensions of incoming residents.

Promotional literature provides some insight into Toluca's early existence, but a more complete picture of the past is found in the firsthand accounts of residents. According to those whose observations were recorded, or those who remained who remembered the mining era, Toluca was in many ways a typically rough-and-tumble mining community. "Toluca was a rough, tough, hardworking, and hard-drinking town made up of Italians, Irish, and Polish people," remarked resident Pete Aimone.[26]

> Toluca was a rip-roaring wide-open town. At one time there were thirty-three taverns, and it was brother against brother. Thursday night was pay night, and women and children stayed off the street because there was bloodthirsty fights, razor fights. There were several murders that took

place. This was quite a town. It looked like a Western town because we had a store called the Great Western and also a cooperative store run by the mine. The miners would go there and buy their things, and they were put on their bill, and then on pay day they would take this out of their pay. Unfortunately, many of the taverns also took plenty of money out of the miners' pay. The women didn't like that too much. The wives were not receptive to that.[27]

Common among resident accounts are stories, often told in a lighthearted manner, of the disorderly nature of the community and the dominant role that Italians played in Toluca's social life. The comments of Jack Gerardo, a retired grocer who lived his entire life in Toluca, provide an example:

Talk about Dodge City, Toluca was a rough old town. . . . It was like Las Vegas or Tombstone or any of those places. Guys would come out 'a taverns with knives in 'em. There was always fight'n over women. . . . I remember one guy took a big knife to the head and came out of a tavern. Died on the sidewalk. There was a black stain on the pavement there for years, bled to death, soaked right into the cement. I used to walk by it everyday on my way to school. Toluca was a wild place and all the mothers would tell their daughters to watch out for them Italians. A lot of girls weren't even allowed in town Thursday and Saturday nights. Oh we had some rough ones here. Holy Christmas! Why I'll tell you, this town really had some hotties.[28]

The comments of Gilbert Flynn, a retired miner from the neighboring town of Rutland, confirm Toluca's boisterous nature: "[T]here were more taverns than anything in Toluca, there was thirty some taverns. The other towns, Wenona, Rutland, Minonk, weren't as bad, Toluca was the worst of the bunch. It was because of the Italians and then the bootlegging days came along and they started bootlegging. . . . [T]his was a tough town." Toluca's notorious reputation is also supported by a claim that during Prohibition, the federal government targeted for cleanup five Illinois cities infamous for bootlegging: Chicago, Peoria, Rockford, Rock Island, and Toluca—the last containing many skilled Italian wine-makers. Although it is difficult to confirm the repeated claim that more than thirty taverns once operated in the community, it is clear that a large number of such establishments were in operation. Sanborn fire insurance maps show twenty saloons operating in downtown Toluca in 1910, seven of which stood on a single block between Railroad and Santa Fe Avenues.[29]

Most historical descriptions of Toluca, particularly those accounts appearing in the newspapers of nearby settlements, contain stories of saloons, bootlegging operations, or the violence common in its streets. Toluca-related stories in the *Lacon Home Journal* during the mining period, for example, are dominated by coverage of Prohibition sting operations, bootlegging arrests, and murder. News from Toluca was rarely positive, and evidence suggests that outside accounts might have been biased by the community's disreputable reputation. The *Lacon Home Journal,* Marshall County's leading newspaper, was selective in the stories it printed about Toluca, favoring reports of outrageous and scandalous events over occurrences with more significant consequences to the town or county.[30] Even at the height of its growth, when its mines were operating at peak production and the town was prospering, Toluca had a difficult time overcoming the stigma associated with mining's influences. Consider the following description that appeared in the *Past and Present of Marshall and Putnam Counties, Illinois,* published in 1907:

> The foreign population is largely of the better class of Italians, although there are enough American residents to give tone to the society. . . . While Toluca is the largest of the towns in Marshall County, containing a population more than three times that of any of the others, it is behind them in embellishments and improvements. The nature of the population being largely miners are more or less shifting all the time and do not take the same interest in their homes and surroundings as do those towns where the inhabitants are more permanently settled.[31]

Archetypal mining town imagery colors historic accounts of Toluca. In fact, stories of Toluca's wild and unpretentious nature are so common that, more than other aspects of its past, they have become ingrained in public memory. Although such perceptions have become an important part of Toluca's internal identity, a conceptualization of place based solely on such imagery is remarkably incomplete. Toluca is remembered as a brawling and boisterous mining camp by residents, but these images have withstood the test of time more readily than others only because they fit mining town stereotypes.

There is another story to be told of Toluca's past. Despite its unruly nature and unostentatious appearance, Toluca held value as a lived-in place. In a 1938 article published in the *Toluca Star-Herald,* H. V. Alexander, the founder of the newspaper, provides a different view of the mining years, one that focuses on favorable aspects of town development and the efforts of residents to build a livable and lasting community:

> A short time after we got things to going good, Postmaster Twist came into the *Star* office. He said: "This town is going to make the big ones stand up and take notice. You can tell them that Toluca is going to have a 'Capitol Hill,' a 'Four Hundred,' and all the high brow stuff that goes with it, and that I am going to start it by building a home that will out-shine them all." Old timers will tell you that Twist did build that home, and that it was the talk of the town for some time. It was too, the starting of Toluca's "Capitol Hill," and there followed many fine new homes. . . . About this time the Santa Fe town site agent let it be known that trees were to be set around all blocks. The varieties selected were ash, black walnut, box elder and silver maple. Everybody volunteered to help set the trees, including myself. . . . The residents of this magic wonder were thrilled when two private rail

cars stopped in front of the Toluca depot. One was of J. W. Reinhart, President of the great Atchison, Topeka & Santa Fe. The other car was that of C. J. Devlin. After thoroughly examining the work at the shafts, they were driven to the bank, the Company stores, all over the town site. Their visit was a revelation to them, and they were not slow, expressing their admiration for the town.[32]

Not as well documented in historical literature, but equally descriptive of life during the mining era, are recollections of mundane aspects of community life. Almost as common in interviews conducted with longtime residents as accounts of taverns, bar fights, and crime are stories related to everyday occurrences: the clouds of dust stirred into the air when cattle were driven down Toluca's unpaved main street; the running of the "doodlebug," a one-car passenger-and-mail train that ran from Toluca to Streator; the sound and sight of miners trudging home in the darkness at the end of the late shift; the ominous blows of the steam whistle sounding at the colliery when an accident occurred underground. Also common, particularly in women's accounts, are lively descriptions of community celebrations: the annual Labor Day parades, Fourth of July picnics, and concerts held Thursday nights by Alphonse Bernardi's Italian Band. Un-extraordinary accounts of town development, the comings and goings of main street businesses, and fond recollections of family and friends are also typical. The pride-felt reflections of longtime resident and funeral director Pete Aimone reveal a more positive side to life in the mining settlement:

> I remember the miners coming home from work and stopping at the coal office. They were lining up for their pay, and they'd be lining up for blocks. A lot of these fellows were drivers of these little mules down below the mine. They had their big black whips and they would snap those whips and we thought they were like Pisarro or something coming in to wreck vengeance on the town. . . . It was a good mine and the Santa Fe railroad stopped every train to get coal and water. We would all go down to the depot to watch the Number Five or the Number Twenty-Two come in. . . . It was a big event. . . . Alphonse Bernardi was the leader of the Toluca Band and it was an excellent band. The band concerts were held on Thursday night . . . right in the center of town. The lumber yard would set up a platform at the corner of Main and Santa Fe. The streets would be lined with cars, and the concert would last two hours. The merchants stayed open and did a land-office-business. The music could be heard up and down at the grocery stores and the taverns. After every number they would all hoot and holler and toot their horns. . . . Many celebrities walked the streets of this town, waiting for the trains to take on water and coal. I remember Pola Negri. She stopped and looked at the marquee on the theatre. One of her pictures was playing. Spencer Tracy also walked these streets, and I'm certain people should know this if they have any knowledge of the history of Toluca.[33]

Resident recollections also include references to a sense of rootedness in place. As is common in mining communities, a portion of Toluca's workforce was transient, coming and going as labor needs at the mine fluctuated. This was especially true of unmarried miners. Many others, however, settled their families in Toluca and established lasting ties to the town. Familial roots ran deep and these bonds to place were strengthened within Toluca's ethnic milieus. Although factions existed, Toluca's ethnic groups, especially the Italians, formed cohesive and nurturing communities. The reflections of Pete Aimone reveal the family ties that bound him to Toluca:

> I remember this town well. My first recollection was when I was a school boy going to school at St Joachim's. It was attached to a little Italian church. My Grandmother was buried there. I have roots in this town. My grandfather and his brother had a business in the old town across the Santa Fe tracks. They later moved down to Main Street and it was called Aimone's Opera House. My father was a barber, a postmaster, county treasurer of Marshall County twice, and also a funeral director and embalmer. I couldn't possibly follow in his footsteps: I took one facet of his work and expanded on that.[34]

Perceptions held of Toluca during the mining years vary substantially. To outsiders, Toluca was a spectacle of debauchery. The view was that of an unadorned, ephemeral, and typically wild mining boomtown. Although this image is also common in resident accounts, their recollections paint a more complete portrait of place as they also include pleasant and everyday memories of community life. Furthermore, residents interpret the town's roughhewn aspects differently than do outsiders, and this difference in interpretation is significant. As is evident in the frequent and often facetious stories told of the town's boisterous beginnings, Toluca had a kind of "rambunctious fraternity," a term coined by scholars who have studied social conditions in mining towns elsewhere.[35] Tolucans are proud that they had the ability to endure the mining way of life. As the comments of miner Joe Vallino reveal, mining was hard and dangerous work but there were advantages to working underground: "Each one of the miners worked individually. . . . [I]t wasn't like working on a bench in a factory, we were independent. If we felt like working we worked, if we didn't we went home. It was up to the miner to produce or he didn't own anything. Oh, it was hard and dangerous work but it was an independent sort of a life. . . . [I]t worked on you in such a way that you begin'ed to have a feeling for it, you enjoyed it in a way."[36]

Vallino's comments also reveal that residents were aware of the negative way outsiders viewed Tolucans. According to Vallino, however, they were an honest people: "Every two weeks the miners would go to the company office. . . . Mr. Martin, the paymaster, he would give us our pay envelope and it was always in cash. I often wondered why it was that he was never robbed. Mr. Martin would go from the bank, pick up this tray of pay envelopes, walk back and pay us all. He walked along there for twenty some years and no one ever bothered him. We were always talked about as being a rough people in Toluca. Hard living, heavy drinking, hard working, but no one ever bothered Mr. Martin. No one ever stuck him up."[37]

There is a duality to the meaning of place in early-day Toluca. Despite its mining town trappings, despite the toil and danger of the mining occupation, the community functioned as a valued home. Pride underlies resident accounts of the past; in this regard, their recollections are the same as one expects to hear recounted in almost any community occupied long enough for residents to lay down roots. Moreover, when the events surrounding mine closure and community survival are analyzed, evidence suggests that these attachments were particularly strong in Toluca. The colliery operated long enough for a second generation of miners to follow their fathers underground. Attachments to place ran deep, and when the mine closed, hundreds of Tolucans were faced with the wrenching decision of choosing between their livelihood and their home. Many chose to stay.

MINE CLOSURE AND COMMUNITY SURVIVAL

In its final years of operation, production and employment in the Toluca mine was relatively high. Annual coal production was greater in the last two years of operation than it had been the previous five years, indicating that there was still plenty of coal in the ground when the decision was made to shut the mine. When closed on May 8, 1924, the mine was running at high capacity, having already produced 221,000 tons of coal that year. Toluca's production had not been decreased over a period of time, as is typical for mines nearing the end of their profitable lifespan. The abrupt halt to production left more than 500 men without work on the day the colliery closed.[38]

Accounts offer various reasons for the mine's closure, and as outside reports of the event show, Toluca's value as a community continued to be overlooked during this difficult period. When the colliery closed, threatening the very existence of Marshall County's largest town, county newspapers focused on the "humorous incidents" that occurred as hoards of panicky depositors pulled their accounts from Toluca's bank. Regional newspapers paid only cursory attention to the cause of mine closure, and, even there, they failed to accurately capture Toluca's plight. An article in the *Henry News Republican,* for example, wrongly claimed that the colliery lost its coal contract with the Santa Fe Railroad.[39]

The primary cause of mine closure was actually a decrease in the operation's profitability, which was strained by a drop in the price of southern Illinois coal and ongoing labor troubles. In March 1924 the value of southern Illinois lump coal dropped seventy-five cents, to $3.00 a ton. For the less-efficient mines in the Longwall District, it was difficult to make a profit at that price. Longwall District miner Gilbert Flynn explained: "They couldn't compete with the big mines in the south. This is only a three foot vein of coal here, and down in the south, they've got eight to ten foot veins. They put machinery down in the mines, but they just couldn't compete around here."[40]

The reduced coal price may well have spelled the end to mining in Toluca; however, some believe that the colliery did not close until labor difficulties forced the mine operator's hand. "I don't want to lay this on the union," stated resident Pete Aimone, "but apparently the Santa Fe decided that the workers contract was getting a little exorbitant. They had a good mine . . . but the Santa Fe decided they had had enough and everything just ceased." William McCall, whose father worked in the mines and was involved in their decommissioning, explains: "[Sharkey Laffins] was the head of the union. He was a tough man. The Santa Fe told him no more strikes, or we're going to close. They went on strike. They closed it down. The next week they were taking the mules out. The week after that they took all the rails out. . . . My dad worked over there for months. They took everything out." It is likely that union troubles played a part in the decision to close the colliery; however, evidence suggests that a shutdown may have already been planned. Attempting to limit losses on their investment in town infrastructure and knowing that the houses would be more difficult to sell once the mine had closed, the Toluca Coal Company offered its company houses for sale to its employees several months prior to shutdown, a practice common to mine operators facing closure. This action suggests that the company was planning to quit the mine well before the union uprising occurred. According to one account, many of the houses were sold. One can speculate that workers who bought houses in the community before losing their jobs faced significant hardship as the decision to close the mine was final. Once the order to quit was made, the mine was quickly disassembled. In addition to mules and track, 580 coal cars and seven mining machines were raised from underground. The rapid dismantling of the colliery nullified any hope of its reopening.[41]

The closing of the mine had a severe impact on the community. According to historic accounts, Toluca lost two-thirds to three-quarters of its population in the year following closure. The census record confirms that the decline was great, although not as high as these estimates. In the 1920 census, the last taken before the mines closed, Toluca's population was listed at 2,503. By 1930 the population had dropped to 1,413, a 43 percent reduction from the mining era population. A decline in the foreign-born population from 36 to 23 percent of residents over the same time period suggests that many of those who left were Italian miners. Generally the poorest with limited prospects for alternate employment, many miners migrated to neighboring mining towns such as Minonk, where collieries were still in operation; to the southern Illinois coalfields; or to urban areas such as Chicago and Peoria.[42]

In May 1925, one year after the mine was closed, the Toluca Coal Company dismantled the hoisting tower over the Number One shaft, the final stage of the salvaging operation, and the mine office prepared to close. At the same time, hearings were held before the Interstate Commerce Commission to consider a plea on behalf of the Chicago & Alton Railroad to allow for the abandonment of their Rutland-to-Granville branch line. Built as a coal line by Devlin and originally named the "Toluca, Marquette & Northern," this line provided the settlement with an important north-south route for grain shipment and passenger service. The hearings marked the beginning of the end for Toluca's second railroad line, and despite attempts by the Greater Toluca Club and other organizations representing communities along the line, the Chicago & Alton quit the road on April 28, 1927. Its loss was another blow to the local economy, which was in the process of making the difficult adjustment back to agricultural production and trade.[43]

Census data, newspaper accounts, and state mine records describe colliery closure, but they provide little detailed information on the hardship Tolucans faced when the mine shut down, a shortcoming that also exists in historical accounts of the event. It is relatively common for mining town histories to overlook mine closure and its aftermath. Historians often view mining settlements as ephemeral "communities of occupation" with few stories left to tell once mines close.[44] Toluca's local histories are a case in point. With the "shaft plugged, the equipment gone, the miners, most of them, scattered to the winds," writes one historian, "a sense of peace and order" descended on the town. In Marshall County Historical Society publications, the post-mining years receive similar cursory attention. A few epilogue-like sentences describe Toluca's resilience: "The Toluca coal mines closed . . . the city's population was reduced by two-thirds. But the city, instead of dying with the mines, made a comeback. . . . The miners' shacks are gone and Toluca is a community of fine homes and thriving business. Like many another community, part of its past was built on a hope and a dream; and like many other communities, it relinquished the dream and built solidly by utilizing opportunities at hand."[45]

The lack of attention to the particulars of mine closure again reveals the influence of the mining imaginary, those popular idealizations of mining and its social and physical influences. Almost exclusively, historians have preferred to remember Toluca as a wild mining boomtown. This incomplete historical record can be partially corrected by exploring the recollections of those who lived through mine closure. Unfortunately, resident accounts are also lacking in detail. When asked about closure, old-timers describe the dismantling of the mine. Some recount the names of those who left. Generally, however, they are unable to recall the period of closure as vividly as they recall the mining era. Why is difficult to determine. Residents may be unwilling to share unpleasant memories of the event, but their memories may also have been affected by the lack of formal interest in the period. So little has been published on Toluca's deindustrialization that a generation has been denied an opportunity to rehearse and recall the events of mine closure. With few occasions to remember this difficult period, many stories have been lost.

What then can be said of mine closure's impact on community life and the meaning Toluca held as a place? With the demise of mining, did the tie that bound residents to the community dissolve, resulting in its ruin? Details may be lacking, but one thing is certain: Toluca did not succumb to ghost town status when the colliery closed. Moreover, the reluctance of many to leave reveals the commitment Tolucans held to place. Many factors enabled Longwall District mining towns to persist, the most important of which was their location in the heart of one of the country's richest agricultural areas. Toluca's trade connection to the Santa Fe and relatively diversified economy, which developed as a result of the colliery's long life, also facilitated the restructuring of the local economy. From a pragmatic standpoint, however, it must have been difficult for residents, especially miners and their families, to remain in Toluca when better paying mining jobs were available elsewhere in the state. The town had lost its primary employer; close to 60 percent of the workforce had been employed by the mine.[46]

Many left Toluca, but more made the decision to remain. For many who stayed, it appears that an important reason for doing so was their unwillingness to abandon their towns. Onetime resident Anna Mae Johnson Terrell sheds light on how Tolucans coped in the years following mine closure. Productive land, she explained, provided a means for survival; however, it was an unwillingness to abandon their community—where friendships and family ties ran deep—that provided a motivation to stay: "Many families went to other areas to work, but for those who stayed, the fertile black soil held the key to survival, not only to the farmers with acres to plant, animals to feed, but also to those who continued to live in the company homes, as there was land enough around them for a big vegetable garden and fruit and nut trees. . . . Many coping skills came into play when the entire town was suddenly out of work. Friendships ran deep—no one locked their doors. Church bells tolled the funerals, rang out the angelus and vespers—everyone was a story teller."[47]

When explored through the eyes of those who lived during the mining era, it is evident that Toluca served as a nurturing home. Mining not only was central to its economic development but, contrary to popular perception, also had a positive influence on the meaning Toluca held as a place. Community and individual identities were rooted in mining's influences, and although deindustrialization severed the industry's economic role in Toluca, it did not break residents' ties to the mining culture. Deindustrialization did not result in the dissolution of community in large part because the social traits that developed during the mining era—an ability to endure hardship and town pride—were unaffected by mine closure. In fact, Toluca's mining culture continues to exert a profound influence on the community even today.

MINING'S LEGACIES

Although Toluca's population was significantly smaller, the community recovered following the initial shock of mine closure. Toluca's average mining era population, measured over three decades, was 2,513. In the eight decades that have passed since mining ceased, its population has ranged between 1,291 and 1,471. Despite a major population decline, economic indicators show that the town has fared relatively well in the post-mining era. It is true that the community has had a long time to recover from mine closure; nonetheless, its survival as an economically viable place defies the notion that mining settlements are, by nature of their nonrenewable resource–based economies, ephemeral places. Indeed, life is comfortable for most Tolucans. Median family income stood at $45,956 in 2000, almost 9 percent higher than the rural national average for towns of similar size. Moreover, the poverty rate in Toluca (4.8 percent) was well below rural national averages (10.9 percent), and the community has developed a surprisingly diverse economy. Agriculture remains a mainstay of the local economy, but more Tolucans now work in manufacturing industries than in any other occupational sector. Toluca boasts garment, sporting equipment, and window manufacturers and an Italian frozen food factory—Bernardi Italian Foods—the largest employer in town.[48]

Toluca has social and economic problems but the same ones confronted in rural communities throughout the country. The town's population, for example, is aged. The 2000 census showed that 27 percent of residents were over the age of sixty-five, well above the national average of 12.4 percent. Moreover, Toluca's 2000 population count of 1,291 is the lowest recorded in its history; a 12 percent decline in population has occurred since 1980.[49] A nationwide rural depopulation trend is affecting Toluca, and the slow but incessant decline in resident numbers has created a variety of challenges, such as the decline in the number of local businesses. Gone are many businesses residents depended on in the mining era, including the Ball and Twist grain elevator, the Fay and Palace Hotels, the Toluca Bottling Works, the Great Western Department Store, a host of dry goods and hardware stores, an auto dealership, and most of the town's saloons. Services, including schools, have also been affected. A significant loss to the community occurred when Toluca High School was closed in 1992. Students now attend high school in nearby Minonk.

Still, in a variety of ways, Toluca remains a healthy community. It maintains elementary and middle schools. It also has a public library, municipal swimming pool, and four churches. Furthermore, although the town's commercial district may be less vibrant today, downtown Toluca remains alive with commerce. Main Street is lined with a bank, bowling alley, farm supply center, post office, several cafes and restaurants, and a variety of other small-town enterprises. Stretching five or six blocks beyond downtown lie Toluca's residential neighborhoods. Most of the original house lots remain occupied by modest, well-kept homes, and, in many respects, Toluca appears to be a typical Illinois farming town. To the discerning eye, however, the cultural landscape reveals legacies of the mining era, such as Mona's and Capponi's Italian restaurants, which were originally established as shot-and-beer parlors in the late 1930s. In the 1960s both eateries came under ownership of the Bernardi family, whose food heritage stretches back to the mining days when they operated the Toluca Meat Market. The two restaurants operate under their original names but are open on alternate days. Serving homemade Italian food, they are immensely popular, drawing visitors from Marshall County and beyond. The success of the establishments spawned the development of Bernardi's Italian Foods.[50]

All founded by Italian immigrants or their descendents, Mona's and Capponi's restaurants and Bernardi's frozen food factory reveal the dominance of Toluca's Italian heritage (Figure 2.5). Italian flags and Virgin Mary statuettes adorn many homes. Evidence that the town was occupied by an array of ethnic groups, not only Italians, is more subtly revealed. Three of Toluca's four remaining churches were established during the mining era. Descendents of Italian and Irish immigrants continue to worship at St. Ann's Parish; those of Anglo American and northern European descent still congregate at the Antioch Christian and St. John's Lutheran churches. The surnames inscribed on the headstones in Toluca's Lutheran and Christian cemeteries and the careful upkeep of the burial grounds show that the descendants of many mining era migrants have remained in the community.

Many structures built in the mining days have disappeared from Toluca, but a number of stately older buildings remain, providing reminders of the substantial economic investment made in the town at the height of the mining era. The old Toluca Public School, an imposing brick structure that once had an enrollment of more than 400 students; the elegant neoclassical First National Bank Building, which now serves as the Toluca Public Library; and the old City Hall with its ground-floor fire station stand in good repair. Among Main Street structures, the building that once housed Tito Palumbo's Tavern still exists. Now operating as the Main Street Pub, the tavern's rustic atmosphere provides an authentic glimpse back to the days when every fourth or fifth downtown business was a saloon. In addition to other mining-era commercial buildings, the community has retained many of its company-built houses. Although some are difficult to identify because of structural modifications, the four-room rectangular houses are typical of the mass-produced company homes built in U.S. mining towns in the early 1900s.

Although remnants of the mining past can be found in Toluca's commercial and residential areas, almost all of the town's mining-related structures have been lost. Salvaged and sold during mine decommissioning, or lost through neglect, all that remains of the hoisting towers, power and fan houses, coal chutes, machine shops, and other industrial features are a few cement foundations. Prior to the summer of 2000, when reclamation activities transformed the old mine site, Toluca's

2.5 The Italian influence remains strong in Toluca. Above, Mona's restaurant. At right, Pete Venturi, son of an immigrant miner, stands with his wife Betty in front of their Toluca home. Photographs by the author, 1998

industrial ruins lay covered under a tangled forest. The foundations of the fan house and water reservoir and a concrete slab sitting atop the opening of the Number One mine were all that remained of the impressive surface structures once used to process coal and transport men and mules from the vast excavation underlying the settlement. Having collapsed into a conical depression and partially filled with debris and trash, the Number Two mine shaft lay hidden in the forested back acreage of the mine yard.

Indeed, the only obvious remnant from Toluca's industrial past are the Jumbos. Visible throughout the community and from many miles distant, Toluca's two piles of mining waste tower over the old mine yard. Often referred to as "slag piles" (slag is a waste produced from smelted metal ore), the Jumbos actually consist of mine gob (small fragments of shale, clay, coal, and other minerals removed from the mine). During the mine's operation, gob was conveyed from the shafts by way of elevated tramways running to the top of the waste piles. The tracks of the tramways were lengthened as the piles grew, resulting in the formation of two elongated conical mounds. Toluca's Jumbos differ in appearance. The north Jumbo, located closest to the townsite, is the larger of the mounds. Prior to being reclaimed, the slopes of the north Jumbo were sparsely vegetated and the feature had a striking red hue, the result of burning and oxidation. In the 1980s the height of the north Jumbo was measured at 110 feet. As locals seldom failed to mention, however, the Jumbo had shrunk considerably since the mining era. Deep gullies along its sides and the thick apron of red alluvium encircling its base showed that erosion was slowly wearing down the Jumbo. The south Jumbo, adjacent to the Number Two shaft, measured ninety-five feet in height, and unlike the north Jumbo, a forest of black locust and cherry trees blanketed its slopes.

The Jumbos are Toluca's most notable landscape features, and the bulk of outside attention the town has received in recent years has focused on the landmarks. A description of Toluca appearing in the *Illinois Guide and Gazetteer* in 1969 read: "Two inverted cones of slag, pink in the rays of sunrise and sunset, tower 200 feet above this central Illinois town, monuments to long-dead coal mines which begot and reared the community." In another account, county historian Eleanor Bussell identifies the Jumbos as one of the region's most significant features. "Consider the county as a living museum," Bussell writes, "have a close-up look at the twin pink and gray slag piles which dominate the skyline and are monuments to those years when coal was industrial king here." A 1999 community editorial appearing in the *Bloomington Pantagraph* opened with the statement: "Toluca usually brings to mind a couple of good Italian restaurants and two huge hills at the south edge of town." Even the *Chicago Daily News,* in reporting the defeat of the Toluca High School basketball team at the 1962 state tournament, made mention of the Jumbos: "No victory fires burned last night on Toluca's mountains—the two huge slag heaps that stand beside the abandoned coal mines that once were the town's major industry."[51]

The Jumbos have become central to Toluca's outside image, as a community exposé written by *Peoria Journal Star* reporter Jerry Klein in 1975 confirms. Klein paints a quaint portrait of the town, one in which the Jumbos play a prominent role. The features are associated with the anticipation experienced by Italian food lovers on their "gustatory pilgrimages" to Toluca. Klein writes: "The great slag pile known as Jumbo still lies beyond the horizon, and there are miles to go before one eats." More significantly, Klein describes the history of Toluca and entwines his narrative with wistful images of the Jumbos: "All that is left of the mine is Jumbo, the red and weathered pile of slag." His regretful account of how Santa Fe locomotives now thunder past this once important train stop also includes reference to the features: "There is the noon whistle again, stirring long echoes. It caroms off the furrowed sides of Jumbo and reverberates off across the prairie."[52]

These accounts of Toluca represent a shift in outside perception. The town's image changed following mine closure; negative outside perceptions faded. No longer burdened by mining's detrimental influences, a positive aesthetic has come to dominate outside accounts of Toluca. Furthermore, external representations, once highly critical of Toluca's mining culture, are now inclined to romanticize the industry's legacies. As reminders of the mining industry were erased from the landscape, nostalgia for what was left set in and Toluca's industrial detritus became quixotic reminders of the town's history. "Big Jumbo and Little Jumbo slag heaps rear their cones high above the prairies," writes a county historian, "sole reminders of the boom days when Toluca was a thriving mining community." Mining's demise and nostalgia for a past way of life may explain the change that has occurred in external perceptions of the town. It is also likely, however, that outside accounts merely came to reflect more accurately the views of Tolucans, who have always respected mining's influences and legacies. Nowhere is such sentiment better revealed than in the community's efforts to protect and preserve the Jumbos.[53]

SAVING THE JUMBOS

Resident Dominic Valesano purchased the colliery property after the Toluca mine closed. An ex-miner, Valesano operated a mule yard and grazed cattle on the site. Following his accidental death in 1939—an incident that has become an important part of town lore—the property was willed on. By the 1980s the heirs to the Valesano trust no longer resided in Toluca. The property lay unused and was frequently trespassed on: refuse was dumped in the area and gob was occasionally removed from the Jumbos. Although such activity was frowned on, Tolucans did not become actively involved in protecting the property until rumors began to circulate in 1985 that the Jumbos were about to be removed. As was evident by the debate that ensued, mining remained central to Toluca's identity.

In 1985, construction was underway on a new interstate highway (I-39) located five miles east of Toluca. Aware that highway contractors were using gob piles in neighboring Minonk for fill material, Tolucans heard rumors that the Jumbos were to be put to similar use. In a front-page article appearing in the *Toluca Star* in October 1985, resident Glenna Schmitt called the community to action: "Rumor is that our two monuments will soon be gone. The state plans to use the shale for landfill for the new state highway. We should not let this happen! All should band together. . . . Write our state officials. Come to council meetings and urge our Mayor to take action. Start now before it is too late!" The first "Save the Jumbos" campaign had begun and residents of all ages joined the fight. Additional letters in support of the Jumbos appeared in the *Toluca Star*. At one point, high school students painted bed sheets with the "Save the Jumbos" slogan and placed them on the side of the north Jumbo. A petition was organized by resident Elton Pearson, who obtained the signature of close to 300 Tolucans demanding that the Jumbos be protected. As a result of these efforts, the Toluca City Council was urged to take action. In November 1985 Mayor Larry Harber announced, quoting written assurances from the Illinois Department of Transportation, that the Jumbos would not be used for highway construction.[54]

Several months later, a letter sent to the *Toluca Star* by Anna Mae Johnson Terrell, Dominic Valesano's granddaughter and part owner of the Jumbo property, revealed that the family had had no intention of selling the Jumbos to the state. The Jumbos were valued by their owners as much as they were by those living in Toluca, and Johnson Terrell encouraged the community to do everything it could to protect the landmarks:

The "Save the Jumbo" campaign has brought attention to the affection all of us have for the Jumbos. We climbed them as children, walked sons, daughters and even grandchildren up to the top to look around. The Jumbos are Toluca. No one wants that lovely wooded area preserved more than the nieces and nephews Barney Valesano willed the land to. We love it! We played there as children, we visit as adults. But we don't live here. Therefore, it is up to the residents of Toluca who care about the area, to see that laws are not broken, that shale is not taken, discards are not dumped, that signs be maintained so strangers do not consider it public property and abuse it. No one in the Valesano trust wants to sell any part of the Jumbo; but sometimes we get discouraged when we see it. The Jumbos need your help. It's up to you to save the Jumbos.[55]

Although the rumored threat to the Jumbos was largely without basis, the rumors of their possible removal and the subsequent fight to protect them heightened awareness of their value to the community. For several years following this event, however, little progress was made in the way of protecting the Jumbos from misuse.[56] It was not until 1995 that such sentiment was reawakened. The City of Toluca had begun searching for a site to construct a new wastewater treatment plant and Elton Pearson suggested buying the Valesano property for this purpose. Of the 101 acres owned by the family, 40 acres were suitable for construction and farming. Pearson suggested that ten of these acres could be used for the water treatment facility and that the city could lease the remaining thirty acres to local farmers. The other sixty-one acres of the mine property, the Jumbo site, could then be set aside for preservation. Pearson's proposal was appealing to the city for the Valesano family was willing to sell the forty acres of prime land and then donate the remainder of the property as a gift to the people of Toluca. Pearson organized a second citizen petition, this time urging the city to act on buying the Jumbo property. Signatures were again collected from nearly 300 residents. Soon after, the Jumbos were purchased by the City of Toluca.[57]

For those concerned with preserving the Jumbos, the city's purchase was viewed as an important accomplishment. Unfortunately, its early stewardship of the area proved controversial. The new wastewater treatment plant was built south of the main Jumbo in 1996. In the process of constructing the plant's access road, however, city contractors removed a large volume of shale from the base of the north Jumbo, leaving an excavation scar on its western slope (Figure 2.6). According to the city, the decision to use the Jumbo for road fill, an action that saved an estimated $30,000 in materials, was a blameless mistake made by the construction firm. Whoever made that decision, however, failed to foresee the outrage it would generate in the community. According to Pearson, the Jumbo had been "defaced." The excavation, which was visible from the townsite, came within several feet of the Jumbo's backbone. Long used as a walking path to its top, the ridge began to crumble into the excavation.[58]

2.6 The excavation scar on the north Jumbo. City of Toluca contractors removed gob from the base of the Jumbo for use as fill material. Photograph by the author, 1998

Once again, letters printed in the *Toluca Star* urged residents to come to the Jumbo's defense. Pearson wrote: "Walk over and see the large gouge visible on the west side of the Jumbo. It is almost impossible to climb to the top anymore. We wanted our elected officials to preserve our Jumbos from others hauling them away. Now our own officials are using them up." In the same edition, Johnson Terrell urged residents to protect the Jumbos before they became "the Toluca mole hills." She wrote: "The City of Toluca now owns the Jumbos. It belongs to the people. If they still feel an affection for them, perhaps it might be time to think once again about saving the Jumbos."[59]

A newspaper reporter from the *Bloomington Pantagraph* was present when Tolucans raised their concerns about the Jumbos at a city council meeting in October 1996. Soon after, the *Pantagraph* ran the Jumbo story under the title "Slag Piles Earn City Heaps of Attention." Articles in the *Peoria Journal Star* and *Chicago Tribune* followed, and after the Associated Press picked up the story, it found its way onto CNN television.[60] The media attention Toluca received was supportive of the residents' cause, and in the midst of this publicity, the city council unanimously approved passage of a resolution recognizing the Jumbos to be part of the community's heritage. The resolution was printed on the front page of the *Toluca Star* on October 24, 1996. It read: "The Jumbos are declared to be part of the heritage of the City of Toluca, to be preserved and protected, and any further diversion is declared to be against the policy of the City."[61]

The city council had issued a formal statement declaring its intent to protect the Jumbos from further disturbance. Concern remained among some, however, that the resolution's non-binding status left the property inadequately protected. As a result, in November 1997, a group of the Jumbos' most vocal advocates created a nonprofit organization called "Toluca Coal Mine Preservation and Development." The group's mandate was to ensure preservation of the Jumbos and to develop the site for the educational and recreational betterment of the community. The organization's short-term plans included a cleanup of the mine property. Their longer-term goals included restoration of the excavation scar and the construction of hiking trails, a picnic area, and, ultimately, a miners' memorial adjacent to the north Jumbo.[62]

Toluca Coal Mine Preservation and Development has actively pursued these goals. Since its founding in 1997, the group has held a membership of approximately thirty-five residents. It has issued regular press releases of its activities, organized community tours of the mine site, and even run a Jumbo float in Toluca's annual Labor Day parade. The organization's primary function is to assist the city in managing the Jumbo property and its members have played a central role in promoting site improvements.

Tolucans have expended considerable effort ensuring that the Jumbos are not disturbed. But why? Why have residents fought to protect and preserve these two piles of industrial waste? Answers emerge from considering the numerous roles the Jumbos have served in Toluca. The Jumbos serve practical needs and have become icons of the town. They also stand as memorials to those who died working in the mine and to a way of life that Tolucans are not willing to forget. More broadly, the Jumbos have become important venues of social meaning, tangible features of the local landscape that help maintain individual identities and a collective sense of place. Several of these functions are evident in "The Jumbos," a poem written by resident Marion Brandt, a former schoolteacher in Toluca:

The Jumbos are our landmarks,
They're really a tradition;
To climb them sometimes during life
Has been each one's ambition.

And when we're at the very top,
So many things we see;
It makes us stop and think
How thankful we should be.

We think about the ones long gone
Who built this little town,
And hope that all who live here now
Will never let it down.

We all do love the Jumbos,
We've loved them through the years;

They've been there in our smiles
And even through our tears.

We hope they're always with us
And we will never part,
For our beloved Jumbos
Are in Tolucans' hearts.[63]

Brandt's poem was designed to capture the feelings of the community when the Jumbos were threatened, and as revealed in the opening stanzas, the landmarks have significant practical value to residents. The relief the Jumbos provide and the wooded mine yard in which they stand are amenities not available in the surrounding countryside. Most Tolucans have climbed to the top of the north Jumbo to enjoy the impressive vista: a 360-degree view over the town and surrounding farmland. On a clear day, gob piles in Wenona, Mark, and Standard, lying as far away as twenty miles to the north, can be seen from atop the north Jumbo, a scene that connects Toluca to neighboring mining communities in the Longwall District. The old mine property also stands as an accessible island of wildness in what is otherwise a landscape of cultivated private landholdings. For many years, residents have been walking the wooded trails that wind through the area, picnicking, playing, and in other ways using the site.

The Jumbo area has been especially well used by children. Although adults often express safety concerns, many admit that the property was their favorite childhood play area. Memories of playing on the Jumbos are common. In winter, children sled down the mounds in cardboard boxes and on discarded car hoods. Jack Gerardo recalled a time when a rope hung from a flagpole erected near the summit of the north Jumbo, providing a terrifying swing over its side. For many years, the site was also home to Toluca's most important recreational amenity, the Legion Swimming Pool. Lying adjacent to the north Jumbo, the pool was built from the remains of the colliery's water reservoir. Brandt fondly recalled, "I remember swimming there . . . floating on my back watching the moon come up over the Jumbo."[64]

In addition to leisure uses, the Jumbos also serve a variety of less tangible functions. The Jumbos have become symbols of Toluca and their iconic value is reflected in the widespread use of their image to represent the town (Figure 2.7). The gob piles adorn the city flag and the town crest worn by municipal employees. The front-page banner of the weekly *Toluca Star* displays a sketch of the Jumbos. They are also prominent on the community's two welcoming signs, where their image declares the uniqueness of the town to visitors. Just as important, the landmarks remind residents that their town is a place set off from the rest.

The Jumbos are locally referred to as Toluca's "trademarks." Indeed, the "Jumbo" name is not used for other communities' gob piles. Although other historic mining settlements in the area have similar features, Tolucans downplay the signifi-

2.7 The Jumbo image appears on Toluca's welcoming signs. Photograph by the author, 1998

cance of their neighbors' gob piles when asked about them. Brandt said that the mound in nearby Wenona, which is also displayed on welcoming signs, "has no name." Moreover, she said that Wenona's gob pile "doesn't have the same feeling like here." The comments of Barney DeRubeis, a founding member of Toluca Coal Mine Preservation and Development, provide further insight: "If you go into other towns that have these Jumbos—well I call them Jumbos—and you say, 'I see you got a Jumbo here in town,' they'll say, 'What's that?' The best thing about our Jumbos is that when you're coming into town, from the north especially, you look right at them; they're the focal point of the road. You see the Jumbos before you see anything else. . . . A lot of these other ones are along the highway off to the side, but in Toluca they're right there. You see them coming in from the east and from the west. You see the Jumbos." As residents young and old attest, the Jumbos are unique markers of their home. Several recounted the strong feelings they experience at the first sight of the landmarks when returning from an extended period away. "When you're coming to Toluca and you see the Jumbos," stated Brandt, "you know you're home!"[65]

The Jumbos also function as historic landmarks. When residents were asked to describe their significance, they almost always recounted Toluca's history. The Jumbos stand as a landscape mnemonic that stimulates memory of the mining past. "At one time we had a population of 5,000 people," stated Pearson, "and it's all because of the Jumbos." The ability of the landmarks to facilitate public memory of Toluca's economic history is obvious and media accounts of the town's efforts to protect the Jumbos have focused on this association. For many Tolucans, however, the Jumbos are more than just symbolic relics of a founding industry; they represent rooted aspects of self and social-group identity. The Jumbos reinforce familial ties to the community and ethnic and class membership. The gob piles were produced from the labor of many relatives. Mayor Larry Harber explained, "[W]ith the ancestors here . . . there's still a lot of memories." For those descended from European emigrants, the Jumbos also represent the beginning of their families' lives in the United States. One resident clarified, "[A]ll the immigrants, the poor people, worked in those mines." Using the mine and its waste pile as a metaphor, he said that the Jumbos represent the immigrants' "getting out of the hole."[66]

The Jumbos also stand as memorials to those who died in the mine. Mayor Harber remarked: "[T]he Jumbos represent all of the men who died in the mine. . . . [M]y wife's father worked in the mine all of his life and my wife's uncle, he got killed in there; he was only twenty-one, got kicked by a mule." Glenna Schmitt recognized the commemorative role of the Jumbos when she wrote, "[T]he Jumbos stand in their glory as a vivid memorial to our descendants who toiled long and hard in the bowels of the earth." The construction of a miners' memorial has long been a goal of Toluca Coal Mine Preservation and Development. In the absence of a formal memorial, however, the Jumbos serve this role.[67]

Literally and metaphorically, the Jumbos serve as elevating features. They are promontories on which Tolucans can gaze at their town. They give Toluca an iconic prominence, standing as symbols of the community's uniqueness. They also serve as beacons of home. So, too, the Jumbos are visible manifestations of the mining past. They facilitate memory of a founding industry and are reminders of those who pursued the mining way of life. In these ways, the Jumbos play a prominent role in facilitating a sense of place in Toluca. Their ability to reinforce social-group identity is further revealed in the stories residents tell about the features.

One of the most frequently shared stories in Toluca involves the disappearance of Dominic Valesano, the first owner of the abandoned mining property. According to town folklore, Valesano disappeared from Toluca in May 1939. "One morning he ate breakfast and they never saw him again," explained Jack Gerardo. After a two-week search failed to locate Valesano, Gerardo speculated that he may have fallen into the unsealed mine shaft adjacent to the north Jumbo. With the help of his brother Frank and his friend Bob Guderjan, Gerardo devised an ingenious plan that not only solved the mystery of Valesano's disappearance but also brought Toluca nationwide attention. The three men assembled a camera and flash unit, attached it to a telephone cable, and lowered it into the mine. Photographs taken at the base of the shaft showed Valesano's body wedged between beams 400 feet below the surface. The mystery was solved and the three young men became instant celebrities. Their story, accompanied by the gruesome photograph, ran in newspapers across the country. The tale of Valesano's disappearance and Jack Gerardo's terrible discovery is legendary in Toluca. As one of the last alive who could recall the mining era firsthand, Gerardo was also viewed as a principal keeper of mining lore. With his passing in 2000, the community lost an important link to its past.[68]

Another story relating to the Jumbos occurred in 1929. In the summer of that year, a tornado moving toward Toluca was allegedly deflected by the Jumbos, saving the town from certain destruction. Jack Gerardo provided the most colorful account: "The tornado came up from the southwest. I saw it up on top of the Jumbo twirling like this here [motions with his hand] and all kinds of dust was coming up. I saw this happen. It looked like the Jumbo saved us I can tell you that. The tornado just stood spinning up there in the dirt. It damaged a few homes around here . . . but the Jumbos were a good thing." Others recalled the tornado story. "That's the day the Jumbos saved Toluca," one resident remarked, and her friend added, "[A]nd that's another reason why we should keep the Jumbos."[69]

In addition to the shared folklore, most Tolucans have personal tales about the Jumbos. Residents convey stories passed down from the mining era and recount memories of childhood experiences playing in the mine yard. Although not all Jumbo references are positive—tales of personal mishap, of packs of coyotes living within the wooded mine yard, and of poisonous gases leaking from open mine shafts are also told—even those with negative stories recognize the Jumbos' value to the community. In addition, a new genre of Jumbo lore—the story of the town's fight to save the features—is now being related. These landscape-centered narratives continue to nurture a sense of place in Toluca. In the stories residents share about the Jumbos, in their daily interaction with these symbolic landmarks, is cultivated a community's identity. Barney DeRubeis stated, "[T]he Jumbos are like one of our kids. . . . [W]e grew up with them." Mayor Harber said, "[T]he Jumbos are a part of us!" This sentiment explains why the surviving mining landscape has been protected in Toluca.[70]

RECLAIMING THE JUMBOS

In a 1996 article covering residents' efforts to protect the Jumbos from disturbance by the City of Toluca, Phil Luciano of the *Peoria Journal Star* wrote: "Outsiders might see the public sentiment as merely making mountains out of coal hills, the waste product from thirty years of mining. But the Jumbos mean much more to Toluca." Luciano predicted that a successful defense of the Jumbos would require city officials to recognize "what the heaps mean to Toluca," and this observation also applied to state bureaucrats in whose hands the Jumbos' fate soon lay. Residents enthusiastically supported efforts to save the Jumbos. Obtaining public ownership of the property and convincing the city that the features should be preserved were significant accomplishments. Once achieved, however, Tolucans were faced with a new set of challenges: namely, balancing the local desire for preservation with state-directed reclamation needs.[71]

Toluca Coal Mine Preservation and Development envisioned preserving the Jumbos and developing the site into a public park, but environmental concerns complicated this task. For Abandoned Mined Lands Reclamation Division officials at the Illinois Department of Natural Resources (hereafter, "DNR"), the Jumbos represented mounds of chemically active, eroding mine waste. The mine site also contained significant safety hazards. Convincing the DNR that energy and capital should be devoted to preserving the area and increasing public access to it would not be easy. The heritage value of mining landscapes is often overlooked in abandoned mine land reclamation planning, as its overriding purpose is to protect public safety and the environment. After conducting early environmental assessments of Toluca's mine land, the state recommended a complete grading of the Jumbo property.

These assessments were done when the DNR conducted environmental inventories of all abandoned coal mining sites in Illinois as required by the Surface Mining Control and Reclamation Act (1977).[72] The goal was to identify and prioritize sites in need of reclamation. The state identified more than 120 gob piles standing in the historic Longwall Mining District. A detailed study of 18 sites showed that acid mine drainage and sedimentation impacts were common problems associated with the mounds, as were public safety concerns. Unsealed vertical shaft openings posed the greatest risk. According to research conducted by the Illinois Geological Survey in the early 1980s, the mine gob could be safely used for construction purposes, including road fill. The research also showed that reducing slope angles and establishing a vegetation cover on gob piles could address acid drainage and sedimentation impacts. These findings guided early reclamation projects conducted by the DNR in the Longwall region. In the 1980s and early 1990s many gob piles in the district—including those near Mark, Morris, Spring Valley, Peru, Ladd, and Standard—were graded or removed through state-funded reclamation.[73]

The Toluca mine site was inventoried by the state in 1981. The environmental assessment identified sedimentation problems on the north Jumbo and revealed that acid discharges were leaching from the gob pile. State investigators recommended that the gob piles be removed, graded, and revegetated. Wildlife habitat was the only post-reclamation land use identified for the area.[74] Had resident input been included in the environmental inventory, however, it is likely that other land use alternatives would have been identified. Likewise, it seems a certainty that Tolucans would have resisted the DNR had it attempted to implement this reclamation plan; after all, they would soon rally to save the Jumbos from a far lesser disturbance by the city. Fortunately, the site's environmental problems were less severe than those existing at other abandoned mine sites in the state and the DNR classified Toluca as a low-priority reclamation site. As a result, nearly two decades passed before reclamation of the Jumbo property was initiated. By that time, the DNR had altered its approach to reclamation in the Longwall District, a change that dramatically altered reclamation plans for the Jumbos. Preservation values were not considered in the initial mine site inventory, but they were to play a central role when the DNR returned to Toluca.

The social and historical significance of Longwall District mine sites was identified in state research conducted in the mid-1980s, but the DNR initially ignored these findings.[75] In so doing, the agency became embroiled in several controversial reclamation projects in the area. In the nearby town of Mark, for example, residents fiercely opposed reclamation of two gob piles. According to local account, the larger of the Mark mounds once stood 500 feet high, making it the tallest in the district. In the mid-1980s, however, in an attempt to stabilize the mine dumps, which were slumping onto adjacent farmland, the DNR merged the two landmarks into a single pile. The mound was then graded down to a height of 135 feet. Longtime Mark resident Ray Justi described how the re-claimed pile was "ugly." He commented: "It's not what the miners created. It's an abortion, a perversion of what it used to be." Justi explained that he would have preferred the state to have completely removed the mounds rather than leave the rounded pile that stands in Mark today. Tolucan Pete Venturi also recalled the Mark project and his comments show that Tolucans were following reclamation projects in neighboring communities. "Over at Mark the state spent 250,000 bucks or more, it was environmental stuff," Venturi said. "The mound at Mark was its original shape outside of erosion. Mark had a beautiful one, shaped real pretty, but the state went over there and put bulldozers on it ... and then they tried to plant stuff on it. Well Mark raised Hell, they didn't want it done. Oh man did they raise Hell but they went and done it anyway. They dressed it all down and planted it."[76]

To be fair, the DNR faced a difficult task; stabilizing the slopes of gob piles and removing safety hazards were difficult goals to accomplish without signifi-cantly altering the mining landscape. It should also be noted that the DNR re-sponded to the problems it experienced in Mark and elsewhere and that today its abandoned mine land reclamation program is one of the most innovative in the United States. More than other state reclamation programs, the Illinois agency has tended to consider alternatives to the standard return-to-original-contour approach that dominates the reclamation field. The DNR's groundbreaking, al-beit controversial, *Effigy Tumuli* project, located on a Longwall area strip mine near Ottawa, Illinois, is an example. Designed by landscape artist Michael Heizer, the project is a tribute to Native American burial grounds; five enormous earthen sculptures—a snake, turtle, catfish, frog, and water strider—have been fashioned from the strip mine spoil.[77]

The DNR learned a valuable lesson from the problems it encountered in early reclamation projects conducted in the Longwall District, and the office developed a greater sensitivity to local desires. In fact, intrusive reclamation projects are no longer being considered at some Longwall sites because of the social value the dumps hold for the communities in which they stand. Mine sites in the towns of Roanoke (located twenty miles southwest of Toluca) and Cherry (thirty miles to the north) provide examples (Figure 2.8). The City of Roanoke flies a U.S. flag on the pinnacle of its gob pile; a lighted cross stands on the peak during religious holidays. Like Toluca's Jumbos, the Roanoke pile stands as a community landmark. Similarly, the gob pile in Cherry has important historical significance. Cherry's mine dump serves as a backdrop for a state historical marker memorializing the 259 miners killed in a fire that swept through the mine in 1909, one of the worst mine disasters in U.S. history.[78]

Now, prior to considering reclamation alternatives at Longwall District mine sites, the DNR waits for a consensus to be reached within affected communities on what type of work is acceptable. Little negotiation is possible, however, when considering mitigation options for high-priority hazards, such as unsealed mine shafts; but the DNR no longer undertakes lower-priority work without first obtaining resident input. This strategy was employed at Toluca, where, by law, the DNR was not obligated to reclaim the Jumbos, which were classified as low-priority hazards. Nevertheless, as high-priority hazards existed at the mine site in the form of two unsealed mine shafts, the state would, in the process of addressing these unsealed shafts, consider local proposals for stabilizing the Jumbos. The DNR did not become involved in reclaiming the features until Tolucans requested their assistance. As a first step, the agency required that the community formulate a vision for the Jumbo property.[79]

Shortly after the city purchased the Jumbo property, the site was leased to the Toluca Sportsmen's Club for a nominal rent of $1 per year for recreational purposes. Under the lease, the Jumbos remained accessible to the public and residents continued to informally use the mine site. Toluca Coal Mine Preservation and Development, however, kept debate over the area's future alive. The group continued to evoke "save the Jumbos" sentiment in the community, this time directed toward formal reclamation and development of the Jumbo property. In March 1998, at the state's urging, the organization conducted a resident survey in which Tolucans were asked to identify potential uses for the site. The variety of responses included creation of a public park with pathways, fishing ponds, and camping sites; construction of a miners' memorial; expanded opportunities for farming; and creation of a municipal dump. Some preferred to leave the site as is, at most only removing trash and debris to improve its appearance. This position was held by the Toluca Sportsmen's Club, whose members favored maintenance of wildlife habitat. Concerns over monetary and legal matters were also expressed. "This site for a park has many drawbacks," wrote resident Leah Bakel in the *Peoria Journal Star*. She explained: "If someone were injured climbing the Jumbo, a lawsuit against the City is certainly a possibility. Another hazard is the main line of the Santa Fe railroad, which runs adjacent to the property. Most people would have to cross the

2.8 The Roanoke (top) and Cherry (bottom) gob piles. Like Toluca's Jumbos, these features stand as community landmarks. Photographs by the author, 1998

tracks to get to the park. . . . We already have a beautiful park in Toluca. Surely for a city the size of Toluca, one park is enough. Lets take care of the one we have. Saving the Jumbo is a worthy cause, but it is not a suitable site for a park."[80]

Although residents disagreed on how the site should be used, Toluca Coal Mine Preservation and Development continued to push for major improvements to the Jumbo property and its enthusiasm for recreational development and historic preservation eventually caught on. In May 1998 the city agreed to consider development plans for the property. Discussions were initiated with the DNR and Prairie Rivers Resource Conservation and Development Council (hereafter "Prairie Rivers"), a state regional development program. Representatives from both state agencies attended town meetings, and in consultation with the city, the Sportsmen's Club, and Toluca Coal Mine Preservation and Development, Prairie Rivers drafted a preliminary reclamation plan, which was then forwarded to the DNR.[81]

The reclamation plan, submitted to the DNR in 1999, called for stabilizing the north Jumbo and sealing the two mine shafts. It also included the construction of walking trails, a pathway to the top of the north Jumbo, picnic and parking areas, and a miners' memorial. The DNR agreed that the smaller south Jumbo did not require reclamation work. The mound had developed a forest cover over most of its slopes and was reasonably stable. Other than sealing the south mine shaft, the southern part of the property would remain untouched, a decision that addressed the Sportsmen's Club's desire to maintain wildlife habitat. The DNR also agreed to preserve the foundations of several mine-related structures and, as was later proposed, create a fishing pond on the site. These design features could be incorporated at no extra cost to the state. The fishing pond, for example, would occupy the borrow pit created from the removal of grading material.

Other aspects of the community's reclamation plan could not be as easily implemented. The DNR did not have the authority to develop walking trails and a miners' memorial; residents would have to find other ways to fund such developments. The most difficult issue to be mediated, however, involved grading the north Jumbo. Limiting alterations to its appearance best preserved the integrity of the Jumbo, but erosion and acid mine drainage problems could not be mitigated unless the feature was stabilized. Accomplishing this task proved problematic. In 1999, the DNR created a computer graphic simulating what the Jumbo might look like after its gullied slopes had been smoothed, graded down, and planted with native grasses. The image was not well received. Barney DeRubeis, president of Toluca Coal Mine Preservation and Development, stated: "We told them that we wanted to save the *slag piles* not the *ant hills*. It looked too much like a hill and there was no backbone on the Jumbo. We wanted to preserve its shape."[82]

Tolucans were unwilling to accept a significant reduction in the elevation of the Jumbo, but preserving its height complicated reclamation objectives as steeper slopes would be more difficult to maintain. Fortunately, a compromise was reached over the grading issue. Standard state practice allowed for no more than a four-to-one slope ratio (that is, no more than one vertical foot of rise for every four feet of horizontal space) when reclaiming area gob piles. The DNR's Abandoned Mined Lands Reclamation Division agreed to allow a three-to-one slope ratio on the Jumbo, provided that the City of Toluca sign a statement relieving the state from responsibility for potential slope failures that might result from the steeper grade. Because the steeper slope grade would barely reduce the overall height of the Jumbo, the city agreed to the DNR's conditions. With the community on board, a final reclamation plan was developed. The city council voted to move ahead with the planned reclamation activity and work began on the project in June 2000.[83]

Reclamation began by clearing away the undergrowth on the 15.5-acre Jumbo property. Forested areas along the stream running adjacent to the feature and on the northeast side of the Jumbo where trees were maintaining slope stability were left in place. The two open mine shafts were filled and closed with circular concrete seals. The Jumbo then was graded to eliminate erosion channels. A layer of lime was laid down on the smoothed-out slopes to neutralize the acidity of the gob. It was then covered with soil. The adjacent mine yard was also cleared and graded. Drainage ditches, lined with acid-neutralizing limestone, were constructed along the base of the Jumbo and the entire area was planted with grass. In removing soil and fill material, a 2.5-acre spring-fed pond was created on the western portion of the property. In addition, the concrete foundations of the fan house and old mine reservoir were left in place. The reservoir was filled to within 1.5 feet of site grade, leaving a rectangular bench to be used as a sitting and gathering place (Figure 2.9).

All reclamation work was completed in the summer of 2000. One year later, the entire site was blanketed with grass, the pond had filled to a depth of more than twenty feet, and bird and aquatic life was recolonizing the area. Other than a significant slumping of soil on the south side of the Jumbo, the mine site had been stabilized.[84] According to officials at the DNR, the reclamation project was a success in terms of addressing public safety concerns. In fact, the two unsealed mine shafts had been a greater public hazard than was first thought. Prior to reclamation, the shafts had appeared to be filled with debris. The DNR had discovered, however, that the material that had been tossed into the mines had created an unstable seal at the surface; the shafts actually had been unfilled to a depth of more than 500 feet. The reclamation work also successfully mediated environmental problems. With the Jumbo slopes smoothed and vegetated, sedimentation and acid drainage problems had been largely eliminated.[85]

The reclamation project also proved to be cost effective. Unexpected mine shaft work increased the costs of reclamation, but project expenditures remained relatively low. The DNR estimated final costs of reclamation to be approximately $300,000, which is lower than other reclamation projects undertaken in the Longwall District. Heavy machinery work, the hauling of fill material, and grading are the most expensive aspects of abandoned mine land reclamation. This type of work was minimized at Toluca. The Jumbo's higher slope grade lessened grading activity. So, too, the transformation of the borrow pit into a pond reduced the amount of hauling work; normally, such depressions would be filled back to site

2.9a The reclaimed north Jumbo stands only ten feet lower than its pre-reclamation height.

grade. In Toluca, preservation considerations and the incorporation of innovative design features reduced reclamation costs. The outcome shows that when carefully planned, community input does not have to increase reclamation costs.[86]

In addition to being an environmental and economic success, the reclamation project received tremendous community support. The DNR achieved reclamation planning's often overlooked goal of maintaining the social and historical significance of the mining landscape. "The people here are really pleased with the project," remarked Pearson in the autumn of 2000. Like many in Toluca, Pearson was tracking the site's rejuvenation in the months following completion of reclamation work and he looked forward to the site's future use. He said: "The new lake has been named the Charles Devlin Lake, after the founder of the mine. It has at least ten feet of water in it. . . . The grass seed has sprouted all over the property and the Jumbo itself is turning a nice green. There are plans for a Halloween powwow and wiener roast for kids at the site of the old reservoir." As Pearson's comments indicate, reclamation dramatically altered the appearance of the mining property. Most residents, however, accepted the area's new look. The Jumbo has a more rounded and softer appearance, and grass protects its once gullied slopes. The mine site, previously covered in scrub, is now park-like and pastoral. Johnson Terrell, onetime owner of the Jumbo property, also approved of the reclamation outcome: "Ever since I was little girl I knew that the Jumbo area could be more beautiful, more useful, and safe." Indeed, the reclamation project has increased

2.9b The preserved foundations of the fan house.

2.9c View of the reclaimed mine yard from atop the Jumbo. Note the fishing pond, named Charles Devlin Lake after the founder of the Toluca colliery, and the rectangular foundation of the mine reservoir, which now serves as a public gathering place. Photographs by the author, 2001

resident use of the area. The reclaimed Jumbo is easier to climb and many have made their first trek in years back to the top of the landmark, which has retained its visual dominance in Toluca.[87]

Unlike other reclamation projects conducted by the DNR in the Longwall District, reclamation was achieved without substantially reducing the height of Toluca's gob piles. The DNR estimated that the Jumbo stands ten feet lower than its pre-reclamation height, an acceptable reduction for most Tolucans. Maintenance of the feature's height was a central issue from the earliest days of reclamation planning, and an incident that occurred when the DNR first moved heavy machinery onto the Jumbo underscored this concern. It was necessary for the state to grade a roadway up the backbone of the mound. A level staging area was then cut at its peak, producing a dramatic change in the Jumbo's appearance. For residents watching the construction process, it appeared that the DNR was breaking its promise to maintain the landmark's elevation. Witnessing the Jumbo's apparent destruction, one Tolucan took action. Barney DeRubeis drove his truck up the base of the Jumbo and purposefully blocked the construction roadway. The standoff ended only after DeRubeis was assured that the height of the feature would be built back up, a promise the DNR fulfilled.[88]

Residents were actively involved in every stage of the reclamation process, never hesitating to act on their concerns regarding reclamation and its implementation. "Many had doubts," recalled Jim Gregg, regional manager of the DNR's Abandoned Mined Lands Reclamation Division. "[I]t stirred up a lot of activity." Gregg viewed citizen involvement, however, as a positive aspect of the reclamation process. "The project brought many people together, and I am pleased with how well it has been received," he said. "[T]he community worked together to improve the site and I am sure it will be enhanced further in the future." As Gregg observed, in continuing to mobilize residents in support of the Jumbo cause, the reclamation project strengthened Toluca's sense of community. Moreover, since reclamation was completed, Tolucans have continued to work together to obtain additional funds for site improvements. In 2001 the Sportsmen's Club led efforts to obtain a DNR grant to stock the new fishing pond. It obtained grants for planting trees and enhancing the pheasant habitat on the Jumbo property in 2002. Toluca Coal Mine Preservation and Development also remained active. The group continued to search for funds to construct walking trails and a miners' memorial, but its most important accomplishment involved obtaining a State Historical Society Marker for the Jumbo site.[89]

In large part, Tolucans fought to preserve the Jumbos because these gob piles stood as markers of the mining past. Although the features long served this role, many in the community felt a need to commemorate mining's history in a more formal way. Indeed, one of the central mandates of Toluca Coal Mine Preservation and Development has been to establish a historical marker on the Jumbo site. Working with the Marshall County Historical Society, the group received approval in 2001 for its historical marker application. The sign's 100-word narrative provides a brief history of the mine, recognizes the community's Italian workforce, and identifies the reclaimed Jumbos as memorials to the region's coal industry. The historical plaque was placed at the base of the north Jumbo. The mound provides an ideal backdrop for the marker (Figure 2.10). As visitors finish reading about the significance of the Jumbos, their eyes naturally fall on the feature and the path rising to its peak.

The historical marker was dedicated in an elaborate ceremony held June 3, 2001. Testimony to its significance, more than 300 people attended the event, which represented the culmination of nearly two decades of community activism directed at protecting mining's landscape legacies. The "Big Jumbo Dedication," as it was called, also provided residents with a formal opportunity to remember the labor of those who built Toluca and to salute the men who lost their lives in the mine. The event began with an assembly of the Toluca Color Guard. After a welcoming statement and invocation prayer was read, the great-granddaughters of Battista Cioni, a resident killed in the mine, placed a wreath beneath the historical marker and a prayer was read for the deceased miners. After speeches were delivered by the mayor and other distinguished visitors, a roll call of the twenty-one men who perished in the mine was delivered. Following the unveiling of the historic plaque, a benediction prayer was read. The event concluded with a firing squad salute and the playing of taps.[90]

Interwoven with somber rituals of memorialization, the Big Jumbo dedication ceremony once again revealed the depth of feeling that Tolucans have for the Jumbos. As Pastor Michael Jones of St. John's Lutheran Church explained in the ceremony's invocation speech, the Jumbos represent sacred ground. His words provided a luminous summary of the historic and social significance of the Jumbos and their role in reinforcing a sense of who Tolucans are.

> When we look back at these two large hills of rock, slag, and debris, we see one of the definite trademarks of our town. . . . They stand before us, silent yet ever-present, as if they are two guardians that watch over our daily lives. . . . And it would not be too much of a stretch to think of them so, as guardians, for these hills in all their height and grandeur bear the indelible stamp of humanity for they are not born of nature, but of the toil and struggle of decades of hard work, work that made this town boom, work that fed the huge iron locomotive leviathans that used to prowl this vast flat prairie land, work that on occasion took life, as men struggled against the rigors of the depths of the earth.
>
> As is most ground, if we just take the time to stop and think and reflect, the land we stand upon here is sacred—that is, to be set apart in our minds and hearts. Whenever people interact and struggle with what life offers, whenever people pour their hearts and years into something grand, something bigger than themselves, something sacred is created. . . . We see such sacredness in our national monuments, and we see it here

2.10 The Toluca Coal Mine Historical Marker. Photograph by the author, 2001

today in Toluca. . . . As ancestors of these miners, or as people who come here today to learn and leave the better for it, our lives are no less important than the miners and citizens of Toluca from years gone by, and indeed it is we who now carry the torch that is life into the future.[91]

The Big Jumbo dedication ceremony provided residents with an opportunity to collectively recognize and celebrate the role the Jumbos serve in defining community and individual identity. In so doing, the gathering reinforced Toluca's meaning as place. "Dear Lord," Pastor Jones prayed in concluding his invocation remarks, "you bring us here today to catch a glimpse of the past. All about us, especially in the symbols that are these two great hills, we see and listen to the stories that define us as who we are."[92]

It is clear that Toluca would be a poorer place had it lost its Jumbo "guardians," which is perhaps the most significant lesson to be learned from the Toluca experience. Residents became active stakeholders in the decision-making processes shaping their environment. Their involvement complicated reclamation of the mining landscape but in a highly productive way. In Toluca, a way was found to accommodate the goals of abandoned mine land reclamation and the community's desire to maintain the integrity and meaning of the mining landscape. Finding this solution was no easy task, but the challenge was worth taking on, for as the late Jack Gerardo had stated, "[W]ithout the Jumbos we would all feel lost."[93]

NOTES

1. *CNN Today,* January 6, 1997.

2. Research on the Longwall Mining District has focused primarily on labor issues in isolated communities. See, for example, Herbert G. Gutman, "The Braidwood Lockout of 1874," *Journal of the Illinois State Historical Society* 53 (1960): 5–28; and Richard Patrick Joyce, "Miners of the Prairie: Life and Labor in the Wilmington, Illinois, Coal Field, 1866–1897" (M.A. thesis, Illinois State University, 1980). A literature also exists on ethnicity and mining disasters. See, for example, Amy Zahl Gottlieb, "British Coal Miners: A Demographic Study of Braidwood and Streator, Illinois," *Journal of the Illinois State Historical Society* 72 (1979): 179–192; and F. P. Buck, *The Cherry Mine Disaster* (Chicago: M. A. Donohue and Company, 1910). John Hoffmann recognized the need for a more comprehensive history of Illinois coal mining in *A Guide to the History of Illinois* (Westport, CT: Greenwood, 1991), 79. I have attempted to address this deficiency in the Longwall area. See David Robertson, " 'Heaps of History': Toluca and the Historic Longwall Mining District," *Journal of Illinois History* 3:3 (2000): 162–184.

3. For the location of waste piles in the Longwall District, see Susan Carol Bradford, "Mining Methods, Geology, and Sampling Procedures Used to Study Colliery Waste from the Historic Longwall Mining District, North-Central Illinois," in *Geologic Study of Longwall Mine Sites in Northern Illinois,* by Illinois State Geological Survey (Springfield: Abandoned Mine Lands Reclamation Council, 1983), 1–30.

4. S. O. Andros, *Coal Mining in Illinois,* Illinois Coal Mining Investigations Cooperative Agreement Bulletin, No.13 (Urbana: University of Illinois, 1915), 1–49, 68; Harry M. Dixon, "The Illinois Coal Mining Industry" (Ph.D. thesis, University of Illinois, 1951), 78–79.

5. Dixon, "The Illinois Coal Mining Industry," 78–81; Howard N. Eavenson, *The First Century and a Quarter of American Coal Industry* (Pittsburgh: Blatimore Weekly Press, 1942), 527–536.

6. Andros, *Coal Mining in Illinois,* 37–38; Gilbert H. Cady, *Coal Resources of District I (Longwall)* (Urbana: State Geological Survey, University of Illinois, 1915), 13; Alburto Bement, *Shipping Mines and Coal Railroads of Illinois and Indiana* (Chicago: Peabody Coal Company, 1903). The Chicago & Alton was the region's most active mine developer, controlling ten mines mostly in the Braidwood region. Other important railroad developers in the district were the Atchison, Topeka & Santa Fe, which controlled nine mines; the Chicago, Burlington & Quincy and the Chicago, Rock Island & Pacific, which each controlled seven mines; and the Illinois Central and the Chicago & North Western, with four mines each.

7. Cady, *Coal Resources,* 14–15, 58–108. The northern Illinois coal district underlies portions of Bureau, Grundy, Kankakee, La Salle, Livingston, Marshall, Putnam, Will, and Woodford Counties.

8. Population estimates based on U.S. census data for thirty-two Longwall Mining District communities. U.S. Bureau of the Census, *Eighth Census of the United States 1860, Illinois,* Washington, DC; U.S. Bureau of the Census, *Ninth Census of the United States 1870, Illinois,* Washington, DC; U.S. Bureau of the Census, *Tenth Census of the United States 1880, Illinois,* Washington, DC; U.S. Bureau of the Census, *Eleventh Census of the United States 1890, Illinois,* Washington, DC; U.S. Bureau of the Census, *Twelfth Census of the United States 1900, Illinois,* Washington, DC; U.S. Bureau of the Census, *Thirteenth Census of the United States 1910, Illinois,* Washington, DC.

9. Grace Abbott, *The Immigrant and Coal Mining Communities of Illinois* (Springfield: Illinois Department of Registration and Education, Immigrants Commission, 1920), 5–9; John H.M. Laslett, "Scottish-Americans and the Beginnings of the Modern Class Struggle: Immigrant Coal Miners in Northern Illinois, 1865–1889" in *Labor Divided: Race and Ethnicity in United States Labor Struggles, 1835–1960,* ed. Robert Asher and Charles Stephenson (Albany: State University of New York Press, 1990), 171–172.

10. Northern Illinois Coal Operators, *Statement of Northern Illinois Coal Operators with Particular Reference to the Mining Machine Differential and Household Coal for Employees* (Chicago, 1923), 2; Abbott, *The Immigrant and Coal Mining Communities of Illinois,* 9.

11. Based on data from the Illinois Department of Energy and Natural Resources, *Directory of Coal Mines in Illinois* (Champaign: Illinois State Geological Survey, 1996), in volumes for Bureau, Grundy, Kankakee, La Salle, Livingston, Marshall, Putnam, Will, and Woodford Counties.

12. S. O. Andros, *Mining Practice in District I (Longwall),* Illinois Coal Mine Investigations Cooperative Agreement Bulletin, No. 5 (Urbana: University of Illinois, 1914), 7–9, 12–38.

13. Northern Illinois Coal Operators, *Statement,* 8; Andros, *Coal Mining in Illinois,* 97, 148.

14. For mine fatality and accident statistics, see Andros, *Coal Mining in Illinois,* 142–143. For more information on the Cherry mine disaster, see Buck, *The Cherry Mine Disaster.*

15. Cady, *Coal Resources,* 15, 111–144; Northern Illinois Coal Operators, *Statement,* 2. Estimates of the number of mines operating in the district are based on data from the Illinois Department of Energy and Natural Resources, *Directory of Coal Mines in Illinois,* for Bureau, Grundy, Kankakee, La Salle, Livingston, Marshall, Putnam, Will, and Woodford Counties.

16. Illinois Sesquicentennial Commission, *Illinois Guide and Gazetteer* (Chicago: Rand McNally & Company, 1969), 501.

17. Marshall County Historical Society, *History of Marshall County, Illinois* (Dallas: Taylor, 1983), 33–34; John Spencer Burt and W. E. Hawthorne, *Past and Present of Marshall and Putnam Counties, Illinois* (Chicago: Pioneer, 1907), 59–61; *Toluca Star,* April 8, 1893, 1.

18. *Toluca Star,* (n.d.) 1895, 1; Marshall County Historical Society, *History of Marshall County,* 33; Burt and Hawthorne, *Past and Present of Marshall and Putnam Counties,* 59; U.S. Bureau of the Census, *Twelfth Census of the United States 1900, Illinois,* Washington, DC.

19. Cady, *Coal Resources,* 64–65. For the description of the Toluca mine, see *Toluca Star,* special Christmas edition, 1895, 3; Judy Paulsen, ed., *Toluca—100 Years: 1893–1993* (Toluca: privately published, 1993), 4–5.

20. Illinois Bureau of Labor Statistics, *Annual Report of the State Bureau of Labor Statistics, Coal in Illinois* (Springfield: The Bureau, 1894–1898); Illinois Bureau of Labor Statistics, *Annual Coal Report of the Illinois Bureau of Labor Statistics* (Springfield: The Bureau, 1900–1910); Illinois State Mining Board, *Annual Coal Report of Illinois* (Springfield: The Board, 1911–1916); Illinois Department of Mines and Minerals, *Annual Coal Report of Illinois* (Springfield: The Department, 1917–1924).

21. Burt and Hawthorne, *Past and Present of Marshall and Putnam Counties,* 61; Jerry Klein, "Here's Looking at Toluca," *Peoria Journal-Star,* February 16, 1975, C-1; Joe Vallino,

interview with Anna Mae Johnson Terrell, Toluca, n.d. Injury and fatality figures are compiled from annual state mine reports (see note 20).

22. Paulsen, *Toluca—100 Years,* 36–37; Jack Gerardo, interview with author, Toluca, Illinois, February 9, 1998; U.S. Bureau of the Census, *Twelfth Census;* Nancy Lutgens, "I Just Came to Look-A: Italian Immigration to Toluca, Illinois, 1894–1918," paper presented at the Illinois History Symposium, Springfield, 1995.

23. Lewis Wabel, *Charles J. Devlin: Coal Mines & Railroads, His Empire,* ed. Doris E. Brown (Henry, IL: privately published, 1991). Production and employment averages are based on data from annual state mine reports (see note 20).

24. *Toluca Star,* April 8, 1893, 1; *Toluca Star,* (n.d.) 1895, 1; *Toluca Star,* special Christmas edition, 1895, 1.

25. *Toluca Star,* April 8, 1893, 1; *Toluca Star,* special Christmas edition, 1895, 1.

26. Pete Aimone, quoted in Paulsen, *Toluca—100 Years,* 128.

27. Pete Aimone, interview with Anna Mae Johnson Terrell, Toluca, Illinois, n.d.

28. Gerardo, interview.

29. Gilbert Flynn, interview with author, Toluca, Illinois, February 9, 1998; Paulsen, *Toluca—100 Years,* 83; Sanborn-Perris Map Company, New York, fire insurance maps for Toluca, 1910.

30. See, for example, "Fines Being Paid: Prohibition Law Violators Plead Guilty," *Lacon Home Journal,* April 19, 1923, 1; "Another Raid on Toluca Bars," *Lacon Home Journal,* August 13, 1925, 1; "Hundreds Hunting Toluca Man-Killer," *Lacon Home Journal,* September 24, 1925, 1; and "Sheriff Has Busy Week with Law Violators," *Lacon Home Journal,* February 4, 1926, 1.

31. Burt and Hawthorne, *Past and Present of Marshall and Putnam Counties,* 60–61.

32. H. V. Alexander, "Echoes of the Past," *Toluca Star,* May 27, 1938.

33. Aimone, interview.

34. Ibid.

35. Ryden, *Mapping the Invisible Landscape,* 181.

36. Vallino, interview.

37. Ibid.

38. Illinois Department of Mines and Minerals, *Annual Coal Report* (Springfield: The Department, 1925), 128; "Toluca Mine Shuts Down," *Henry News Republican,* May 8, 1924, 11.

39. "Toluca Banks Avert Disaster," *Henry News Republican,* May 22, 1924, 11. See also, "Toluca Banks Avert Disaster," *Lacon Home Journal,* May 8, 1924, 1; "Cut Coal Price," *Lacon Home Journal,* March 27, 1924, 1.

40. Flynn, interview.

41. Aimone, interview; William McCall, interview with author, Toluca, Illinois, February 9, 1998; "Toluca Mine Shuts Down," *Henry News Republican,* May 8, 1924, 11.

42. "Clean Up of Toluca Coal Mine Continues," *Henry News Republican,* May 22, 1924, 4; Gerardo, interview; U.S. Bureau of the Census, *Fourteenth Census of the United States 1920, Illinois,* Washington, DC; U.S. Bureau of the Census, *Fifteenth Census of the United States 1930, Illinois,* Washington, DC.

43. The rail line continued operating through Toluca under new ownership but with limited service until December 1937. See Wabel, *Charles J. Devlin,* 71–102.

44. See James D. Muhly, "Foreword," in *Social Approaches to an Industrial Past: The Archaeology and Anthropology of Mining,* ed. A. Bernard Knapp, Vincent C. Pigott, and Eugenia W. Herbert (New York: Routledge, 1998), xv.

45. Klein, "Here's Looking at Toluca," C–1; Marshall County Historical Society, "Toluca Built on Devlin's Coal," *Heritage Sampler No. 2* (Lacon: *Henry News Republican,* 1965), 54. See also Marshall County Historical Society, "From Coal Mining to Salad Dressing," *Marshall County Historical Society Newsletter,* January 19, 1956; Marshall County Historical Society, *History of Marshall County,* 33.

46. The percentage of the workforce employed in the Toluca mine was estimated by comparing town population in 1920 (2,503) to the state average for proportion of the population gainfully employed (40.5 percent). With an estimated workforce in 1920 of 1,013 and an average mine employment of 600, it can be estimated that approximately 59 percent of Toluca's workforce was employed in the mine. See U.S. Bureau of the Census, *Fourteenth Census*; Illinois Department of Mines and Minerals, *Annual Coal Report of Illinois 1920.*

47. Anna Mae Johnson Terrell, letter to author, May 7, 1999.

48. U.S. Bureau of the Census, *Census of the United States, Illinois* (1910 to 2000), Washington, DC.

49. U.S. Bureau of the Census, *2000 Census of the United States, Illinois,* Washington, DC.

50. Paulsen, *Toluca 100—Years,* 119–121.

51. Illinois Sesquicentennial Commission, *Illinois Guide and Gazetteer,* 500; Eleanor Bussell, "A Sunday Tour in Summer," *County Chaff* (Lacon, IL: n.p., 1960); "Toluca residents are tackling Jumbo problem with pride," *The Pantagraph,* Bloomington, Illinois, February 13, 1999, A-12; William Gleason, "A Small Town's Big Dream Ends in Stream of Tears," *Chicago Daily News,* March 15, 1962, n.p.

52. Klein, "Here's Looking at Toluca," C-1.

53. Marshall County Historical Society, "Toluca Built on Devlin's Coal," 54.

54. Glenna Schmitt, "Toluca's Monuments In Jeopardy," *Toluca Star,* October 17, 1985, 1; "Toluca Jumbo Safe," *Toluca Star,* January 30, 1986, 1; Elton Pearson, interview with author, Toluca, Illinois, February 11, 1998.

55. Anna Mae Johnson Terrell, letter to the editor, *Toluca Star,* July 24, 1996, 2.

56. In 1993, negotiations occurred between the Valesano trust and the Prairie Rivers Resource Conservation and Development Council. A concept plan was drawn up to develop the Jumbo property into a recreation and wildlife preservation zone, but no headway was made in furthering these plans.

57. Elton Pearson, letter to author, January 27, 1998.

58. Larry Harber, interview with author, Toluca, Illinois, February 12, 1998; Pearson, letter to author.

59. Elton Pearson and Anna Mae Johnson Terrell, letters to the editor, *Toluca Star,* October 3, 1996, 8.

60. Greg Stanmar, "Slag Piles Earn City Heaps of Attention," *Bloomington Pantagraph,* October 30, 1996, n.p.; Phil Luciano, "Toluca Man Takes on Jumbo Project," *Peoria Journal Star,* November 15, 1996, n.p.; Wes Smith, "Heaps of History Captured in Piles of Coal Mine Rock," *Chicago Tribune,* December 2, 1996, n.p.; *CNN Today,* January 6, 1997.

61. *Toluca Star,* October 24, 1996, 1.

62. "New Organization in Toluca Dedicated to Saving the Jumbo," *Toluca Star,* November 20, 1997, n.p.; Pearson, letter to author.

63. Marion Brandt, "The Jumbos," in Paulsen, *Toluca: 100—Years,* 126.

64. Gerardo, interview; Marion Brandt, interview with author, Toluca, Illinois, February 12, 1998.

65. Harber, interview; Brandt, interview; Barney DeRubeis, interview with author, Toluca, Illinois, February 12, 1998. Other associations of home connected to the Jumbos were also observed. In a Toluca High School yearbook, for example, the graduating class photograph shows students posing on the north Jumbo. In maps drawn of the town by grade-school students, the Jumbos were also prominently displayed. See *Toluca High School Yearbook,* 1986, n.p.; David Robertson, "Enduring Places: Landscape Meaning, Community Persistence, and Preservation in the Historic Mining Town" (Ph.D. thesis, University of Oklahoma, 2001), 82.

66. Pearson, interview; Harber, interview; Brian Ricconi, "Jumbos Being Saved," *The Streator Times-Press,* July 26, 2000, n.p.; *CNN Today.*

67. Harber, interview; Schmitt, "Toluca's Monuments in Jeopardy," 1.

68. Gerardo, interview. See also Paulsen, *Toluca—100 Years,* 8–13.

69. Gerardo, interview; Resident interviews (names withheld) with author, Toluca, Illinois, February 10, 1998.

70. DeRubeis, interview; Harber, interview.

71. Luciano, "Toluca Man Takes on Jumbo Project," n.p.

72. U.S. Public Law 95-87, August 3, 1977, Surface Mining Control and Reclamation Act of 1977, Title IV.

73. I. G. Krapac and C. A. Smyth, "Geochemical Evaluation of Colliery Waste from the Historic Longwall Mining District, North-Central Illinois," in Illinois State Geological Survey, *Geologic Study of Longwall Mine Sites in Northern Illinois* (Springfield: Abandoned Mine Lands Reclamation Council, 1983); Susan Carol Bradford et al., *Characteristics and Potential Uses of Waste from the Historic Longwall Coal Mining District in North-Central Illinois,* Environmental Geology Notes 118 (Champaign: Illinois State Geological Survey, 1987); and *Geological Study of Longwall Mine Sites in Northern Illinois* (Champaign: Illinois State Geological Survey, 1983).

74. "Abandoned Mined Lands Inventory and Assessment," file document PU-094 (Springfield: Illinois Department of Natural Resources, 1981).

75. A 1987 Illinois Geological Survey publication showed that waste piles were often of local historical value. The study described how the gob piles were relics of an important era in the industrial history of the state, and that many of the mine sites served as tributes to the men who worked in the mines. See Bradford et al., *Characteristics and Potential Uses of Waste from the Historic Longwall Mining District,* 14–15.

76. Ray Justi, quoted in Jessica L. Aberle, "Reddish Mountain Majesties," *Peoria Journal Star,* May 20, 2001, n.p.; Pete Venturi, interview with author, Toluca, Illinois, February 9, 1998.

77. For additional information on *Effigy Tumuli,* see Douglas C. McGill, *Michael Heizer's Effigy Tumuli: The Reemergence of Ancient Mound Building* (New York: Harry N. Abrams, 1990); Frederick C. Klein, "Moving Earth for Art's Sake," *The Wall Street Journal,* June 12, 1985, n.p.; Erika Lee Doss, *Spirit Poles and Flying Pigs: Public Art and Democracy in American Communities* (Washington, DC: Smithsonian Institution Press, 1995).

78. James (Jim) Gregg, telephone interview with author, Norman, Oklahoma, 18 February, 1999; Aberle, "Reddish Mountain Majesties," n.p.

79. Gregg, telephone interview.

80. Toluca Coal Mine Preservation and Development Committee, "Development Survey Response" (Toluca: unpublished document, 1998); Leah J. Bakel, "Toluca Has One Park, Slag Pile Shouldn't Be Another," *Peoria Journal Star,* November 26, 1996, A-4.

81. "Toluca City Council Hears Presentation on Concept Design for Coal Mine Area," *Lacon Home Journal,* January 21, 1999, n.p.

82. James (Jim) Gregg, interview with author, June 25, 2001; Barney DeRubeis, interview with author, Toluca, Illinois, January 26, 1999.

83. Gregg, interview, 2001.

84. The slope failure was determined to be the result of unusually wet weather conditions rather than from the steep slope grade; thus, the DNR returned to fix the slump in 2001.

85. Gregg, interview, 2001.

86. Ibid.; Problem Area Summary, Toluca Coal Company, Abandoned Mine Land Inventory System (AMLIS), Office of Surface Mining Reclamation and Enforcement, Department of the Interior, Washington, DC.

87. Elton Pearson, letter to author, October 20, 2000; Anna Mae Johnson Terrell, letter to author, September 2000.

88. Gregg, interview, 2001; DeRubeis, interview with author, Toluca, Illinois, June 3, 2001.

89. Gregg, interview, 2001.

90. "Big Jumbo Dedication," Program Brochure, privately printed, Toluca, Illinois, 2001; "Ceremony on Sunday Designates Toluca Jumbos as a State Historical Site," *Toluca Star Herald,* June 7, 2001, 1, 9.

91. Pastor Michael S. Jones, St. John's Lutheran Church, "Dedication at the Jumbos Invocation," Toluca, Illinois, June 3, 2001.

92. Ibid.

93. Jack Gerardo, quoted on *CNN Today.*

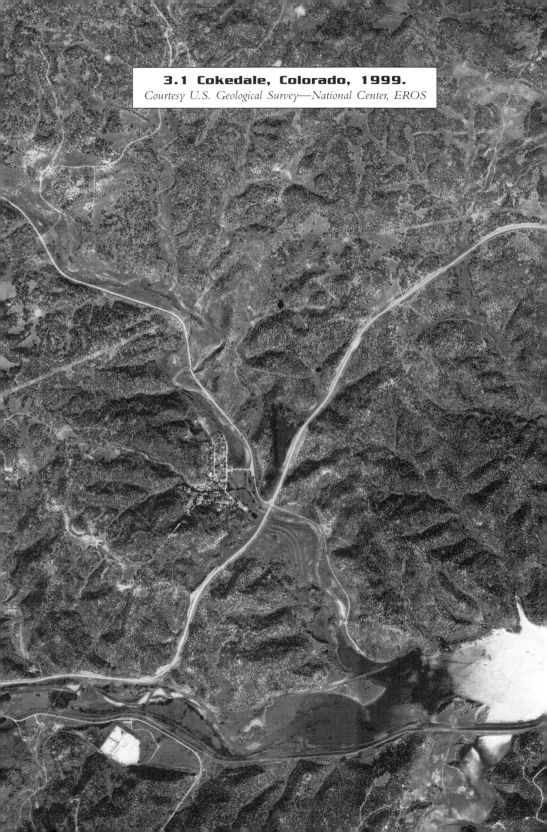

3.1 Cokedale, Colorado, 1999.
Courtesy U.S. Geological Survey—National Center, EROS

Cokedale

STATE HIGHWAY 12 RUNS WEST FROM TRINIDAD, COLORADO, CLIMBING INTO the pinyon-speckled foothills of the Sangre de Cristo Mountains. As the road tops a rise eight miles west of Trinidad, a wall of black coal waste interrupts the verdant scenery. The highway parallels the bank of mine tailings as it descends into the valley. To the south of the highway lie two rows of crumbling coke ovens. In their ruin, the oven arches resemble an ancient Roman viaduct. To the north, at the base of the spoil pile, a gravel road runs up the canyon. At the intersection sits a sign: "Cokedale—National Historic District." Built on Reilly Creek in 1907 by the American Smelting and Refining Company (ASARCO), Cokedale is the only company town in the Trinidad area to survive mine closure. It is among the best-preserved company mining towns in the western United States.

Cokedale lies hidden beneath a canopy of elm trees (Figure 3.2). Only after crossing the bridge that spans the creek does the town come into full view. A parking area marks the entrance to Cokedale. Here, pinned to a bulletin board, is a guide for a self-guided walking tour of the community; complimentary copies sit in a brochure holder.[1] Leaving cars behind (the best way to experience Cokedale

3.2 View of Cokedale looking across Reilly Creek. The large structure on the left is the old company store building. On the far right stands the schoolhouse. Photograph by the author, 1999

is on foot), visitors begin the walking tour by heading north to Spruce Street. Standing to the right is the old icehouse, which is difficult to recognize as it has been converted to a home. To the left, a dozen cottages of similar design front the dirt road. Like all of the town's company-built houses, the cinderblock structures have metal-clad roofs and are two rooms wide. One is in disrepair and lies abandoned but the majority of Cokedale's old company houses are well kept. The road curves and climbs up to Elm Street. At the junction, a road leads north to an elegantly restored schoolhouse, where, the walking tour brochure explains, the sons and daughters of three generations of miners once attended first through eighth grades. Both sides of Elm Street are lined with cottages. Those nestled into the canyon wall are larger than the others, and all of the homes on Elm are occupied. Behind low fences lie carefully tended gardens. Beside the front doors of many are woodcut signs bearing the names of the homes' occupants.

Cokedale's town center lies at the southern end of Elm Street. Here stand the community's largest structures: the company store, bath and boarding houses, the doctor's and superintendent's homes, and the mine office. All but the company store serve as homes and in front of each building is a small sign identifying its original use. Next to the steps of the restored company store—known as the Gottlieb Mercantile when it served as bank, post office, and dry-goods, grocery, and furniture store for mining-era residents—stands a sign declaring this the home of the Cokedale Miners' Museum. (The tour brochure points out that the mercantile was not a company store in the truest sense as miners were paid in cash, not scrip.) All that remains of the walking tour is the town's south-side residential area. Sightseers are guided to the top of Church Street where they find the Sacred Heart of Jesus and Mary Church, a structure built from two unused company houses in the 1930s. Backtracking down to Pine Street, the shady streetscape appears less tidy than other areas of Cokedale but the majority of homes remain in good condition.

The thirty-minute walking tour returns to the town center. If visiting during the summer season, the inquisitive visitor may, however, visit the miners' museum where a copy of *Cokedale 1907–1947: Anatomy of a Model Mining Community* can be purchased. Skimming through the community history, the reader learns that Cokedale was a model mining camp. Allegedly, it was a harmonious place run by a caring operator, and it differed from other company towns in the area. One learns that Cokedale provided a higher quality of life than other mining towns in the area and that the community survived because it was a utopian-like company town, a place residents refused to abandon when the colliery closed in 1947.[2]

This romantic story of the town's past would seem to be confirmed by the visitor's stroll through Cokedale. The community appears to have changed little in the course of nearly a century of habitation and it is orderly and pleasant. Indeed, if modern intrusions like automobiles are ignored, it truly seems like one is walking through a living, early twentieth-century company town.

Yet, its current appearance and local history provide an incomplete impression of the town's past and do not adequately convey its meaning as a place. Neither book nor tour reveals the hardship of life in the mining era or the challenges residents faced following mine closure. The walking tour brochure claims that a visit to Cokedale is akin to taking a step back into the past, but the community is not a living history museum where time has stood still. During the mining era, the population was more than five times what it is today. The town was larger, grittier, and faster paced. True, residents found a home in Cokedale and were proud of the lives they led there, but these attachments to place were cultivated in the midst of a factional, hardworking industrial community that was governed and controlled by restrictive company rule. Theirs was not an ideal existence and, following mine closure, Cokedale's population plummeted, portions of the town were demolished, and what was left fell into disrepair. A small group of dedicated townsfolk kept the community alive but its survival had little to do with exceptional living conditions or company altruism. Cokedale struggled on through three decades of dereliction before changing economic conditions and preservation efforts stimulated the rejuvenation that is evident in the landscape today.

As with many historic mining towns, Cokedale has proven susceptible to myth and misconception. Cokedale's utopian image fails to communicate a sense of the town's true character and the complex meaning it has—and continues to hold—as a lived-in place. It also fails to explain why it was the only company town in the Trinidad Coal Field to survive mine closure. Moreover, the belief that living and working conditions were superior in Cokedale has influenced preservation efforts. As a result, the contemporary landscape falls short in communicating significant elements of the community's past.

THE TRINIDAD COAL FIELD

The Raton Mesa coal region straddles the eastern slope of the Sangre de Cristo Mountains. The region is split approximately in half by the Colorado–New Mexico state boundary, which serves as the dividing line between New Mexico's Raton Field and Colorado's Trinidad Coal Field. Commercial coal mining began in the Trinidad area in the 1870s. The Colorado Fuel and Iron Company (CF&I) developed the first collieries. The district contained a high-grade coking coal and was the chief producer of coke west of the Mississippi. The product fueled the furnaces of a growing steel industry in nearby Pueblo, Colorado, and metal smelting industries elsewhere in the West. Output of coal grew over the first four decades of the field's operation, peaking in the decade of 1910–1920.

The rise of the mining industry brought dramatic change to southern Colorado. Prior to the onset of commercial coal mining, Las Animas County contained approximately 4,000 residents. By 1920 close to 39,000 people called the county home, and the town of Trinidad, once a rail and ranching outpost, had boomed into a mining metropolis of 11,000. The Trinidad Coal Field attracted a sizable number of Anglo and Hispanic workers from other parts of Colorado and New Mexico, but miners also came from farther afield. The two largest groups of foreign-born workers came from Mexico and Italy. Also present were Austro-Hungarians, Slavs, Poles, Greeks, Germans, English, Irish, Scottish, Canadians, and Japanese.[3]

The Trinidad Coal Field lay within an Anglo-Hispanic frontier made more diverse by the migration of foreign-born coal workers. The mining towns and their workers moved into a landscape dotted with Hispanic settlements, but as rail, coking, and mining operations spread, the old village life was destroyed.[4] Hispanic settlement was subsumed by more than two dozen company-owned mining communities built along expanding rail networks north of Trinidad along the front range of the Sangre de Cristo Mountains, to the south up Raton Pass toward New Mexico, and to the west along the Purgatoire River (Map 3.1).

The Trinidad field became Colorado's most productive coal mining region but the area is best remembered as the site of one of the bloodiest labor disputes in U.S. history. The coal miners' strike of 1913–1914 was not the area's only instance of labor unrest, but in shaping the identity of the mining region, the Great Coalfield War, as it has come to be called, was the most significant. Delegates of the United Mine Workers of America (UMWA), representing the camps of the Trinidad

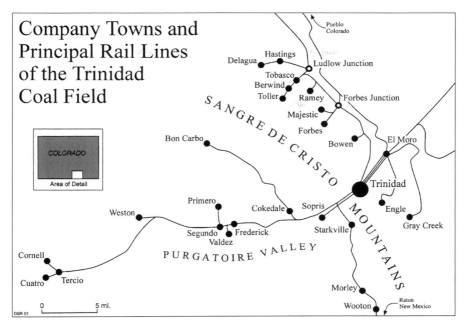

Map 3.1 *In the early 1900s more than two dozen company towns were in operation in the Trinidad Coal Field.*

field, unanimously approved a motion to strike on September 16, 1913. Workers had several demands, the most important of which was union recognition, but operators like the CF&I—the union's fiercest opponent—showed little interest in negotiation. Their response was to evict all strikers and union sympathizers from the company towns. The evicted workers and their families established tent colonies near the mouths of the canyons leading into the settlements. The largest tent colony, at Ludlow Junction, housed more than 1,200 inhabitants. As the strike continued, the towns and tent colonies became guarded military zones. Hoping to quell tensions, the State of Colorado ordered the National Guard into the strike zone in November 1913. Charged as an impartial peacekeeping force, the National Guard was welcomed at first by strikers, who thought that state intervention might help their cause.[5]

Unfortunately, National Guard occupation only amplified the dispute. Siding with the coal companies, the National Guard disarmed and harassed strikers, facilitated the importation of strikebreakers, and deported union organizers. The strike evolved into a violent standoff that came to a head on April 20, 1914, at the Ludlow tent colony. Much has been written of the "Ludlow Massacre," but the details surrounding the event are still uncertain. Shooting began in the morning and by dusk the tent colony was ablaze. One militiaman perished in the battle and at least five strikers were killed. More alarming, in the aftermath of the fire the lifeless bodies of two women and twelve children were found in an earthen cellar beneath a burnt-out tent.[6]

The Ludlow incident sparked an armed rebellion in the coal field. Finally overcoming his reluctance to interfere, President Woodrow Wilson ordered the Army into the field. With the arrival of federal troops the state military was ordered out and both sides were disarmed. As the dispute moved toward its second winter, however, the union cause began to weaken as federal troops continued the state militia's policies. Strikebreakers continued to be protected by government soldiers and production continued at most collieries. By November 1914, with strike funds exhausted, the executive board of the UMWA terminated the strike.[7]

None of the union's demands was achieved. Nevertheless, although workers lost the labor battle, they won the propaganda war surrounding it. The strike and Ludlow Massacre received widespread national press, much of which was critical of mine owners and their resistance to improving living and working conditions in the camps. John D. Rockefeller Jr., principal shareholder and president of the CF&I, received especially harsh treatment. A well-publicized congressional investigation also was conducted into the strike, drawing attention to the brutality of company control. This publicity bolstered the cause of workers. Life remained hard, but living and working conditions improved in the wake of the strike and union organization was eventually permitted in the camps. The events of 1913–1914 furthered growing public sentiment against company towns, and the camps of the Trinidad field have come to be widely vilified in the works of novelists and labor historians.[8]

Output of coal from the Trinidad field fell during the Great Depression. The 1940s saw a slight rebound in production, but by the 1950s the Trinidad field was mostly played out. At its height (1910–1920), more than seventy collieries operated in the district; by the midpoint of the 1950s only seven remained. The high cost of underground mining, a general decline in the price of coal, and increased labor costs contributed to the field's decline. As collieries closed, the company towns disappeared. Buildings and mine equipment were moved to other camps. Operators salvaged structures in an attempt to recover capital investments in town infrastructure. All of the company towns were razed with the exception of Cokedale.[9]

Built in 1907, Cokedale was developed to provide coking coal to ASARCO's El Paso copper smelter in west Texas. It was ASARCO's only operation in the Trinidad Coal Field. Operated by the Carbon Coal and Coke Company (an ASARCO subsidiary), Cokedale was sited on the west slope of Reilly Canyon, a mile from the entrance to the Purgatoire Valley. The town was carefully planned (Map 3.2). Three rows of houses were built parallel to the creek. The top row, on Elm Street, was dubbed "Silk-Stocking Row" because it contained larger houses built for professional-class employees. A second group of houses, located south of

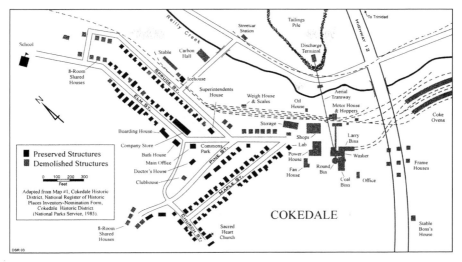

Map 3.2 Cokedale town plan showing original buildings and industrial features that remain standing along with those that have been demolished or lay in ruin, as of 2001.

Elm along Pine and Maple Streets, followed an arroyo into the west side of the canyon. Cokedale's public buildings—the Gottlieb Mercantile, mine office, and boarding, bath, and doctor's houses—were erected at the center of the community. The schoolhouse anchored the north end of town and a community hall, icehouse, stable, and baseball field sat on the eastern side. The company planted elm trees and maintained public spaces, giving the camp a pastoral atmosphere. ASARCO enforced a uniform aesthetic standard. Residents were not permitted to paint, repair, or in any way change the appearance of their homes.[10]

ASARCO built eighty-six single-family, cinderblock cottages in Cokedale; eighteen wood-frame cottages; and two one-story and twenty two-story, multiple-family duplexes (Figure 3.3). Modest in appearance, all houses had hipped or pyramidal roofs and were finished with a plain stucco finish. Trim and roofing was painted a uniform dark green. The houses ranged in size from one to four bedrooms and were equipped with coal-burning stoves and electricity. Only the community buildings and homes located on the top row of Elm Street had indoor plumbing.[11]

Cokedale's mining and coking operation was located on the southern end of the community. Although a small cluster of housing was built on a bench above the coke ovens, industry was otherwise separated from residential areas. An imposing powerhouse and washery-tipple complex sat on the western slope of the canyon. An aerial tramway carried washery waste to the tailings pile located on the eastern slope. Cleaned coal was transported by rail to the coke ovens: a double row of 350 beehive ovens built along the curve of Reilly Creek. Cokedale contained the

3.3 Portions of a panoramic photograph taken of Cokedale, circa 1910. The top photograph shows Pine and Maple Streets. Note the large two-story houses in the foreground; these multi-family homes were demolished following mine closure. The bottom photograph shows portions of Spruce and Elm Streets and the collection of community structures, the largest being the Gottlieb Mercantile, located in the town center. Courtesy, Carnegie Public Library, Trinidad Colorado

largest set of coke ovens in the Trinidad District, begetting the community's name.

Coal was initially extracted from two drift mines sunk into the west side of Reilly Canyon. The Number One mine was located above the washery, and the Number Two near the southern end of the coke ovens. The Number One was abandoned after the workings ran into property boundaries, and Number Two's poor production forced ASARCO to search for a new source of coal. In 1918 a third mine was opened at Bon Carbo, located nine miles up Reilly Canyon. The company built a small camp at the new mine site but most miners continued to live in Cokedale. Workers and coal were transported to and from Bon Carbo on a spur of the Denver & Rio Grande Railroad. The Bon Carbo collieries remained in operation for close to thirty years until increased production costs and depressed coal prices resulted in their closure in 1947. ASARCO pulled out of Cokedale the same year.

A MODEL COMPANY TOWN

At the turn of the Twentieth Century, company controlled mining communities throughout the nation were plagued by intolerable working and living conditions. Substandard housing, disregard for sanitation, oppressive company control, company indifference to the safety of the workers, and limited opportunities for constructive social activity were widely prevalent. Cokedale, however, was an exception.[12]

The preceding passage appears in *Cokedale, 1907–1947: Anatomy of a Model Mining Community*. Written by historian Holly Barton, it is the community's most extensive and influential local history. Uniform in its praise of living and working conditions, the book portrays Cokedale as a utopian company town.

Local newspaper accounts produced at the time of Cokedale's founding serve as the starting point in Barton's analysis. *Anatomy of a Model Mining Community* begins by referencing the article "Riley [*sic*] Canon Will Be Model Camp of State," printed in the *Trinidad Chronicle News* in January 1907. The newspaper claimed that an unprecedented one million dollars was being invested in the camp's construction. ASARCO, it was explained, was equipping the town with every convenience: solidly built and affordable homes, a clean water supply, a well-stocked general store, a school, and fire department. A city was being built "where every man was to be paid a fair price for his hire." Cokedale would soon "pour its smoke of progress and send forth hundreds upon hundreds of filled cars of coal and coke."[13]

The *Trinidad Chronicle News* was an ardent promoter of local mining interests and it followed events in Cokedale closely, including visits made by industry and government officials. In March 1907, W. L. Bretherton, financial representative of the noted Montana "copper-king" and U.S. senator William A. Clark, toured the community. Bretherton's goal was to gain insight into the workings of a "model coal and coke camp." According to newspaper accounts, he came away impressed. "I regard this Riley [sic] Canon camp as one of the very best I have ever seen," he stated, "It is an ideal camp."[14] In August of the same year, U.S. vice-president Charles Warren Fairbanks visited the district. A large gathering greeted the vice-president at the Cokedale depot. The *Chronicle News* described Fairbanks's tour:

> After making an address the Vice-President was taken over the little town. For once the smile that had played over his features vanished, usurped by a look of wonderment. He glanced at the library, at the general club rooms, at the concrete dwellings and at the clean, well-kept streets and he exclaimed, "wonderful, wonderful!" It was up to the Vice President to look amazed. He had been in coal camps before, but this was the first time he was ever in a Colorado model camp. "These people must be happy," he said as he surveyed their pretty little homes and their model institutions.[15]

Cokedale's status as a model mining camp also was established by descriptions appearing in state coal reports and industry journals. In 1908 the *Thirteenth Biennial Report of the State Coal Mine Inspector* contained an overview of the new Cokedale mine. It praised its operation. ASARCO, it explained, "has stepped out of the beaten track regarding houses for their workmen," making Cokedale "one of the prettiest mining camps in the state." Other industry reports extolled the town's cleanliness and its exceptional array of civic features, which, it has come to be believed, reflected the humanitarian concerns of Daniel Guggenheim, then president and director of ASARCO. This opinion is based on testimony Guggenheim gave at a hearing held by the Federal Commission on Industrial Relations in 1916, where, as quoted in *Anatomy of a Model Mining Community*, he stated: "I do not think there can be too much legislation along humanitarian lines. Surely no man who has been successful can be happy when he realizes the conditions of the workers. We must see that the worker not only gets sufficient wages but also gets some of the comforts and luxuries of life. I have always felt that way. I believe in the democratization of industry."[16]

In local histories, Guggenheim serves as the benevolent founder of Cokedale, and his status and that of the town are bolstered through contrast with the most reviled operator in the Trinidad District, the CF&I's John D. Rockefeller Jr. "If ASARCO's record in Colorado were judged from on high," writes one historian, "it might have qualified for industrial sainthood. . . . If the verdict were delivered by a jury of southern Colorado coal miners, the judgment would be simple and direct: 'Go straight to hell, Rockefeller! Thanks, Guggenheimer!'"[17]

Allegedly, residents had much to thank Guggenheim for. Barton writes: "Cokedale was responsibly planned, offered substantial, comfortable homes, good community facilities and services, attractive surroundings, satisfactory working conditions, and an atmosphere that encouraged a healthy community spirit." In most ways, she concludes, Cokedale stood apart from other company towns in the Trinidad Coal Field. Its housing could be rented at the lowest possible rates. Provision of sanitation, water, and electricity—services reportedly unavailable in other camps—were company priorities. Residents were provided with a clean and healthy living environment. A company doctor delivered care for a nominal monthly fee. A regular maintenance regime including house painting, and electrical and carpentry work were supplied free of charge. A camp beautification program, which included the planting of shade trees and grass, helped retain an orderly appearance, and the town earned a reputation as "the most attractive mining camp in the area." The company also provided an elementary school, "one that compared favorably with similar schools found in cities of ten thousand."[18]

It is claimed that one of Cokedale's most outstanding amenities was its company store (Figure 3.4). Usually, company stores were loathed institutions but Cokedale's Gottlieb Mercantile was reputedly an exception. ASARCO owned the store. According to historians, however, its operating philosophy differed from that of other companies. ASARCO leased the building to an independent proprietor, a merchant named David Gottlieb, who set the store's prices. Supposedly, ASARCO had no desire to expand its economic control by forcing employees to trade at the store; residents traded wherever they wanted to, and scrip (a company coupon redeemable only at the company store) was never issued in lieu of cash on paydays.[19]

According to historical accounts, ASARCO's concern for resident well-being created a harmonious and tolerant community. Drinking and disorderly conduct were believed to be rare, as was conflict among the town's various ethnic groups. Barton claims that the Cokedale town constable had "the easiest job in town. . . . [D]espite the incredible variety of ethnic backgrounds, people got along remarkably well." Purportedly, this amicable atmosphere also extended into the workplace. Early newspaper accounts and industry literature heaped praise on ASARCO's safety standards and fair wage scales. The picture painted is one of a company that cared for its workers; miners were satisfied with working conditions and ASARCO fostered good management-employee relations. As an example, Barton describes ASARCO's willingness to help employees during the Great Depression by ignoring rents that couldn't be paid, donating groceries to families in need, and providing domestic coal free of charge. She also asserts that fair treatment of workers was an effective antidote to unionization. Worker grievances were "few" and "insignificant." For most of its operation, she presumes, Cokedale avoided unionization. As a result, it is widely believed that the community was unscathed by the labor war of 1913–1914 and that Cokedale remained distant from the tragedy at Ludlow Junction.[20]

3.4 The Gottlieb Mercantile, circa 1910. Owned by ASARCO but leased to an independent operator named David Gottlieb, the company store contained groceries, dry goods, furniture, and hardware. Courtesy, Cokedale Miners' Museum

The events surrounding mine closure have also become an important part of Cokedale lore. As described in *Anatomy of a Model Mining Community,* newly hired men, familiar with union activities in other camps, brought labor organization to the colliery late in its operation. Reportedly, unionization increased production costs and forced ASARCO to close operations in 1947. Soon after, ASARCO sold its Cokedale property to Florence Machinery and Supply Company, a Denver salvaging firm. Allegedly, at ASARCO's request, the sale agreement included a provision allowing residents to purchase their homes. Ostensibly, residents expressed a desire to stay and houses were made available for purchase. In 1948, residents incorporated the town.[21] The story of Cokedale's persistence, then, is also tied to its utopian character. The community's survival is attributed to the belief that unlike other company towns in the Trinidad Coal Field, Cokedale was a desirable place to live and work. Residents grew attached to the community and, with ASARCO's assistance, purchased their homes following mine closure.

THE UTOPIAN MYTH

The historical narrative is consistent: Cokedale was a paradise—a utopian mining camp—compared to other company towns. Unfortunately, however, the town's idyllic image does not stand close scrutiny. The familiar story of Cokedale lacks historical context.[22] The promotional sources used to interpret early conditions in the camp are misleading; the industry's underlying rationale for constructing "model" company towns must be considered.

Model company towns were being built across the U.S. industrial landscape in the early decades of the twentieth century. Although commonly promoted as places built by operators with an altruistic interest in worker well-being, company towns generally were not constructed for humanitarian reasons. For industrialists, use of the "model" label was a good public relations move, because in the early 1900s company towns were increasingly being perceived as exploitive places. More significantly, model company towns directly served the economic interests of industry. An environmentalist philosophy underpinned their construction: operators believed that favorable living conditions would yield a loyal workforce and that company paternalism, operating in a carefully designed environment, could be used to maintain control over labor. At the time Cokedale was founded, a need for such measures was substantial. Poor conditions in neighboring camps were being investigated by the state in the wake of the field's first general strike (1903–1904). Furthermore, by 1907, labor interests in southern Colorado were reorganizing. With the more radical Industrial Workers of the World gaining a foothold in the area, incentive existed for operators such as ASARCO to attempt to minimize union activity. The model camp served this purpose.[23]

ASARCO's decision to build a state-of-the-art industrial settlement was guided by the belief that by increasing worker productivity and subverting labor unrest, expenditures in town infrastructure would prove to be a wise investment. Regrettably, the historical record lacks such critical appraisal. Instead, as previously mentioned, the town is said to embody the humanitarian concerns of Daniel Guggenheim on the basis of questionable use of his testimony to the U.S. Commission on Industrial Relations in 1916. At the hearing, which was held in the wake of the Ludlow Massacre, Guggenheim expressed his sympathy for the worker and his deposition generated favorable press. Yet, Guggenheim was ordered to appear at the inquiry because of ASARCO's history of labor troubles and the notoriously poor conditions that existed at its smelters and mines. An astute businessman, Guggenheim was aware that the hearings provided an opportunity to sway public opinion of company operations, even if his stated concern for worker welfare was not representative of the company's practices. Looking more critically at the facts, biographer Harvey O'Connor suggests that Guggenheim turned the commission into a sounding board designed to undo the mischief caused by a generation of unfavorable publicity. Indeed, Guggenheim made no direct mention of Cokedale at the hearing. This omission is significant considering that he had been asked to detail measures the company had taken to improve living and working conditions at its U.S. facilities.[24]

Of all the various claims about this supposedly utopian mining town, the notion that living conditions were better in Cokedale holds the most truth. ASARCO devoted considerable resources to community upkeep and the town's organized layout and tidy appearance set it apart from other company towns in the Trinidad Coal Field. Moreover, at the time of construction, Cokedale's housing was superior to that of adjacent camps, many of which had been in operation for several decades. In the early 1900s it was common for Trinidad-area mining families to be living in dirt-floored shacks. Cokedale could boast the absence of such conditions. Living conditions in Cokedale, however, were exceptional only in the town's early years; conditions in the camps of the Trinidad Coal Field did not remain constant over time. Generally, civic infrastructure was deplorable at the time of the 1913–1914 strike, but in its wake, public scrutiny and political pressure forced operators to implement changes as a wave of corporate liberalism swept through the mining field. In the CF&I camps, reform came by way of Rockefeller's Industrial Representation Plan. Although criticized for not significantly altering power relations between capital and labor, Rockefeller implemented reforms that resulted in improved camp conditions. The CF&I replaced dilapidated housing with structures comparable to those found in Cokedale. Like ASARCO, the CF&I also instituted community beautification programs. Many of Cokedale's other amenities were the same as those provided by operators in other towns. Virtually all of the camps had elementary schools and provided recreational facilities. Services such as garbage collection, company doctors, and company stores were also standard. As a result, for most of its operating lifespan, Cokedale contained few amenities that were not available in other company towns.[25]

Even Cokedale's much-hailed housing situation was not much different from other towns in the field. Contrary to the belief that housing in Cokedale was of a better quality and that ASARCO charged lower rents, an investigation of area housing conditions conducted in the 1920s shows that similar cinderblock homes were being rented at identical rates ($2 a room per month) elsewhere in the field. Boarding rates were also comparable; rooms in ASARCO and CF&I boardinghouses rented for $25 and $26 per month, respectively. Whether Cokedale's company store operated differently in terms of the use of scrip, the pricing of merchandise, and the degree to which workers were expected to trade at the establishment are also open to debate. In an interview conducted in 1978, longtime resident Horace Hurtado confirmed that scrip was used as a means of pay early in the camp's operation. He also said that workers who chose not to trade at the company store often lost their jobs.[26]

Another aspect of Cokedale's past that has received little attention is the state of living conditions that existed at Bon Carbo, an integral part of the Cokedale operation. The few written accounts that exist of Bon Carbo portray it in an unflattering light. The company built offices, a schoolhouse, a company store (a branch of the Gottlieb Mercantile), and more than a dozen cottages at Bon Carbo. At its peak, 200 residents lived in the camp. Unlike Cokedale, however, Bon Carbo also contained a shantytown where ASARCO miners lived in ramshackle hovels. Living conditions were poor and the settlement had a notorious reputation; it is best remembered for its rowdy saloon and dance hall. Longtime resident and former Cokedale mayor John Johnson stated that Bon Carbo was a "rough place" reserved primarily for bachelor miners, many of whom were of Slavic descent. The poor living conditions at Bon Carbo fail to uphold ASARCO's image as a benevolent operator.[27]

Division and conflict along ethnic and class lines were common in the company towns of the Trinidad Coal Field and, once again, Cokedale was no exception. Area historian Rick Clyne describes how workers of Asian and Hispanic descent were common targets of discrimination. Clyne also relates how Cokedale's Japanese workers, a group employed in the community in the early years of its operation, were completely segregated both above and below ground. They were barred from the bathhouse and had a separate entry into the mine. He also reveals that an active chapter of the Ku Klux Klan existed in Cokedale in the 1920s and that cross-burnings were commonly held on company property. Moreover, unlike the CF&I, ASARCO had an unwritten company rule that banned African Americans from employment. Clyne quotes resident Frank Wojtylka to support this claim: "They [ASARCO] just wouldn't hire them. . . . You never saw a colored man working here in this mine. . . . They work in CF&I [mines] . . . but not at Cokedale."[28]

Analysis of census data confirms that Cokedale was an ethnically diverse place. Manuscript census schedules from 1920 show that of the town's 142 homes, 48 contained heads of households of Anglo American ancestry, 33 were Hispanic, 24 were Italian, and 23 were Mexican. The remaining households contained residents of various European ancestries. Spatial plotting of these households reveals that the community was segregated along ethnic lines between Cokedale's northern and southern residential districts. To the north, along Elm and Spruce Streets, lay 65 percent of the town's Anglo American households. Homes on Elm Street were 80 percent Anglo American and only one home on Silk-Stocking Row (the west side of Elm Street) contained a non-Anglo head of household. By contrast, to the south, mixed together on Pine, Maple, and Church Streets, were 83 percent of the community's Italian households and 70 percent of its Hispanic-headed households. The census also reveals that the town's multiple-unit houses were dominated by residents of Hispanic and Mexican ancestry.[29]

Ethnicity also played a role in the occupations held by Cokedale residents. In 1920, 75 percent of miners—the largest occupational class and the lowest paid workers—were of Hispanic and Mexican ancestry. Only Italians and Hispanics, the former dominating in number, worked the coke ovens. In addition, of the roughly twenty managerial or professional positions in the camp, only two were held by non-Anglos: the coke oven foreman and the section boss, both of whom were Italians. Almost all of Cokedale's positions of power—camp marshall, school principal, store manager, camp superintendent, and shift bosses—were held by Anglo Americans. As a result of these ethnic occupational biases, a north-south cleavage existed in class structure. In 1920 more than 60 percent of north-side homes were occupied by managerial or professional-class workers. The occupations of those living on Silk-Stocking Row (chemist, foreman, accountant, camp physician, and safety inspector) reveal that this area was reserved almost exclusively for this group. In contrast, the majority of the town's lower-paid workers resided south of the town center.[30]

Like other operators in the Trinidad Coal Field, ASARCO controlled housing and job assignments, and segregation along ethnic and class lines was intentional. Interviews conducted with longtime residents confirm that Cokedale was a divided community. Notable tension existed between residents living on the north and south sides of the community. A longtime resident of Elm Street imparted the following childhood recollection: "They're real negative over there on Maple Street. When we were kids we used to fight with them, with those people from over there. One night we were playing marbles under the arc lights and a gang from over there came by and started harassing us. I was a feisty one and I got a baseball bat. I said leave or someone will get hurt. I hit one guy with the bat and they took off. This guy was Polish or Czechoslovakian."[31]

Another resident described the lasting nature of ethnic and class conflict in Cokedale. His comments also reveal how the town's layout and atmosphere have helped to maintain polarized attitudes.

> There has been a lot of divisiveness. It goes back to the coal mining days. On one side was Silk-Stocking Row. Maple Street was the poor area. The town center was a dividing line. This is still uppermost in many people's minds. At first, I couldn't understand this conflict. Why couldn't these people get along, and why was there so much animosity and hatred? Part of it is ethnic, but Maple Street was also closer to the coke ovens and the machine shop, so it was noisier and dirtier. On Maple Street it's still the pits. It gets dark very early. . . . When I walk around town I almost never walk down Maple. I find that the people who live there, if I was to characterize them, which is probably very unfair, are not very civil or friendly. I don't know what it is, there's vibes or something in the air.[32]

True to historical claims, Cokedale had one of the best-equipped mining operations in the Trinidad area. The quality of working life, however, has been overstated. Pay scales, working conditions, and ASARCO's general policies regarding labor were not exceptional. In 1917, the State Inspector of Coal Mines published a comparative listing of wages paid in the Trinidad Coal Field. As was standard practice, ASARCO miners were paid for each ton of coal they dug. ASARCO paid fifty-eight cents per ton, the same rate paid by the CF&I. Moreover, ASARCO's pay rate was exceeded at ten collieries operating in Las Animas County. Although data is scarce, a glimpse into the economic existence of the Cokedale worker is provided by the monthly payroll statement of miner Jacob Game, dated February 10, 1913. The statement was submitted at a 1914 congressional investigation into working conditions in the Trinidad Coal Field. Game was paid $29.15 for loading coal and brushing shafts. Following deductions for living and working expenses, he was left with a paltry $1.70 in take-home pay.[33]

ASARCO's mines were also as dangerous as any in the Trinidad Coal Field. Between 1911 and 1929, sixty-two men died in the Cokedale and Bon Carbo mines. In ten of these years, the fatality rate for ASARCO miners (one fatality per 148,000 tons of coal produced) was higher than that of the CF&I (one fatality per 244,000 tons). In addition, like other operations, the ASARCO mines were vulnerable to disaster. On February 9, 1911, an explosion ripped through the Cokedale Number Two mine, killing seventeen workers. As was standard practice, a state investigation of the mine disaster was conducted. Evidence suggested that ASARCO should not have ordered workers into the mine, because an inspection by the fire boss prior to the explosion had revealed the presence of volatile gases in the shafts. Nevertheless, state investigators laid blame for the accident on worker negligence; the explosion was deemed the result of an overcharged shot. (Most accidents were blamed on the workers.) What appears to distinguish Cokedale from other mining camps is the residents' reaction to this accident, which reveals the degree of control that ASARCO held over its workforce. Previous disasters in the field had been marked by protests as grieving family members and surviving miners flocked to accident sites to express their dissatisfaction with mine safety. As reported in the *Trinidad Chronicle News,* however, ASARCO displayed firmer control over Cokedale's residents. "A similar heartrending scene was not enacted in Cokedale," the newspaper explained, "where the guard lines have been closely drawn and the utmost order prevails."[34]

According to resident John Johnson, one of the community's last surviving miners, working life was hard. His account of working conditions differs markedly from those appearing in local histories. When asked if workers could make a decent living in Cokedale, Johnson remarked: "You could if you were a company man, they were on a wage. The coal diggers had to make their own money. What ever you loaded, that's all they paid you. If you got a good place to dig you could make money, if you didn't you suffered. There were a lot of complaints especially at Bon Carbo. It was a lousy mine. The company, they didn't help out much. They'd tell you there it is—go at it." Regarding claims that ASARCO donated food and coal and did not collect rent from residents during the Great Depression, Johnson remembers things differently:

Coal miners had tough times, especially during the Depression. It was really tough. Only one day a month could you go to work at the mine. Maybe load one or two cars of coal. When you'd go by the company store and ask for something to eat they would ask, "How many cars did you load?" They would give you that amount and no more. The company didn't help. We had to pay for our own lights and for our coal. There was a group of people that had money. They were involved with the company, bosses and town clerks, they were OK. . . . This was a dead place during the Depression. No money coming in, grocery man wouldn't give you credit. We didn't get anything for free that's for darn sure. If we did, I didn't get any of it. Hell no! Not even when they were going full blast, they wouldn't give you nothing. Give you a lot of Hell if you weren't doing what they wanted you to do. A typical coal mining camp.[35]

As confirmed by the comments of onetime oven worker Emilio Ferraro, ASARCO ruled Cokedale with absolute authority. "They had the law. The company officials, they had the law on hand. They would come to tell you something and you'd be obedient and go ahead with what they were telling you."[36]

These firsthand accounts contradict claims that workers were content, and evidence suggests that ASARCO experienced its share of labor troubles. Although ASARCO maintained production during the 1913–1914 strike, coal output and employment dropped during these years (Figure 3.5). And contrary to popular belief, Cokedale miners were unionized. When the strike was called at a convention held in Trinidad on September 16, 1913, the community had UMWA representatives in attendance. Cokedale's five representatives gave it as large a voice in the strike vote as any town in the Trinidad Coal Field. In fact, at a second UMWA convention held in September 1914, the town exceeded its allotted quota of delegates.[37] How Cokedale's representatives voted at these conventions is unknown, but testimony given by delegate Tony Lamont at the 1913 meeting suggests that they supported the strike. Lamont detailed the poor conditions that existed in the ASARCO mines with unfair rates charged for supplies and paltry pay scales. According to Lamont, a living wage was not paid in Cokedale and the company's attitude to union organization was oppressive:

Every man is closely watched and if the guards suspect him of belonging to the organization, he is discharged. . . . The boss said he would have me fired because I was a member of the union, and I told him he was behind the times; that everyone was a union man now, but he notified the superintendent to give me my time. . . . They keep the miners very close in the camp. . . . They get very poor food and some of the children are dressed in clothes made of gunny-sacks and their fathers are working every day.[38]

The comments of resident Horace Hurtado, interviewed in 1978, also suggest a high level of union membership: "If you came in here when they had a strike and you were not a union man you were in for trouble." UMWA records show that in

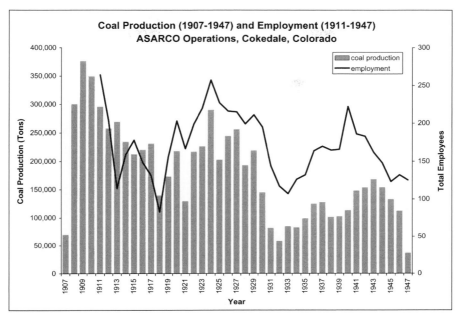

Coal Production (1907-1947) and Employment (1911-1947)
ASARCO Operations, Cokedale, Colorado

3.5 Coal production peaked at Cokedale in 1909 (376,196 tons). The highest employment levels on record occurred in 1911 (264 employees). Coal production and employment fluctuated throughout Cokedale's forty years of operation in response to shifting conditions in the metals market and, to a lesser extent, changing labor relations in the Trinidad Coal Field. A significant drop in production and employment, occurred during the 1913–1914 strike. Data from Bien-nial *and* Annual Reports of the State Inspector of Coal Mines, *1907 through 1947*

the post-strike year of 1915, the Cokedale local had ninety-eight members, a figure representing more than half of ASARCO's workforce.[39]

Like other operators, ASARCO maintained coal production during the 1913–1914 strike by hiring nonunion workers. Mexicans and Hispanics commonly were used as strikebreakers in the Trinidad Coal Field, and comparison of Cokedale's ethnic makeup prior to and following the strike suggests the importation of such workers. In 1910 only 20 percent of miners were of Mexican or Hispanic descent; by 1920 they composed 75 percent of the mining workforce.

To maintain production, like other camps, Cokedale became a guarded military zone during the dispute. According to various accounts, the state militia joined company guards in patrolling the community and established a militia camp near the mouth of Reilly Canyon. A fence was erected around the mining property, searchlights were installed on a cupola above the washery, and a locomotive was parked on the road to prohibit traffic in and out of the town. Such measures belie the notion that Cokedale was a haven of labor peace.[40]

Although Cokedale held aesthetic advantages over neighboring mining towns, beneath this veneer lay an industrial community built and operated for the profitable production of coal and coke. Living and working conditions were not exceptional; in most ways life was as difficult as that experienced in other company towns. Why then has Cokedale been portrayed as a utopian community? The answer lies in exploring the challenges historians faced in coming to terms with Cokedale's meaning as a mining town as well as a lived-in place.

Cokedale's idyllic image is influenced by the mining imaginary—popular idealizations of mining landscapes—and by company town stereotypes.[41] Commonly thought of as boisterous, transient, and dilapidated, mining towns are widely thought to have offered their residents difficult and unrewarding lives. Although these generalizations have not been directly applied to Cokedale, they still influence its image as Cokedale is considered an exception to the norm, a place where industrial exploitation and resident hardship—believed to be central aspects of life in other company towns in the Trinidad Coal Field—did not exist. This counterintuitive view dominates historical interpretations of the town and is dependent on the acceptance of established stereotypes.[42] It is difficult to accept Cokedale's utopian image without first accepting the dystopian image that dominates accounts of neighboring company towns. Unfortunately, just as a purely hellish view of these places is inaccurate, so, too, is one of a mythic ideal. A truer account of life in Cokedale lies between these extremes.

It is true, for example, that many in Cokedale established a bond to the community. Although claims of community cohesiveness have, in terms of ethnic and class relations, been overstated, the fact remains that residents were engaged in community life. Numerous church, school, and recreational organizations existed in Cokedale. Social events such as the annual Fourth of July field day, Labor Day celebrations, and Sunday afternoon baseball games were well attended. Longtime residents expressed considerable community pride. "It was just so pleasant to live here," remarked Gertrude Ferraro. "People were very friendly. . . . [W]e had a lot of doings. . . . [I]n those older days nobody had a lot of money but we had good times." In describing his family's tenure in Cokedale, genealogist Rollie Schafer stated, "[F]amilies have a golden time when life falls into place in a proper and satisfying order." For the Schafer family, Cokedale served as that place.[43]

Resident accounts show that many grew attached to Cokedale, but residents were aware of the town's shortcomings. When asked to describe his attachment to Cokedale, John Johnson claimed that it was, indeed, a "model community" and a good place to live. In discussing the details of daily existence, however, he said that the town was a "typical coal mining camp" and that ASARCO was as tough an operator as the CF&I. Resident Bette Arguello, who grew up in the nearby CF&I camps of Segundo and Valdez and moved to Cokedale in her teens, expressed similar ambivalence, but she described her preference for Cokedale. Arguello felt affection for the town but she also explained that life could be unforgiving. In many ways, she explained, daily existence was a challenge. For Johnson and Arguello, Cokedale held value as a community and home and they both had sentimental attachments to the town, but their comments reveal a competing sentiment: knowledge that Cokedale was a difficult place to live and work.[44]

A more accurate account of Cokedale's past would show that there was a duality to place meaning: life was hard and yet many developed an intense bond to place. Such an account would serve the community better than its utopian narrative, which, it could be argued, represents a form of community boosterism, a common fault of the local history genre. Viewing works like *Anatomy of a Model Mining Community* in this way, however, is too simplistic for it discounts the challenges historians faced in coming to terms with Cokedale's past. Without question, negative details were omitted from local histories, but how else were their authors to come to terms with the affection residents expressed for the community? The easiest way for historians to explain this sentiment was to show that Cokedale was somehow different or better than other company towns in southern Colorado. Indeed, the stereotypes that surround these settlements leave little room for other interpretations. It seems logical to think in one of two ways: either Cokedale was a typical company town, an exploitive place despised by its residents and subsequently abandoned when its colliery closed, or it was a more humane and appreciated place that survived because it was a better community in which to live and work. Faced with the challenge of trying to make sense of this paradox and influenced by the mining imaginary, historians searched for a story that seemingly explained resident attachments and the town's survival. The notion of Cokedale as a utopian town served this role.

MINE CLOSURE AND COMMUNITY SURVIVAL

Cokedale's utopian mythology fails to convey an authentic sense of the town's character and identity. It also fails to explain one of the most unique aspects of the town's past: its survival following mine closure. Historians have attributed this community's persistence to three factors: ASARCO's creation of a more livable and humane environment, the development of a unique community spirit and residents' subsequent refusal to quit the town, and ASARCO's plan of disinvestment that reportedly allowed residents to stay in the community. None of these claims, however, adequately explains the town's survival.

Cokedale did not become the Trinidad Coal Field's sole surviving company town because it was a better place to live and work. Such an explanation is entwined in a faulty utopian mythology. What then can be said of the other factors implicated in Cokedale's endurance? Was an attachment to place unique to this community and, if so, does it explain the town's persistence? *Anatomy of a Model Mining Community* highlights this thesis, which also appears in National Register documents citing a "cradle-to-grave" sense of contentment and loyalty to community as key contributors to the town's survival.[45]

Many of Cokedale's residents developed an emotional tie to place, a bonding that at first seems unusual given the nature of life and landscape in mining communities and company towns. Such sentiment, however, was common in the Trinidad Coal Field. Historian Rick Clyne describes how life in these company towns led their residents to develop a strong sense of community: "The coal towns were isolated, populated largely by immigrants, and driven by a dangerous activity— mining coal. These characteristics colored all relations among camp residents and contributed to a shared sense of community. . . . A sense of community could not be imposed from above. It was created and maintained by camp residents, who relied on it for defense against the company, against isolation, and against the traumatic nature of mining coal."[46]

Anecdotal evidence suggests that residents living in other mining towns also may have resisted abandoning their communities following mine closure. The comments of Bette Arguello, who moved to Cokedale from Valdez, a nearby CF&I company town, describe her mother's wish to stay in Valdez for as long as she could. Arguello explains: "I left Valdez after the mines closed. They started selling houses and they took them to La Junta. My mother wanted to stay there and she wouldn't get out. Pretty soon the electricity was off and the water was off. They were moving houses and there were foundations all around. . . . Finally I convinced her to move down to Cokedale. There's not much you can see in Valdez now."[47] Although Cokedale would not have endured without a commitment by some to stay, the likelihood that similar bonds to place existed in other company towns makes this explanation of community survival problematic. Thus, Cokedale's status as the area's only surviving company town cannot be fully explained by the allegedly distinctive ties residents established to place.

Cokedale's survival has also been attributed to the role ASARCO played in assisting residents to stay following colliery closure. Reportedly, ASARCO engaged in a thoughtful plan of property disinvestment that aided the community's continuation, but the actual events of mine closure do not support this claim. In the final years of operation, rising production costs had decreased the profitability of the Bon Carbo mine. Because ASARCO could no longer afford to supply its distant El Paso smelter with Colorado coke, Bon Carbo was closed on May 9, 1947.[48] Five days after mine closure ASARCO sold its Cokedale and Bon Carbo properties (land and buildings) to the Florence Machinery and Supply Company of Denver. The fact that ASARCO sold its property to an independent salvaging firm, effectively washing its hands of the decommissioning project, was unusual. Mine operators usually salvaged what they could before quitting the company towns and they often retained ownership of the land. ASARCO, however, had no local operations where infrastructure could be moved. Nor did the company have a need to maintain ownership of mineral rights in the area. For these reasons, ASARCO chose to sell its Cokedale properties outright.[49]

Florence Machinery bought the ASARCO properties for $225,000. Even though the actual details of the transaction are unknown, it is assumed that ASARCO negotiated a provision in the sale agreement whereby residents were allowed to purchase their homes. Local historian Patrick Donachy writes, "[W]hen ASARCO closed its operations people envisioned another ghost camp beset with grotesque foundations where homes once stood. . . . [B]ut the company allowed what most companies wouldn't—the camp would remain if people wanted to buy their homes." The fact that Florence Machinery immediately began dismantling the town, however, casts suspicion on this claim. Most of Cokedale's industrial infrastructure was salvaged. More significant, all of its two-story shared housing structures, twenty in total, were demolished, significantly reducing the housing stock. Florence Machinery also pulled up and sold the town's municipal water pipes. Had the salvaging firm been planning to maintain the community it seems unlikely that housing and vital civic infrastructure would have been removed. Residents at the time remembered feeling great uncertainty regarding their tenure in Cokedale. "At first we didn't know what the company was going to do with the houses," explained Emilio Ferraro in an interview conducted in 1978, "they first said they were going to tear them all down." Likewise, resident John Johnson confirmed that the town's future was in doubt at this time: "It was a very sad time. I was on the State Legislature and the phone was ringing every day for me. People were asking what are we going to do, what are we going to do? I had no idea what to do. I was in the same shape that they were—wondering were in the Hell to go. A lot of the old-timers, especially the old-timers, were scared."[50]

Florence Machinery was dismantling Cokedale and the majority of the community's approximately 800 residents were forced to leave. "A lot of people left, they had to go," stated Johnson, "some went up to Valdez where the mines were still working. A lot went over to New Mexico to the York mine near Raton." A small number of residents, however, stayed on and Florence Machinery employed some in demolition work. All paid rent to the salvaging firm. Witnessing their community being torn down around them, those residents that remained began considering ways to save their homes. Father Haller, priest of the Cokedale Church, formulated a plan. He proposed pooling residents' resources into a cooperative fund that would be used to purchase the town's remaining structures. Florence Machinery was willing to consider offers to sell its properties and halt further demolition. Unfortunately, to the dismay of many, Florence Machinery's asking price of $32,000 was too high and the co-op plan fell through. Haller's efforts, however, appear to have strengthened residents' resolve to save the community.[51]

Thus, contrary to conventional wisdom, ASARCO played no role in preserving the town; Cokedale's fate lay in the hands of Florence Machinery. Why the salvaging firm decided to sell the remaining houses, rather than continue to demolish the town, is not precisely known but it is likely that Florence Machinery determined that more money could be made selling the houses that were left. It was clear that potential homebuyers existed in Cokedale. Furthermore, unlike other company towns, most of which lay in remote mountain canyons, the community was easily accessible by road to the city of Trinidad where a larger market existed for affordable housing. Had these economic and spatial factors not existed, residents' desire to stay in Cokedale would have been inconsequential; like other company towns in the Trinidad field, the settlement would have been demolished. More than any altruistic desire to save the community, a business decision made by Florence Machinery, based on the town's favorable location, facilitated Cokedale's survival.

Florence Machinery sold Cokedale's housing at a standard rate of $50 per lot and $100 per room. Although the Trinidad Public School District assumed ownership of the schoolhouse, other company structures—Gottlieb Mercantile, mine offices, bathhouse, boardinghouse, and ice house—were put up for sale. By the end of 1947, Florence Machinery had disposed of approximately thirty properties. According to land deeds, fifty property transactions were made in 1948. It is unclear how long Florence Machinery served as landlord for renting residents but the company continued to sell off their Cokedale properties for close to forty years, selling their last properties in the 1980s.[52]

LIFE AND LANDSCAPE IN THE POST-MINING ERA

Residents began organizing to incorporate Cokedale shortly after the first homes in the town were sold. The first formal community meeting was held on October 3, 1947. Not only was town incorporation discussed, but residents also began to develop plans for a volunteer fire department and PTA. One week later, residents adopted a resolution to incorporate the town, but taking control of the community proved to be a daunting task. Municipal services needed immediate attention. Town maintenance ceased when ASARCO abandoned the community and Florence Machinery's gutting of vital infrastructure compounded problems. "We had so much to contend with, we weren't prepared," stated Johnson. "We had outhouses that were beginning to get bad. We had no telephones. We needed water for the schoolhouse and we had to create a school board." Florence Machinery's removal of the water system had created a major problem and a concerted effort was required to reestablish water service. The state provided funds for new water pipes and, for a nominal fee, the city purchased an obsolete water tank from the Santa Fe depot in Trinidad. The tank was erected above the townsite by resident volunteers. Later, federal loans were used for new sewers. Again, residents provided the labor to put the sewers in place.[53]

Company paternalism had left residents with little experience in civic governance but a culture of hard work made up for their inexperience. With considerable effort, community services were reestablished and, other than a general decline in the town's appearance, living conditions were brought back to mining-era standards. There was a certain continuity to life in the post-mining era. Cokedale's single-family houses and the majority of its community structures remained standing. By 1950, three years after the mine had closed, the town had a population of 214. Although significantly reduced in size—at its height it contained more than 1,000 residents—the community was hanging on. In 1952 the *Trinidad City Directory* listed seventy-two residences in Cokedale, indicating that the majority of its remaining houses were occupied five years after colliery closure. Many of those who stayed on purchased the same homes they had occupied in the mining era. As a result, social divides in the community were preserved. In addition, the mining way of life had not been entirely abandoned, as a number of residents found employment in other area collieries still in operation.[54]

Despite these continuities in lifestyle, the community was experiencing considerable change. In the decade following mine closure, a transformation occurred in the social characteristics of the community. Cokedale remained an ethnically diverse place but an influx of newcomers was altering social identity. The exact number of residents who remained following mine closure is unknown but a rough estimate can be calculated by analyzing rural directories prior to and following colliery closure. A comparison of resident listings in 1935 (the last directory printed in the mining era) and 1948 reveals that 25 of the town's 64 homes were headed by families who lived in the community twelve years prior to ASARCO's pullout. By 1952 the number had fallen to 14, revealing an increase in the number of newcomers to the town.[55]

For the first time in its history, Cokedale was home to a largely non-mining population. Affordable housing attracted many of these newcomers. In particular, some students from nearby Trinidad State Junior College found that it was cheaper to purchase a home in Cokedale for two or three years than to rent in Trinidad. In 1948 Joan Reese of *Rocky Mountain Empire Magazine* described the attraction Cokedale held: "Four-room house and lot for $450! And 72 houses available, all for the price of $100 per room and $50 for the land." Reese's description, however, also documents a transformation of the town's image. Cokedale, she explained, provided only "adequate living." Homes lacked indoor plumbing and forty years of "hard living" had taken a toll on the structures. Fences and windows needed to be replaced, and "the abandoned smelter, rows of gaping coke ovens, and other useless equipment, still need to be cleared away."[56]

"Cokedale is far from being the model town of its origin," wrote Reese only a year after ASARCO had abandoned the community. This statement is surprising as basic living conditions had not significantly changed. Nevertheless, the town was no longer viewed as a desirable place. Reference to the community's struggles and a detailing of inadequate living conditions dominate the handful of outside accounts of Cokedale in the early years of incorporation. With mine closure, ghost town imagery began to pervade outside perceptions.[57]

This transformation in Cokedale's image occurred, in part, because the community was no longer serving the function for which it was built. Although living and working conditions in U.S. company towns were obviously difficult, these conditions were frequently justified on the basis that they offered the only efficient means of extracting natural resources from remote areas. Viewed as necessary evils, mining towns like Cokedale were tolerated as long as they served their primary function. Without mining, no justification remained for defending their existence. More significantly, however, negative accounts of the town emerged as a result of relatively superficial changes to its appearance. Journalists had long been enamored with the camp's tidy appearance and had ignored the details of life beneath this aesthetic facade. Once ASARCO had ceased to maintain the community, this veil was lifted and more critical accounts of the town emerged.

The Trinidad area was entering a period of deindustrialization and this change compounded Cokedale's growing image problem. Increasingly, residents were struggling to survive in an economy that lacked local employment. Work in the mining industry was unreliable; labor disputes and temporary shutdowns plagued the few collieries still in operation. The Frederick Mine at Valdez closed in 1960, putting many Cokedale residents out of work. The last area colliery, the Allen Mine, struggled on intermittently until 1982. As the economy soured, Cokedale's population declined. The town fell off the federal census record after 1950. Population figures reappeared in 1980, at which time only ninety permanent residents remained. By most accounts, the town was succumbing to dereliction. "The 1950s and 1960s weren't kind to Cokedale," writes historian Patrick Donachy, "people found it necessary to sell their homes and relocate. Empty houses were plentiful and were being placed on the sale block for a proverbial song." Many homes fell into receivership with residents unable to pay mortgages.[58]

By this time, town infrastructure was in significant decay and the Cokedale Town Council was struggling to maintain services on a limited budget; meager property and water taxes provided the bulk of municipal income. Doug Holdread, an art instructor at Trinidad State Junior College and one of the few to settle in Cokedale during this period, described the town:

> When I first moved here, Cokedale was perceived as a dump and it *was*
> pretty dumpy. The places that were maintained stuck out like a sore
> thumb because they looked out of context. It really did look like a ghost
> town. Of course it wasn't, there was just a lot of people sort of hanging
> out here. They were retired from the mines, or they were people like me
> who thought that Cokedale was a cheap place to live and that it was kind
> of funky. . . . I just felt that there were a lot of people who were kind of
> old, kind of tired and poor, who just wanted to be left alone.[59]

Holdread's comments describe a perception, widely held at the time, that Cokedale was teetering on the verge of death. The comments of resident Richard Bell confirm this viewpoint. Bell moved to the community in the mid-1980s. His wife grew up in Trinidad and she held strong preconceptions of what the town was like. Bell explains:

> The mine office in Cokedale was for sale and we looked it over. But Cokedale had a very dismal reputation as a place to live at that point in time. My wife in particular was very cold to the idea of coming to Cokedale even just to look at something, but I thought the house sounded interesting. It had a lot of character to it. She said, "You've got to be kidding." She grew up in Trinidad and since the mines had been closed, Cokedale was not thought of as an attractive place to live. Just a lot of old houses. At that time many were for sale.[60]

To outsiders, Cokedale had become a derelict place. For residents, however, the town still held considerable value. Although internal factions existed, on the whole Cokedale remained a close-knit community. "You could feel some of the tensions," Holdread said, "but as far as living here and relating to people I experienced it as a fairly friendly community. I had to pass muster with some of the old-timers but over-all I felt pretty accepted." Residents would routinely gather at the post office, located within the old company store building. "The post office was the best place to find out what was going on in Cokedale," Holdread recalled. "[I]t was the community meeting place. It had a wood stove and everyone would come in and sit around, wait for the mail, and talk." In other ways, too, residents remained engaged in community life. "We had people doing a lot of volunteer work," Johnson explained. "We were a small town and we didn't have a lot of money. People would help cutting lawns and trimming trees."[61]

Bette Arguello described how Cokedale remained a "tight" community where residents remained committed to helping each other out. "People would do anything for you," she stated. That the community remained cohesive with many retaining a fondness for the town in these difficult years is also confirmed by the comments of Tony Massarotti. A onetime oven worker, Massarotti moved to Trinidad following mine closure. He was interviewed in 1999: "[I]t was great growing up in the camp," he said. "[E]verybody looked out for everybody else." Massarotti described how he often returned to Cokedale: "I used to go to Cokedale and reminisce with a lot of friends who are now gone. We'd talk about all the good times we used to have up there. Those were the good times, the good days with a lot of good people. That was the key. There were a lot of real great people. Those were the happy days. I feel very fortunate to have lived them."[62]

Further evidence of residents' engagement in community life was their involvement in civic politics. Residents, however, had little experience managing community affairs and governance issues tended to bring community factions to the fore. For example, despite vocal opposition, the town council passed strict maintenance ordinances similar to those that had existed under ASARCO's control. Designed to maintain Cokedale's aesthetic order, the most contentious of these ordinances required regular cutting of weeds and lawns. Newcomers to the community, who viewed this ordinance as too restrictive, fiercely opposed the yard maintenance law. "People wanted things done but the income we had wasn't enough," remarked Johnson, who was then mayor of Cokedale. "It was difficult to do anything and people were always hollering at me for doing this and not doing that."[63]

Not only did tensions develop between old and new residents, but the divide that existed between residents living on the north and south sides of the community continued through town incorporation. Politically, power remained in the hands of the historically more affluent north-siders: a group of longtime residents, headed by Mayor Johnson, who came to be known as the "old guard." Many felt that the old guard was undemocratically enforcing its will, much as company officials had once done. Johnson served as mayor of Cokedale for twenty-five years and opposition to his governance was constant. During his tenure, one of the major disputes concerned water issues. Although a new water delivery system had been built, the town was still relying on the original spring and reservoir system put in place by ASARCO, a system that was not maintaining a constant and clean water supply. On one occasion, the National Guard was called in by the state to bring emergency water rations to the town; a permanent solution to the water problem was required. The old guard, living primarily on the rocky slopes of the north side of town, favored constructing a pipeline from the Purgatoire River. The scheme would be financed by a municipal water tax. South-siders, however, were opposed. Many of those living along the creek paralleling Pine and Maple Streets had access to groundwater and wanted to be exempt from paying water fees to the city.

After a lengthy debate the old guard's pipeline and tax scheme was established, but the dispute amplified tensions along the community's north-south divide. Having long felt marginalized, first by company management and now by the old guard, south-side residents continued to view the north as the governing elite. In contrast, from the north-side of town, south-siders were viewed as unjustly critical and demanding. Johnson stated: "The other side of camp was always opposed to every damn thing. They always objected to things that were good for the town."[64]

The negative legacies of the mining era—company paternalism, community factions, and the boom-and-bust nature of the mining economy—had a lasting influence on Cokedale. However, although Cokedale's depressed condition was tied to its company town and mining origins, old-timers were in no way eager to discard these legacies. To the contrary, the old guard resisted most changes that were perceived to be altering the town's mining-era character. Cokedale's company town and mining legacies were not viewed as obstacles to be overcome. For old-timers, the past and the landscape that reflected it were viewed in a positive way.

This sentiment was so strong that community politics and town management were dominated by the old guard's desire to maintain Cokedale more or less as it had been during the mining era. Not surprisingly, a common criticism of the old guard's governance and one that grew as the number of newcomers increased, was their resistance to change, causing improvements in town infrastructure and services to come slowly. The town council was restricted by its limited budget, but newcomers claimed that the old guard displayed little will to make improvements. "When I moved to the community the old-timers were still very much in control," explained Richard Bell. "I saw this as a community with so much potential and I thought I had all kinds of good ideas but I was met with resistance." Bell described how he and several other newcomers struggled to implement changes, such as altering landscaping, bettering roads, and placing playground equipment in Cokedale's Commons Park:

> A few of us were able to get onto the town council but we encountered a great deal of resistance to anything new. . . . [T]he old guard wanted to maintain everything exactly the way it was, they didn't want to see change—what we thought were improvements. They were able to get a handful of people together on the council who would all agree to vote the same way. This all started back in the coal camp days when decisions were made by the company. They [the old guard] didn't have the background or experience to implement change. . . . They just saw this as a very poor community and they feared anything that would cost money; it was a very conservative viewpoint.[65]

The comments of Pat Huhn, who moved to the town in 1990 and later became mayor of Cokedale, provide further insight into the attitudes of old-timers:

> I lived in coal country before, in Pennsylvania and here, and it seems to be a common characteristic. There is too much of an emphasis on this one industry, coal mining. What I see is a fatalistic attitude. The idea that there can only be this one industry. That if we don't have this big industry we're nothing and we'll never get any better. There is this perception that we were good when coal was here and we will never get any better—things will stay the same. It's not true of course, but that's one of the sources of conflict between people coming in and people who have been here.[66]

According to Huhn, old-timers could not envision a future beyond coal mining. The old guard, however, had another, more important reason for resisting change. As resident Doug Holdread explained, the Cokedale landscape held different meaning for old-timers. This contrast in perception underlay many of the conflicts that developed between older and newer residents:

Some people had the mindset to build a better community. But the town was permeated with people talking about the old days, of what it was like when the mines were going. There was a lot of that. That was the character of the community. All these people hanging around remembering, and they didn't really have much of a view of the future; it was more looking back. Probably this attitude was a little negative in the sense that you could see how run-down the community was, but I don't think they saw that. That was the tension. When I first came, there were outhouses everywhere; some people thought that was fine but others didn't. Some people liked Cokedale the way it was, others saw possibilities.[67]

For the old guard, the landscape provided a venue for remembering the mining days. They fought to retain control in order to maintain a sense of what Cokedale had been. The old guard was protective of the town's antiquated atmosphere because it provided a link to its meaning as a place. It also reminded the old guard of who they were as individuals. Although it had succumbed to dereliction, the company town landscape affirmed the community's reason for being and, in turn, residents' place in the world. Cokedale's future was uncertain but the past was secure and could be experienced in a landscape that remained unaltered. Patricia Schorr, who moved to Cokedale in 1992, explained:

The town was falling apart but they [old-timers] were trying to hold on to the idea that this was their little town. They were the ones who had hung onto it at first when the mines closed. They felt a kind of paternalism of their own for the town; they had hung onto it, they really wanted to stay, and I think that's a part of why they didn't want it to change. They were afraid that it would just get too much like anywhere else if they didn't hang on to some of these old thoughts for a long time.[68]

The old guard's conservative ways had a mixed effect on the community. Deindustrialization had taken a toll and little had been done to fight Cokedale's decay. The town developed a pitiful outside image and by socioeconomic measures it was a poor place to live. Its population had steadily declined following mine closure. The town operated on a limited budget, the quality of housing stock had deteriorated, and few opportunities existed for local employment. Nevertheless, despite Cokedale's woes, an intimate attachment and commitment to place was being maintained. Cokedale held a positive image in the eyes of many of its inhabitants. For old-timers, continuity with a past way of life was more important than community rejuvenation. Moreover, in refusing to alter the town's physical character, the old guard had maintained the town's identity and preserved its historic integrity. A modest rejuvenation would come to Cokedale, a renewal made possible by the fact that its company town atmosphere had been protected. In taking a cautious approach to change following incorporation, the old guard had maintained the settlement's physical and cultural uniqueness, which served as the foundation for preservation efforts in the 1980s and 1990s.

As described in the walking tour brochure of Cokedale's historic district, the town provides an opportunity, in a sense, to "step back in time."[69] Yet, much of what is experienced in Cokedale today is the product of changes that occurred in the decades following mine closure. Major changes came about when the Trinidad Dam was built on the Purgatoire River, five miles downstream of the town. A large recreation and flood control project completed in 1977, the dam created a reservoir, which flooded Reilly Canyon's junction with the Purgatoire Valley. At high-water level, the Trinidad Reservoir comes within several hundred yards of the southern end of Cokedale's oven complex. As a result, State Highway 12, which originally ran along the floor of the Purgatoire Valley, was re-routed. Prior to dam construction, the town lay hidden from the highway and was accessible only by a mile-long gravel road. In the mid-1970s Highway 12 was routed through the southern end of the community, now running between Cokedale's residential area and the coke ovens (see Map 3.2). The town lost much of its isolated mining-era character when the highway bisected the town.

With dam and highway construction, newcomers began to come to Cokedale in greater numbers. Homes were bought by outsiders for use as holiday retreats and some real estate speculation occurred; Cokedale was the closest community to the reservoir, which was promoted in local newspapers as southern Colorado's answer to Lake Tahoe. By 1985, 36 of the town's 101 house lots were owned by individuals whose permanent residency lay outside the Trinidad region but not all newcomers were second-home buyers. The town's proximity to Trinidad, its low real estate prices, and, above all, its unique atmosphere attracted a diverse group of outsiders. Cokedale continued to draw individuals employed in Trinidad, where the economy was slowly improving. The town was also popular among faculty from Trinidad State Junior College. In addition, a number of alternative-lifestylers came to town. The Trinidad area gained a reputation as a place of refuge for artists, members of unconventional religious groups, and hippies, a few of whom found their way to Cokedale.[70]

Population decline in Cokedale was reversed by this influx of newcomers. Between 1980 and 1990, the population grew from 90 to 116. By 2000, 139 permanent residents resided in the community, a 35 percent increase in population through the 1980s and 1990s. More than 22 percent were over the age of sixty-five, but this percentage was down from 28 percent in 1990. Although the community remains aged, the trend is easing and Cokedale is evolving into a more diverse place. A greater array of young and old now live in the town and a professional class of residents, many employed as teachers and health-care workers in Trinidad, has diversified the traditional working-class economy. In fact, median family income in Cokedale now stands at more than $40,000. Although well below the state average, that income is 15 percent higher than the average for Las

Animas County. In 2000, poverty rates in Cokedale stood at 7.3 percent, close to the state average, but almost half the county average. Regionally, the Cokedale economy is faring well.[71]

Economic and social diversification has continued to alter social relations in Cokedale. The old animosity that existed between north- and south-siders has weakened. "There are factions that I don't even know about because they go so far back into the history of the community, families that have had tensions," Holdread said. "[B]ut I don't think at this point most people are very aware of it anymore. It's confused enough today that old-timers have to work pretty hard to maintain animosities." Many of the old-timers, he explained, are gone or they just "don't have the fight left in them."[72]

Unfortunately, as old community divides faded, tensions grew between long-time residents and newcomers. According to Holdread, this conflict had a variety of causes. Many newcomers were intent on improving conditions in the community and these changes continued to be resisted. The conflicts that arose, however, were not solely the result of differences in opinion regarding community improvements. Many newcomers, Holdread explained, refused to pay their "dues" to old-timers or in other ways recognize their authority. Holdread also believed that new residents represented outside Anglo control, something that old-timers had resented since the mining days: "Outsiders, who were mostly Anglos, were identified with the company and the management. They were buying up the big houses, the mining office, the mercantile, and the other buildings that symbolized outside authority. There was a lot of resistance and resentment. Many of them were trying to do good things for the town but they weren't paying deference to the old-timers." New arrivals also tended to be wealthier and they were altering the structures of power in Cokedale. Control of the community had remained with the old guard since ASARCO's pullout, but a transition was underway that was threatening their ability to dictate the town's atmosphere. As Holdread observed, especially threatening for old-timers was seeing many of the community's most notable structures—the Gottlieb Mercantile, mine office, doctor's house, superintendent's house, bathhouse, and boardinghouse—fall back into the hands of an elite.[73]

As the old guard became more elderly, their hold on municipal politics weakened. Newcomers were elected to the town council and had a greater say in community affairs. Still, despite their attrition, the old guard continued to exert significant control. Testimony to their influence was their continued ability to resist change, which frustrated novice town council members to the point that several quit midway through their terms. It wasn't until 1998, when John Johnson retired as mayor, that control of the community passed into the hands of the next generation of residents.

With a weakening of the old guard's influence, Cokedale's appearance began to change. A number of new residents were repairing and remodeling town structures. Unlike old-timers, they had both the desire to improve their properties and the financial means to do so. Run-down cottages began to receive foundation work, new roofs, and fresh coats of paint. Yards were cleaned out, patio decks were built, and driveways were graveled.

Rejuvenation was a mixed blessing. Although Cokedale's general appearance was being improved, its mining-era character was being lost. Not held back by a sense of what Cokedale was like during the mining era and unaware of or indifferent to the town's historical significance, many newcomers were altering the town in intrusive ways. Siding and new color schemes were replacing the stucco finish and uniform trim of the company-built houses. Several were altered beyond recognition by building additions. Moreover, most of the old company maintenance structures—stables, sheds, and workshops—were torn down, as were several houses deemed too dilapidated to restore. Johnson described the situation: "People were changing the décor of the town and I didn't appreciate it. But they bought the house, you couldn't stop them, there was no zoning ordinance in town. We attempted to make building ordinances but we were never successful. People objected, they wanted to do what they wanted to do with their houses." The old guard expressed concern over the direction of development, but, as referred to by Johnson, with no zoning or building ordinances in place few means existed to fight these changes. Planning ordinances were a topic of debate in town council meetings throughout the 1980s but too much opposition existed for even minor restrictions to be put into law. A mobile home even appeared in Cokedale, a structure that the town council fought unsuccessfully to remove. Increasingly, however, a number of new residents also became concerned with preserving Cokedale's mining past. Some even aligned themselves with what remained of the old guard. At the same time as the town was being transformed by development, a counterforce was developing to preserve the company town's heritage.[74]

According to an article appearing in *The Pueblo Chieftain* in 1976, newcomers were responsible for introducing a preservation ethic: "[N]ewcomers have recognized the value of Cokedale as a landmark of coal mining history. Now some of the old-timers are beginning to appreciate this too." This statement reveals a lack of understanding of the different ways these groups viewed the community, and the role both played in development and preservation initiatives. The old guard held intimate knowledge of Cokedale's past. Although some were indifferent to formal preservation efforts, this apathy was not the result of a lack of interest in the town's heritage. For old-timers, formal preservation was not a prerequisite for valuing the local landscape; they were comfortable with the community in its deteriorated condition. To them, the landscape provided continuity to a past way of life. The old guard did not object to preservation per se, but they did resent outside interference in community affairs. Moreover, although the town had deteriorated under the old guard's watch, on the whole it was the actions of newcomers—particularly their remodeling of homes and other structures—that posed the greatest threat to Cokedale's historic integrity.[75]

Old-timers played a central role in raising initial awareness of the community's historical significance. In August 1976, Cokedale's first reunion of old-timers was organized. Invitations were sent to approximately 300 former residents, who were invited to celebrate the sixty-ninth anniversary of the community's founding. The reunion was highlighted by an arts and crafts festival, a field Mass, and an exhibit of coal mining artifacts. In a newspaper article promoting the reunion, the *Trinidad Chronicle News* reported that advance sales were being taken for Holly Barton's *Cokedale 1907–1947: Anatomy of a Model Mining Community,* which would be released on the day of the reunion. The event triggered interest in Cokedale's past and, with the release of Barton's book, the first extensive history of the town was made available. Despite its shortcomings, *Anatomy of a Model Mining Community* had a positive influence. Barton showed that the town's past should be treasured, a point being overlooked by those intent on improving the look of the community and increasing property values.[76]

In the years that followed the reunion, interest in local history and preservation grew. Residents formed the Cokedale Historical Society, whose members included both old and new residents. The organization's first order of business was to place a historical marker in Cokedale's Commons Park. At about this time, state officials came to Cokedale, generating further interest in preservation. In 1980, officials from the Mine Land Reclamation Office conducted a hazard survey of the old mine workings. As a part of the abandoned mine land survey, a cultural resource inventory was also conducted. Focusing their attention only on those areas containing mining hazards (the town and coke ovens were not included in the survey), the state officials determined that the foundations of the aerial tramway located on the tailings pile and the remains of the fan house were of historical significance as engineering artifacts. Although the initial hazard inventory recommended re-grading the tailings pile, reclamation was not undertaken in deference to the feature's historical significance.[77]

Soon after the reclamation office conducted its cultural resource inventory, the Colorado Historical Society showed interest in the town. At a town council meeting held in November 1983, resident Gladys Davis, representing the Cokedale Historical Society, explained that state officials were urging residents to nominate the town to the National Register. One month later, state representatives met with the town council to field questions regarding historic district designation. Of concern were potential building restrictions. It was explained, however, that unless individuals received federal restoration grants, historic district status would not restrict remodeling. At the same time, residents were cautioned that, if too pervasive, remodeling could result in a delisting from the register.[78]

Before proceeding with nomination procedures, the community was required to show that local support existed for historic district designation. In January 1984 the town council reviewed the results of a community poll and found that the majority of property owners had consented to the proposal.[79] Holdread provides insight into residents' views of historic district designation:

> The historical society group and some outside interests that I think might have had roots in the area were really involved. It was kind of funny. It was all driven by a sense of pride in the town but there was a lot of passivity about it as well. It was a combination of some people who thought it would be cool without really thinking about why it would be so cool: like why would we want more people driving through town? Others looked at it more in terms of whether it was going to cost us anything, is it going to impinge upon our rights? As long as they felt like it wouldn't do any harm they would go ahead with it. I don't think anyone really had any specific idea of how Cokedale would benefit.[80]

Within a year, funds had been raised to hire a preservation consultant to inventory community structures, and historic district nomination forms were sent to the National Register in Washington, D.C. Cokedale received National Historic District designation in 1985.

The following excerpt, taken from Cokedale's National Register of Historic Places Inventory Nomination Form, explains the town's historical significance and the justification for its inclusion in the National Register: "While most similar coal camps were dismantled as mines ceased operation in the Las Animas–Huerfano district, Cokedale continued to thrive. . . . The perception of the residents of Cokedale, and the entire Trinidad District, that the camp was a desirable place to live and work, coupled with a company philosophy differing from the theories prevalent in the area, created an environment in which Cokedale could remain intact. . . . The town remains the best example of an intact coal camp in Colorado." From this reading, it is evident that the utopian myth played an important role in historic district designation. Unfortunately, however, evidence also suggests that this inaccurate historical narrative has shaped preservation practice in problematic ways. The perception that Cokedale was an idyllic company town has limited the types of landscape features that have been preserved. The town's utopian image has also reinforced a misperception that the community stands as an intact company town. Moreover, it has shaped interpretation of the preservation landscape in misleading ways.[81]

What is experienced in Cokedale today, like what is read in its local histories, tells only part of the town's story. Its quaint, contemporary atmosphere fails to communicate, without considerable imagining, the way of life that existed in the mining era. Cokedale's quiet streetscape conveys little sense of the town's industrial origins. The double row of crumbling coke ovens, the impressive tailings pile, and the ruined foundations of the tipple and washery are significant landmarks, but they only hint at the extent of industrial operations that existed in the community (Figure 3.6). And the town does not resemble the derelict place it was

3.6 Two views from atop Cokedale's tailings pile looking toward the old washery and powerhouse. The top image, circa 1910, shows the scope of industrial operations that existed on the town's southern margin. Not shown is the mine and coke oven complex, which lay to the left of the photograph (south). The bottom image shows the same area in 1999. On the left stand the concrete foundations of the larry bins. The conical structure at center is the round bin. Photographs from Carnegie Public Library, Trinidad, Colorado (top) and by the author (bottom)

no more than twenty years ago when most of its structures were vacant or in disrepair.

It was hoped that historic district designation would raise local awareness of the importance of preservation, but it did not halt intrusive development. Johnson stated: "People kept extending their houses, building them differently. Originally, when we got appointed a historical district, they didn't want us to do anything like that, they wanted everything as it was. If they were to come back now and take a look they'd be disappointed. They came in and spread it on to us, told us all about it. They took pictures of every house and they warned us not to change their décor but they've been changed." Nonetheless, National Register status did facilitate significant restoration work. The most faithfully preserved features in Cokedale, and its most complete category of original structures, are its community buildings. Although direct involvement in preservation by the town council was limited by budget constraints, protection of two community buildings—the Cokedale Schoolhouse and the Gottlieb Mercantile—was facilitated through municipal ownership.[82]

Following mine closure, the Trinidad Public School District took control of the school. The facility was closed after several years of operation because of low enrollment, and in the 1960s the school district sold the structure to the town for one dollar. The town used the school for community events, but by the 1980s the structure was in disrepair and a contentious debate occurred to determine its future. In the wake of historic district designation, some wanted to restore the school but this was a difficult task. Johnson explained: "The school was sitting there doing nothing, deteriorating. Bats had moved in on it and were tearing it apart. I went to the council and said we got to get rid of that building its costing us money. . . . I said let's sell it. We had a big town meeting about selling the schoolhouse and the opposition even hired an attorney to come to the meeting to stop us from selling it. They wanted to keep it as a landmark for the historic district. I said the thought was well but how are we going to keep it up, how are we going to afford it? There were heated meetings." The old guard was sympathetic to preserving the structure but viewed city involvement as an unwise expenditure. Fortunately, a compromise was reached. In 1989 the school was sold to Christ of the Canyon's Ministries, an interdenominational Christian church. Under terms of the sale, a provision was made that the ministry repair and restore the building. By most accounts, the transaction proved to be a good solution. Today, Christ of the Canyon's Ministries maintains ownership of the schoolhouse, one of the town's most exquisitely restored buildings (Figure 3.7).[83]

After ASARCO abandoned Cokedale, the Gottlieb Mercantile, the town's largest structure, was abandoned. A small portion of the old company store was leased from Florence Machinery for use as a post office, but the building otherwise lay unused. In the mid-1970s the building was purchased by resident Gary Coulter, who converted it into an old-time buggy museum. After several years of

3.7 The Cokedale Schoolhouse circa 1940 (left) and 1999 (right). Ownership of the structure was transferred to the Trinidad Public School District following mine closure. The school operated until the mid-1960s. Christ of the Canyon's Ministries, its current owner, restored the building in the 1990s. Photographs from Cokedale Miners' Museum (left) and by the author (right)

operation, however, the mercantile fell into receivership. In the late 1980s Mayor Johnson negotiated with Trinidad National Bank to finance Cokedale's purchase of the mercantile. Johnson claimed that the town's primary interest in purchasing the structure was to maintain the post office.[84]

The town of Cokedale bought the mercantile for $7,000, but it soon become apparent that structural problems needed to be addressed to save the building from condemnation. In 1989, Vernon Williams, who owned property in Cokedale and had been a seasonal visitor since 1968, came forward with a plan. Williams, a faculty member in the Department of History at Abilene Christian University (ACU), envisioned restoring the mercantile and converting it into a mining museum. ACU would develop a history field course that would provide student and faculty assistance. The town council approved Williams's proposal in 1991 but the politics surrounding implementation of the museum project were contentious; not all in the community were supportive. Although old-timers were proud of the museum, they were uneasy about having outsiders in charge of its operation. Also frustrating for some was the view that the mercantile now was unavailable for community use. The building, however, rarely had been used prior to its restoration and may have been demolished without the involvement of ACU. Nonetheless, community access and control over the building remained issues. Even though they contributed greatly to preserving Cokedale's heritage, many of those spearheading the museum project were viewed as outsiders and this weakened support for their efforts. The museum remains an ongoing project. An impressive collection of mining-era artifacts and photographs now stand professionally displayed in the building.[85]

A handful of individual residents have seized the opportunity to restore Cokedale's other community buildings. The mine office, boardinghouse, and

3.8 *The restored Cokedale boardinghouse. One of the community's largest buildings, the board-inghouse had twenty-two bedrooms, large dining and public rooms, a kitchen, and quarters for the manager. Unmarried miners occupied the building, which now serves as a private home. Photograph by the author, 1999*

doctor's and superintendent's houses were listed in good condition at the time of National Register designation in 1985. The icehouse and bathhouse were listed in fair condition. Of these structures, the doctor's house and icehouse have since been altered to the extent that their original function is now difficult to recognize. The mine office, bathhouse, boardinghouse, and the superintendent's home, however, were remodeled with relatively little change to their exteriors (Figure 3.8). They now stand in excellent condition.[86]

More intrusive development and structure loss has occurred to Cokedale's housing stock. A substantial portion of Cokedale's original housing—all but one of its twenty-two shared-housing structures—has been demolished (see Map 3.2). One single-story duplex remains; it serves as Town Hall. Florence Machinery demolished the wood-framed, multiple-family homes, once occupied by lower-class Hispanic and Mexican residents, shortly after mine closure. As a result, what remains of Cokedale's housing is only its more comfortable and better-built homes. In addition, of the ninety-eight houses listed in Cokedale's 1985 National Register nomination form, twenty-three were deemed noncontributing features of the historic district. Inappropriate development was the primary cause. Fortunately, despite the fact that few of the cottages have remained unchanged, most

3.9 Most of Cokedale's single-family dwellings remain standing and the majority retain original design elements. Shown are examples of standard four-room (top) and five-room (bottom) cottages. The structures are built of cinder blocks fashioned from coking waste. Photographs by the author, 1999

have retained original design elements. A small number have since been faithfully restored to mining-era condition (Figure 3.9).[87]

Unlike some mining-era structures, Cokedale's industrial infrastructure has received little attention. Most elements of the town's industrial heritage—landscape features that stand as explicit reminders of Cokedale's reason for being—have been demolished or lay in ruin (see Map 3.2). Although ten industrial features were recognized by the National Register as contributing structures in the historic district, none—including the remains of the coke ovens—has received restoration work. The largest set of coke ovens in the Trinidad field, the ovens have rapidly deteriorated. At the time of their listing to the National Register, many of the beehive ovens had complete roofs; all have now collapsed (Figure 3.10). Moreover, since 1985, several of Cokedale's industrial structures, including the oil house and machine shop, have been demolished. Like most of the town's original infrastructure, Cokedale's industrial features lie on private land. Unlike the owners of community and residential buildings, however, industrial property owners have not had a practical or perceived need to engage in preservation activities, nor has the community or any outside organization stepped forward to assist in doing so. Most of what remains of Cokedale's mining and coking operation, once the most dominant aspect of its cultural landscape, lies deteriorating behind barbed-wire fences and "no trespassing" signs.

Thus, the claim that Cokedale represents an intact company town has been overstated. Although most of its community structures remain standing, only a portion of its original housing stock remains. Furthermore, the town's picturesque contemporary atmosphere fails to convey historic conditions in the community. During the mining era the population was seven times greater than it is today. The town was larger and faster paced. Cokedale was built for the efficient production of coal and coke, but this purpose is not reflected in the present-day landscape. Also not conveyed is the lengthy period of decline experienced following mine closure. Cokedale's tidy appearance today is the product of a relatively recent rejuvenation and contains little evidence of the community's near-death in the post-mining era.

Furthermore, preservation efforts in Cokedale have failed to fully interpret the town's social history. In large part, this deficiency is attributable to the utopian narrative that still dominates interpretations of Cokedale's past. Historians have mostly ignored the similarities that existed between Cokedale and adjacent company towns in the Trinidad Coal Field. Because their histories have guided preservation initiatives, so, too, does the preservation landscape. Attention has been paid to restoring community structures and the settlement's quaint single-family cottages because these features suit its image as an idyllic place. Likewise, the impression of intactness exists, because what remains standing is precisely what one would expect to see in a utopian company town: substantial community structures and comfortable homes. Practical issues are also at play as, generally, habit-

3.10 Little attention has been paid to preserving Cokedale's impressive array of coke ovens. The most extensive coke oven complex in the Trinidad Coal Field, the structures were an integral part of ASARCO's industrial operation. The brick beehive ovens with concrete facing walls are rapidly deteriorating. Photograph by the author, 1999

able structures have received restoration work and inhabitable structures have not. It is telling, however, that little attention has been paid to interpreting features that fail to fit Cokedale's utopian image. Signs have been placed in front of most of the town's community structures, identifying their original function, but no such signs have been placed in industrial areas of the community or in the locations where the remains of shared housing structures can be found. Furthermore, not a single stop in Cokedale's historic walking tour is devoted to these landscape elements.[88]

Although its contemporary landscape fails to convey a complete sense of the town's past, it would be unfair to overly criticize the community's preservation accomplishments. There is no denying that Cokedale was a company town and that its residents lived modest, working-class lives. Enough mining-era structures have been preserved that the town's original layout and streetscape have been retained. Original architectural design elements remain apparent in most of its structures, as does the town's planned uniformity. Overall, Cokedale's array of civic structures makes it one of the best-preserved company towns in the western United States.

It should also be noted that if a timely reinterpretation of public history takes place, the opportunity remains for preservation priorities to be refocused in productive ways. There is a pressing need to protect Cokedale's industrial heritage, a need that is of both historical and emotional significance. As the comments of residents attest, Cokedale's industrial features play a central role in maintaining individual and social-group identities. Johnson, for example, described the sadness he felt in seeing the coke ovens deteriorate: "They are landmarks. . . . [T]he name of the town is 'Cokedale' and it wouldn't be the same without them."[89] Other remnants of the town's mining industry are also valued. Cokedale's massive tailings pile is a common focal point of attention, as is evident in the comments of resident Patricia Schorr: "When we first moved here there was not a spot of growth on the old slag pile. It was just slick and black and shiny. It amazes everybody to see that grass is starting to grow on it. In the winter time it's beautiful with the snow sitting on it." Like those of Johnson, Schorr's comments reveal the pain felt in seeing the slag pile and other industrial features come under threat:

> There was some talk at one time about the county digging the slag pile out and using it for the roads, but that's a part of Cokedale! . . . I just fell in love with the old machine shop we used to have. It was a huge tin building. I used to sit, especially when it was snowing, and just watch it. The snow changed the look of that building, it was beautiful. I just loved to watch it change. It took a bulldozer most of the day to knock it down; it was very sad. It was privately owned; we couldn't do anything about it.[90]

These comments reveal that the landscape's mining and company town impress are central to Cokedale's identity, but this notion is nothing new. Old-timers resisted change in the years following mine closure; they sought to preserve the town's historical integrity and maintain its meaning as a place. For the same reason, a need now exists for old and new to fight to control change. Whether today's residents will prove to be as committed as the old guard in maintaining the town's heritage landscape, however, remains unknown, but there is reason for optimism. In 1998 the town council once again visited the building ordinance issue. Under Mayor Pat Huhn, Cokedale passed its first building restrictions, banning mobile homes on the basis that their presence threatened the town's historic district status and character. If protection of Cokedale's industrial features also becomes a priority, and if ways can be found to better interpret the community's social history and incorporate it into preservation practice, then today's residents will have earned a right to consider themselves the "new guards" of Cokedale.

Before the last of the old guard passes on, it would be wise for newcomers to note their predecessors' commitment to the town. The old guard's resistance to change allowed Cokedale to retain its mining-era features. Their protective ways enabled elements of the past to be preserved. It now lies in the hands of newcomers to call for a reinterpretation of the community's history. A new story is needed, one that explains how Cokedale, despite its company town failings, served as a valued home. Indeed, in many ways, the community's survival is made more remarkable by recognizing the hardships residents faced in the mining era and beyond. The next generation has an obligation to ensure that the old guard's efforts to maintain the community's links to its past were not in vain.

The value of Cokedale's mining heritage is explained by resident Joyce Holdread. In an unpublished essay titled "The Town That Wouldn't Be a Ghost Town" lies both a fitting conclusion and a starting point from which to begin to build a new story of place and identity in Cokedale:

> Cokedale was a town consigned to the scavengers of the coal industry's played-out holes, but in the spring of 1947 life emerged from its dark humus in the united cry of its inhabitants to save their town. . . . Because of the united refusal of its diverse populace to fade into history, Cokedale has remained one of the few "coal camps" preserved in the United States today, thus earning its listing on the National Register of Historical Places. The continual mosaic of people from different ethnic, religious, and cultural backgrounds, united by shared concerns, make Cokedale one of the best and most unique American small towns.[91]

NOTES

1. Cokedale Tourism Committee, "Cokedale: A Historic Coal Mining Camp," walking tour brochure (University of Colorado at Denver, n.d.).

2. Holly Barton, *Cokedale 1907–1947: Anatomy of a Model Mining Community* (n.p. :privately published, 1976).

3. Marius R. Campbell, "The Trinidad Coal Field, Colorado," in *Contributions to Economic Geology,* United States Geological Survey Bulletin 381 (Washington, DC: GPO, 1910), 434–437; Ross B. Johnson, *Coal Resources of the Trinidad Coal Field in Huerfano and Las Animas Counties, Colorado,* United States Geological Survey Bulletin 1112-E (Washington, DC: GPO, 1961); U.S. Bureau of the Census, *1920 Census of Population,* 6:3, Washington, DC.

4. Sarah Deutsch, *No Separate Refuge: Culture, Class, and Gender on an Anglo-Hispanic Frontier in the American Southwest, 1880–1940* (New York: Oxford University Press, 1987), 87–106.

5. George S. McGovern and Leonard F. Guttridge, *The Great Coalfield War* (Boston: Houghton Mifflin, 1972), 42; Priscilla Long, *Where the Sun Never Shines: A History of America's Bloody Coal Industry* (New York: Paragon House, 1989), 273–292; *Trinidad Chronicle News,* "Militia Will Occupy All Camps," November 8, 1913, 1.

6. Long, *Where the Sun Never Shines,* 281–282, 292–294. For further discussion of the Ludlow Massacre, see Howard M. Gitelman, *Legacy of the Ludlow Massacre: A Chapter in American Industrial Relations* (Philadelphia: University of Pennsylvania Press, 1988).

7. Long, *Where the Sun Never Shines,* 295–304; McGovern and Guttridge, *The Great Coalfield War,* 250–267.

8. United States Commission on Industrial Relations, *Final Report and Testimony,* Senate Doc. 415, 64th Cong., 2d Sess., Washington, DC, 1916; United States Congress,

House Subcommittee on Mines and Mining, *Conditions in the Coal Mines of Colorado,* Pursuant to H.R. 387, 63rd Cong., 2d Sess., Washington, DC, 1914. Upton Sinclair wrote two quasi-fictional novels documenting oppressive conditions in the company towns: *King Coal* (New York: Macmillan, 1917) and *The Coal War: A Sequel to King Coal* (Boulder: Colorado Associated University Press, 1976).

9. Another reason that company towns were demolished by operators was to reduce property tax burdens. Lee Scamehorn, letter to author, June 27, 1999.

10. Gary L. Lindsey, "Creating Presence: The Early Twentieth Century Company Store in Three Coal Mining Towns in Southern Colorado" (M.A. thesis, Abilene Christian University, 1998), 193; National Park Service, National Register of Historic Places Inventory Nomination Form: Cokedale Historic District (Washington, DC, 1985), 7; Barton, *Cokedale 1907–1947,* 30–41.

11. Lindsey, "Creating Presence."

12. Barton, *Cokedale, 1907–1947,* 1.

13. *Trinidad Chronicle News,* "Riley Canon Will Be Model Camp of State," January 15, 1907, 3.

14. *Trinidad Chronicle News,* "Will Spend Millions to Develop New Camp," March 6, 1907, 1, 4.

15. *Trinidad Chronicle News,* August 29, 1907, 1.

16. W. B. Lloyd, "The Cokedale Mine," *Thirteenth Biennial Report of the State Coal Mine Inspector,* Denver, 1909, 152–156; Kenneth S. Guiterman, "Mining Coal in Southern Colorado," *The Engineering and Mining Journal* 87:21 (1909): 1009–1015; Barton, *Cokedale 1907–1947,* 5. Guggenheim's original testimony appears in United States Commission on Industrial Relations, *Final Report and Testimony,* Vol. 8, Senate Doc. 415, 64th Cong., 2d. Sess., Washington, DC, 1916, 7559–7579.

17. Rollie Schafer Jr., *The Schafers of Cokedale, A Century in America* (Trinidad, CO: privately published, 1993), 41.

18. Barton, *Cokedale 1907–1947,* 1, 30–70.

19. Ibid., 62–65. See also Gary L. Lindsey, "Creating Presence," 211–214; Schafer, *The Schafers of Cokedale,* 48.

20. Barton, *Cokedale 1907–1947,* 43–44; Guitterman, "Mining Coal in Southern Colorado," 1009–1015; Lloyd, "The Cokedale Mine," 152–156; "Riley Canon," *Trinidad Chronicle News,* 4.

21. Barton, *Cokedale 1907–1947,* 19–23; Schafer, *The Schafers of Cokedale,* 91.

22. Scholarly research conducted in the Trinidad Coal Field has been dominated by the works of labor historians who deal almost exclusively with labor conditions in the camps of the CF&I. One notable exception is historian Rick J. Clyne's *Coal People: Life in Southern Colorado's Company Towns, 1890–1930* (Denver: Colorado Historical Society, 1999), in which Clyne considers community life in the company towns. *Coal People* is a valuable addition to the literature, but Cokedale receives only minor attention in this work.

23. John S. Garner, *The Company Town: Architecture and Society in the Early Industrial Age* (New York: Oxford University Press, 1992), 4; Anne E. Mosher, "'Something Better than the Best': Industrial Restructuring, George McMurtry and the Creation of the Model Industrial Town of Vandergrift, Pennsylvania, 1883–1901," *Annals of the Association of American Geographers* 85:1 (1995): 84–107; John S. Garner, *The Model Company*

Town: Urban Design through Private Enterprise in Nineteenth-Century New England (Amherst: University of Massachusetts Press, 1984).

24. United States Commission on Industrial Relations, *Final Report and Testimony;* Harvey O'Connor, *The Guggenheims: The Making of an American Dynasty* (New York: Covici Friede, 1937), 316–322.

25. Long, *Where the Sun Never Shines,* 308–323; H. Lee Scamehorn, *Mill & Mine: The CF&I in the Twentieth Century* (Lincoln: University of Nebraska Press, 1992), 57–67.

26. Leifur Magnusson, "Company Housing in the Bituminous Coal Fields," *Monthly Labor Review* 10:4 (1920): 215–222; Horace Hurtado, interview transcript, May 24, 1978, Eric Margolis Collection, 14-3, Archives, University of Colorado at Boulder Libraries.

27. Leslie K. Beck and Mike Kirchereds, *Down Home in Bon Carbo: Memories of a Dream* (Trinidad: Paperworks, 1988), 29–60; John Johnson, interview with author, Cokedale, Colorado, July 26, 1999.

28. Deutsch, *No Separate Refuge,* 94–95; Frank Wojtylka, interview transcript, University of Colorado, Institute of Behavioral Science, Coal Project, Norlin Library, Western Historical Collections, Boulder, Colorado, quoted in Clyne, *Coal People,* 49.

29. U.S. Bureau of the Census, *Manuscript Census 1920, Colorado: Las Animas County.*

30. Ibid.

31. Interview (name withheld) with author, Cokedale, Colorado, 1999.

32. Ibid.

33. "Mining Prices Paid at the Various Coal Mines in Colorado, January 1, 1917," *Fourth Annual Report of the State Inspector of Coal Mines, 1916* (Denver: Smith-Brooks Printing, State Printers, 1917), 14–17; United States Congress, *Conditions in the Coal Mines,* Part 9, Exhibit M47, 2582. The deductions listed on Jacob Game's 1913 payroll statement are store, $16.00; bath, $0.50; electric lights, $1.05; coal, $2.00; carbide, $0.40; hospital, $1.00; rent, $6.00; and smithing, $0.50.

34. *Biennial* and *Annual Reports of the State Inspector of Coal Mines,* 1911 through 1929 (Denver: Smith-Brooks Printing, State Printers: various dates); *Trinidad Chronicle News,* "Gas in Entries of Cokedale," February 15, 1911, 1; "Report on Cokedale Explosion," *Fifteenth Biennial Report of the State Inspector of Coal Mines, 1911–1912* (Denver: Smith-Brooks Printing, State Printers), 26–30; *Trinidad Chronicle News,* February 10, 1911, 1.

35. Johnson, interview.

36. Emilio and Gertrude Ferraro, interview transcript, May 22, 1978, Cokedale, Colorado, Eric Margolis Collection, 9-8, Archives, University of Colorado at Boulder Libraries.

37. UMWA documents, Edward Lawrence Doyle Collection, Western History Department, Denver Public Library, Folder 10, Envelope 9.

38. Tony Lamont, testimony, Edward Lawrence Doyle Collection, Western History Department, Denver Public Library, Folder 10, Envelope 9.

39. Hurtado, interview transcript; UMWA documents, Edward Lawrence Doyle Collection, Western History Department, Denver Public Library, Folder 10, Envelope 9.

40. See Deutsch, *No Separate Refuge,* 94; and Long, *Where the Sun Never Shines,* 253. U.S. Bureau of the Census, *Manuscript Census 1910 & 1920, Colorado: Las Animas County*; Hurtado, interview transcript; Johnston, interview; Barton, *Cokedale 1907–1947,* 19–22; Schafer, *The Schafers of Cokedale,* 40.

41. For discussion of the U.S. company town and societal perceptions, see James B. Allen, *The Company Town in the American West* (Norman: University of Oklahoma Press, 1966); John S. Garner, *The Company Town: Architecture and Society in the Early Industrial Age* (New York: Oxford University Press, 1992). The best analyses of company towns in the Trinidad area are provided by Scamehorn, *Mill & Mine*, and Clyne, *Coal People*.

42. Mining towns in the Trinidad Coal Field have been described as oppressive, fading relics that lacked a mining-related community identity. See, John L. Keane, "The Towns that Coal Built: The Evolution of Landscapes and Communities in Southern Colorado," *Yearbook of the Association of Pacific Coast Geographers* 62 (2000): 70–94.

43. Barton, *Cokedale 1907–1947*, 46–60, 70–76; Ferraro, interview transcript; Schafer, *The Schafers of Cokedale*, vii.

44. Johnson, interview; Bette Arguello, interview with author, Cokedale, Colorado, June 15, 1999.

45. Barton, *Cokedale 1907–1947*, 1, 23; National Park Service, National Register of Historic Places Inventory Nomination Form: Cokedale Historic District, 3.

46. Clyne, *Coal People*, 42–43.

47. Arguello, interview.

48. Mine closure may also have been stimulated by the state's temporary shut down of Bon Carbo because of unsafe working conditions a week earlier; see *The Trinidad Chronicle News*, "Las Animas County Coal Mines Closed As Unsafe," April 3, 1947, 1.

49. Barton, *Cokedale 1907–1947*, 20–23; *Trinidad Chronicle News*, "Cokedale Coal Mines Operation to Be Abandoned," April 10, 1947, 1; *Trinidad Chronicle News*, "Cokedale–Bon Carbo Properties Sale Is Reported," May 16, 1947, 1.

50. Schafer, *The Schafers of Cokedale*, 91; Patrick Donachy, *Coal the Kingdom Below* (Trinidad: Inkwell, 1983), 16; Ferraro, interview transcript; Johnson, interview.

51. Johnson, interview; Barton, *Cokedale 1907–1947*, 23.

52. Index to property deeds, Cokedale, 1947–1983, Trinidad Abstract & Title Company, Trinidad, Colorado.

53. *Trinidad Chronicle News*, "Cokedale Folks Hold First Town Meeting," October 4, 1947, 1; *Trinidad Chronicle News*, "Cokedale Plans Incorporation," October 10, 1947, 1; Johnson, interview.

54. U.S. Bureau of the Census, *U.S. Census of Population: 1950*, 1:6 (Washington, DC: GPO, 1952); *Trinidad City Directory, 1952* (Colorado Springs: Rocky Mountain Directory, 1952); Johnson, interview.

55. *Polk's Trinidad City Directory, 1935*, 17 (R. L. Polk Directory, 1935); *Trinidad City Directory, 1948* (Colorado Springs: Rocky Mountain Directory, 1948).

56. Joan Reese, "4 Rooms and a Path," *Rocky Mountain Empire Magazine*, May 23, 1948, 4.

57. Ibid.; O'Connor, "Lights Burn Bright in Cokedale."

58. Scamehorn, *Mill & Mine*, 201; U.S. Bureau of the Census, *1980 Census of Population, Colorado*, Washington, DC; Donachy, *Coal—The Kingdom Below*, 17.

59. Doug Holdread, interview with author, Cokedale, Colorado, July 15, 1999.

60. Richard Bell, interview with author, Cokedale, Colorado, July 13, 1999.

61. Holdread, interview; Johnson, interview.

62. Arguello, interview; Doc Leonetti, "Cokedale Holds History for Massarotti," *Trinidad Plus Hometown Spotlight,* http://www.trinidadco.com/plus/spotlight99/ massarti.html (accessed May 17, 2001).

63. Johnson, interview.

64. Ibid.

65. Bell, interview.

66. Pat Huhn, interview with author, Cokedale, Colorado, July 14, 1999.

67. Holdread, interview.

68. Pat Schorr, interview with author, Cokedale, Colorado, July 14, 1999.

69. Cokedale Tourism Committee, "Cokedale: A Historic Coal Mining Camp," n.p.

70. Levinson, "Cokedale Awakening," 3A; National Park Service, National Register of Historic Places Inventory Nomination Form: Cokedale Historic District, 2–4; Beck and Kirchereds, *Down Home in Bon Carbo.*

71. U.S. Bureau of the Census, *1980, 1990 & 2000 U.S. Census of Population, Colorado,* Washington, DC.

72. Holdread, interview.

73. Ibid.

74. Johnson, interview.

75. Arlene Levinson, "Cokedale Awakening from 29-Year Nap," *The Pueblo Chieftain,* June 14, 1976, 3A.

76. Johnson, interview; Arlene Levinson, "Cokedale Reaches 69th," *Trinidad Chronicle News,* July 21, 1976, 4.

77. State of Colorado, Department of Natural Resources, "Close-Out Report: Cokedale Project," Denver, n.d.; State of Colorado, Department of Natural Resources, "Colorado Inactive Mine Inventory Problem Area Date Forms: Cokedale Problem Areas," Denver, 1980; State of Colorado, Department of Natural Resources, Inactive Mine Program, *Their Silent Profile: Inactive Coal and Metal Mines of Colorado* (Denver: The Program, 1982).

78. Minutes, Town Council Meeting, Cokedale, Colorado, November 11 and December 8, 1983.

79. Minutes, Town Council Meeting, Cokedale, Colorado, January 12, 1984.

80. Holdread, interview.

81. National Park Service, National Register of Historic Places Inventory Nomination Form: Cokedale Historic District, Item 8, n.p.

82. Johnson, interview.

83. Ibid.

84. Johnson, interview; Lindsey, *Creating Presence,* 225; Kit Miniclier, "Coulter Reviving Romance, Practicality of Horse-Drawn Vehicles," *The Denver Post,* October 20, 1980, 2.

85. Vernon L. Williams, personal correspondence, December 8, 1999; Huhn, interview.

86. National Park Service, National Register of Historic Places Inventory Nomination Form: Cokedale Historic District.

87. Ibid.

88. Cokedale Tourism Committee, "Cokedale: A Historic Coal Mining Camp," n.p.

89. Johnson, interview. See also Keane, "The Towns That Coal Built," 79.

90. Schorr, interview.

91. Joyce Holdread, "The Town That Wouldn't Be a Ghost Town," unpublished essay, n.d.

4.1 Picher, Oklahoma, 2002.
Courtesy U.S. Geological Survey—National Center, EROS

CHAPTER FOUR

Picher

FEW HISTORIC MINING TOWNS IN THE UNITED STATES ARE PLAGUED BY MORE severe environmental problems than Picher, Oklahoma. In fact, when the Environmental Protection Agency (EPA) compiled its initial list of Superfund sites in 1983, the community was designated as one of the agency's highest priority cleanup areas. At the time, the environmental problems afflicting Picher were considered more serious than those at Love Canal, the EPA's most infamous hazardous waste site. Unlike its ill-famed contemporary, however, many of Picher's environmental hazards remain uncontrolled more than two decades later. Named after the stream that runs through the Picher area, the Tar Creek Superfund Site extends over forty square miles. It is one of the oldest and most costly Superfund sites in the nation.[1]

In the early twentieth century, Picher was the largest mining town in the Tri-State Mining District, once the world's most productive lead and zinc mining field. Ore was discovered in the Picher region in 1914 and within three years, the settlement's population exceeded 20,000. A quintessential boomtown, Picher captivated its earliest visitors with its remarkable growth. Mines were opening at a feverish pace and outsiders marveled at how quickly the mine derrick and ore mill, unquestionable symbols of prosperity, had come to dominate the prairie landscape. Community accolades quickly turned to antipathy, however, after the novelty of the mineral discovery faded. The intrusive nature of industrial development, the lack of basic civic amenities, and Picher's ramshackle appearance were impossible to ignore, and although some sympathized with the plight of its residents, most simply voiced disdain for the community. This external perceptual legacy is one Picher has found difficult to discard. The last of Picher's mines closed more than thirty years ago, but consistent with the mining imaginary, most outsiders still view the town as a hopelessly despoiled place.[2]

In looking at Picher today, it is difficult to argue that its negative reputation is not deserved. Deindustrialization and population loss have devastated the local economy, as the decayed state of town infrastructure attests. Many houses and commercial structures lie abandoned or stand in noticeable disrepair. The run-down condition of the built landscape, however, is overshadowed by the presence of mining-related features. Residential and industrial development occurred side by side in Picher and the remains of mines and ore mills, with their giant piles of gray-colored mining waste (locally know as "chat"), litter the townscape. Streets wind around the mountains of debris, many of which stand more than 200 feet tall, and houses huddle beneath their slopes (Figure 4.2). Mining has ravaged the environment and left poverty in its wake, and Picher's dilapidated, chat-covered landscape produces a kind of "scorched-earth" reaction in most first-time visitors.

Although mining's aesthetic impact on Picher is striking, the town's appearance is a relatively minor concern compared to the environmental disturbances the industry has wrought. For decades, Picher has been beset by mine subsidence as surface collapses are caused by the caving of mines lying beneath the community. When the Tar Creek Superfund Site was created in the 1980s, however, environmental concerns centered on acid mine drainage problems. Acidic, metal-laden mine water was flowing to the surface from mine shafts, abandoned water wells, and bore holes in and around Picher. The discharge killed aquatic life in Tar Creek and migrated into the town's water supply, an aquifer underlying the mining zone. The EPA attempted to mitigate these problems but the results were disappointing. Residents remained plagued by rust-tainted drinking water, and after failing to improve water quality in Tar Creek, the EPA concluded that its contamination was irreversible.[3]

Water pollution remains an issue in Picher today; however, a greater threat to public health now garners more attention. In the mid-1990s health researchers discovered that the community had the highest incidence of juvenile lead poisoning in the nation. Chat was soon identified as the source of lead contamination. Chat piles had long served as playgrounds for Picher's children, and widespread use of the waste for local landscaping and road surfacing had increased residents'

4.2 *A chat pile stands as backdrop to a Picher home. Photograph by the author, 2000*

exposure to the toxic metal. Lead now was pervasive in the Picher environment and, in 1996, the EPA began a second phase of its Superfund program aimed at addressing the problem. Chat-contaminated soil was removed from more than 2,000 public and residential properties, an action that has reduced blood lead levels in area children. Sadly, however, the incidence of lead contamination in Picher remains well above state and national averages.[4]

These remediation failures coupled with skyrocketing cleanup costs—more than $100 million has already been spent at Tar Creek—have eroded residents' faith in government and its ability to address their problems. Resident misgivings, however, are also the product of a history of external derision. Picher has long been viewed as a spectacle of hopeless dereliction, a perception that has hampered efforts to address the town's problems. True, for the first time in history, lawmakers are now showing a commitment to resolving Picher's plight. Unfortunately, the solution that is gaining momentum, a series of voluntary resident buyouts, is fraught with problems, many of which are rooted in a persistent belief that Picher is an irreparable place.

Without question, the landscape Picherites inhabit is detrimental to their physical health and many are expressing a desire to leave based on health concerns. Yet, resident well-being is also a product of mental health, and a substantial number are refusing to consider relocation because of the emotional bonds they hold to place. Despite its economic and environmental problems, Picher retains value as a community and home for many. As in many historic mining settlements, self and social-group identity remains tied to mining and its social and physical legacies, which, despite being the source of most of the town's problems, are central to its meaning. These enduring attachments raise a host of problems for implementing an effective and fair resident buy-out program, and mistakes of the past threaten to be repeated in this long-marginalized community should lawmakers remain ignorant of Picher's value as a lived-in place. Cultivating such understanding begins by gaining a sense of who Picherites are and by exploring what they and their community have experienced.

THE TRI-STATE MINING DISTRICT

The Tri-State Mining District was a unique mining field. Extending over more than 1,100 square miles, the district embraced portions of southwest Missouri, southeast Kansas, and northeast Oklahoma (Map 4.1). According to historian Arrell M. Gibson, a distinctive mining economy existed in the Tri-State district. The shallowness of the ore and the opportunities available for workers to acquire mining properties made it possible for wage earners to become operators. This "poor man's camp" characteristic, as Gibson calls it, was central to the district's identity; workers had an opportunity for upward mobility, creating a sprit of individualism and egalitarianism that other U.S. mining districts lacked. As Gibson recognizes, however, the poor man's camps dissipated as the field evolved, a fact confirmed by labor historian George G. Suggs, who showed that as the focus of mining turned to the deeper lead and zinc deposit in Oklahoma, larger and more heavily capitalized companies came to dominate production. According to Suggs, the Picher Field was not a place where poor men could easily improve their economic status, and a spirit of fair treatment did not exist between operators and workers. To the contrary, even more than in most historic mining districts, the area was inhabited by a poor and burdened workforce.[5]

Another distinct aspect of the Tri-State Mining District was that its workers were drawn from a relatively homogenous local labor force. North America's historic mining fields often served as foci for European immigration and, thus, became centers of ethnic diversity. The Tri-State district was an exception. Most of its workers came from adjacent Ozark Mountain territory and U.S.-born whites accounted for approximately 98 percent of the district's population. In fact, Tri-State mining towns were widely known as "white man's camps," and this image was perpetuated by the xenophobic attitude that prevailed among its native-born miners.[6]

According to Suggs, Tri-State's nonunionized metalworkers were an anachronism. Not only was ethnic diversity absent in the workforce, but also lacking was a strong labor movement. "Unlike their counterparts in the hard-rock camps of Colorado, Idaho, and elsewhere," Suggs wrote, "workers rejected unionization

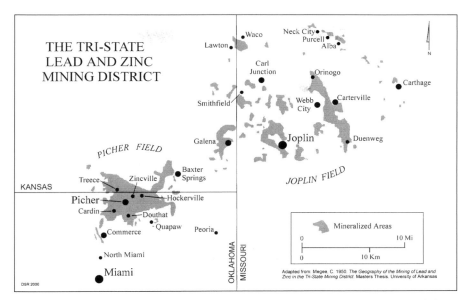

Map 4.1 *The Tri-State Mining District of Oklahoma, Kansas, and Missouri was divided into two mining fields. The region's first commercial lead and zinc mines were developed in the Joplin Field in the 1850s. Mineral development in the Picher Field, which contained the district's most productive mines, began in 1914.*

as a panacea for their problems." The Tri-State district was periodically organized; most notably, a strike shut down operations in the field in 1935. Unionization was never widely accepted, however, and various explanations have been offered to explain this resistance. Early industry accounts focused on the domestic nature of the workforce to explain this phenomenon. Unionization was viewed as an "un-American" concept by pro-industry observers, and Tri-State laborers, they alleged, had a more individualistic "American" ethos. Industry also claimed that having come from the backwoods of the Ozarks, Tri-State workers were more accepting of difficult living and working conditions. Gibson has asserted that workers did not unionize because they were unsympathetic to the union cause, in part because of their independent spirit but also because many had, at one time or another, been operators. Although Suggs recognizes worker independence as a potential inhibitor to unionization, as his work details, heavy-handed opposition to unionization by industry and government also played a central role in inhibiting labor organization in this district.[7]

The Tri-State Mining District was also unusual in that it stretched across the boundaries of three states and five counties. In addition, much of the field lay on Indian land and Gibson asserts that few mining areas could match the Tri-State district in complexity of land tenure. Most of the mining settlement in the Oklahoma portion of the district, for example, was located on Quapaw tribal land, which was administered by the Bureau of Indian Affairs (BIA). A branch of the Siouan family, the Quapaw were relocated from the Mississippi River Valley of Arkansas to Indian Territory in the mid-1830s. Beginning in 1893, the Quapaw Reservation was fragmented into hundreds of individually owned allotments under the Dawes Severalty Act. Deemed "restricted lands" by the BIA, the Quapaw were prohibited from selling their property or using it in certain ways. Use by non-Indians was also restricted, but the BIA maintained the right to negotiate farming, grazing, and mining leases to these lands.[8]

Small quantities of lead and zinc were extracted from the yet-to-be named Picher Field as early as the 1890s. The full extent of the mineral deposit was unrecognized, however, until 1914. In August of that year, the Picher Lead Company of Joplin, Missouri, had dispatched a prospecting rig to Commerce, Oklahoma. Traveling across roadless Quapaw land in Ottawa County, the rig became anchored in mud near Tar Creek. With its rig mired down several miles short of its destination, the company ordered the rig's crew to drill a wildcat hole to occupy their time. After cuttings showed signs of a rich ore deposit lying at 270 feet, the Picher Lead Company approached the BIA and obtained mineral leases to 2,700 acres in the prospect area.[9]

By September 1914, the Picher Lead Company was developing four mines in the Tar Creek watershed. The first workers came from established Tri-State mining towns in Missouri and Kansas, and as additional mines came into operation, a settlement began to form. Most structures sat on BIA leases. Typically, the company purchased forty-acre mineral leases from the BIA. These sections were then divided into smaller plots that were subleased to workers and merchants for housing and commercial purposes. Mineral development had priority on the company-controlled subplots, and the leases could be terminated with thirty days' notice.[10]

Because of this unusual leasing system, Picher grew haphazardly. Although the Picher Lead Company erected a handful of buildings and surveyed a rudimentary town grid, the company played a minor role in the town's structural development. Most residents lived in small shanties adjacent to the mines. Many of these dwellings were constructed from scrap material (Figure 4.3). Because of the short-term nature of the leases and because houses and other structures were often moved to make way for new or expanding mines, workers had little incentive to construct more substantial housing. The uncertainty of leases also affected the quality of commercial structures. After fire destroyed several commercial buildings in 1918, for example, the renamed Eagle-Picher Lead Company gave notice that no new structures were to be erected if they could not be removed with thirty days' notice.[11]

Poor living conditions were common in mining boomtowns; during the mining rush, infrastructure development often lagged behind population growth.

4.3 Miner's Home, Picher, 1936. Library of Congress, Prints & Photographs Division, FSA-OWI Collection, reproduction number USF34-004136-E DLC

Unfortunately, the circumstances that first created substandard housing in Picher—the temporary nature of leases and the lack of industry involvement in infrastructure development—did not significantly change as the town grew; and grow it did. Picher's population was listed at 9,676 in the 1920 federal census, the first conducted in the town. This total did not include, however, thousands of residents who were living in unincorporated towns on the community's margin—settlements like Douthat, Hockerville, Treece, and Zincville—or those residing in small squatter camps on the field's periphery. Population estimates for the Picher Field at this time exceed 20,000, a remarkable number considering that the settled area was only six years old and that newcomers faced extraordinarily difficult living conditions. The Picher townsite developed as mine encampments coalesced. Settlement was unorganized because of the mixing of mines and residences, and most lived in drafty, dirt-floored hovels. There was a chronic lack of food and civic services were few. Initially, Picher had no sewer system, garbage collection, public utilities, schools, or city government, and according to an account published in the *Daily Oklahoman* in 1917, the Eagle-Picher Company acted as a "feudal" overlord of the camp. The only service the company provided was primitive water delivery. Homes were equipped with water barrels that the company charged twenty-five cents to fill. Frequent conflagrations of the miners' shacks and periodic epidemics of pinkeye and smallpox added to the hardships early residents faced.[12]

With the town's incorporation in 1918, some shortfalls in municipal services were addressed, but improvements came slowly. More than one billion dollars of lead and zinc were produced from the Picher mines; however, industry invested little of this wealth in the community. Likewise, little was shared with those who labored under difficult and often lethal working conditions to produce Picher's metal riches. Low wages were a long-standing problem for Tri-State workers. Moreover, because employment was tied to fluctuating market demands for lead and zinc, worker income was never ensured; mines slowed production or shut down when metal demand fell. Occupational hazards were also a burden and workers faced many perils. More than one-half of all mine fatalities occurred from falling roof rock. Mines in the Picher Field contained vast chambers, some with ceiling heights greater than ninety feet. Even small rock falls from such heights often proved fatal. Unwise use of explosives and hauling and hoisting accidents also claimed many lives. The most serious occupational hazards, however, were dust-induced respiratory diseases. Silica dust was prevalent in the mills and mines, and over time its inhalation produced silicosis, a disease that afflicted an estimated 30 percent of the Picher workforce. Although silicosis could itself be fatal, it also predisposed its sufferers to tuberculosis, a highly infectious respiratory disease. Indeed, the crowded and unsanitary living conditions in which residents lived created a tuberculosis epidemic in Picher, and in the 1930s, Ottawa County had the unenviable distinction of having the highest tuberculosis fatality rate in the nation. Respiratory diseases had a profound impact on the health of miners and their families, and the disabilities and dependencies they caused represented serious social problems.[13]

Mine production in the Picher Field was closely tied to the price of zinc, its most valuable mineral commodity (Figure 4.4). Development of the ore body coincided with the outbreak of World War I, and as zinc was a component in artillery shells and cartridge brass, Picher supplied a significant volume of ammunitions metals for the war effort. Metal prices were high during the war and in the first five years of the field's operation (1915–1920), lead and zinc production rose from 21,125 to 350,365 tons. At this time, Oklahoma was the nation's leading

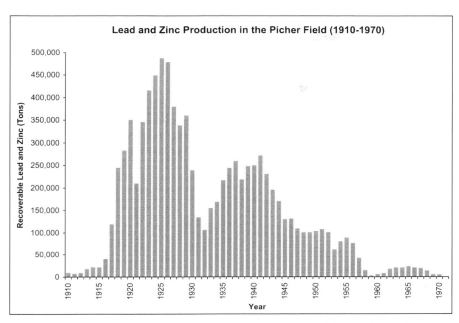

Lead and Zinc Production in the Picher Field (1910-1970)

4.4 Lead and zinc production in the Picher Field peaked in 1925. After a decline in the 1930s, production rebounded with the development of new ore-processing technologies. Mine production again declined following World War II. All of the field's large-scale commercial mines were closed by 1960, but small amounts of metal continued to be produced for several more years through small-scale contract mining, locally known as "gouging." Data from Edwin T. McKnight and Richard P. Fischer, Geology and Ore Deposits of the Picher Field, Oklahoma and Kansas, *89–90; and United States Bureau of Mines,* Minerals Yearbook.

zinc-producing state. In fact, from 1920 to 1930, the area produced more than 70 percent of all U.S. zinc and 35 percent of the metal mined worldwide. Peak production occurred in 1925 when 387,002 tons of zinc and 100,838 tons of lead were extracted from the Picher Field.[14]

Picher had grown into a substantial city by the 1930s. Its corporate limits extended over twelve square miles. The business district occupied nine square blocks centered on Main Street. Buildings remained of low-quality frame construction, and a disorganized mix of mines, mills, chat piles, and residential areas surrounded the downtown core (Figure 4.5). Picherites were serviced by more than 100 small businesses, including two banks and four funeral homes; undertaking was a profitable business because of miners' high fatality rates. In addition, more than forty boardinghouses and seven hotels, occupied mostly by bachelor miners, were in operation. For recreation, Picher boasted four movie theaters, a dance hall, and ten billiard parlors. Dozens of bootlegging establishments and bordellos also existed. The community had a vibrant underground economy

4.5 A panoramic view of Picher looking north from atop the Premier Mine chat pile, 1931. More than thirty mines and their adjacent chat piles are shown in the photographs. Main Street, Picher's commercial center, is shown at top. At this time, an estimated 20,000 people occupied the Picher Mining Field, the world's most productive lead and zinc mining area. Western History Collections, University of Oklahoma Libraries

and it is alleged that mining officials named many of Picher's streets—such as Francis, Emily, Ella, Mabel, Gladys, and Pearl Streets—after their favorite "girls downtown."[15]

In 1929, more than 7,000 workers were employed in the Picher Field. Almost all were of Anglo descent. Although Picher lay on allotted Quapaw land, few tribal members actually lived in the town or worked in the mining industry. Most resided in the nearby town of Quapaw, several miles to the southeast, but Picherites generally accepted the Indian population. As mineral royalties had made some allotees extraordinarily wealthy, the Quapaw held a relatively high social status. They frequented Picher businesses and their children attended community schools. Other minority groups did not have the same status, however, and racism was rampant. Indeed, the Ku Klux Klan was influential in local politics and a customary law existed, barring foreign-born Europeans and African Americans from living and working in the region, and few did.[16]

In the 1930s, the zinc industry was severely affected by the Great Depression. In 1932 the price of zinc concentrates fell to below $20 a ton (it had exceeded $50 in the mid-1920s) and annual production fell to 89,686 tons. Thousands lost their jobs as mines shut down or slowed production; it was at this time that workers unionized in greatest numbers. Labor unrest culminated with the bloody Tri-State Metal Workers' Strike of May 1935. Organized by the International Union of Mine, Mill, and Smelter Workers, the strike effectively shut down mineral production in the district for approximately three weeks. An industry-led back-to-work movement and military intervention by the Kansas and Oklahoma National Guards finally broke the strike.[17]

Zinc prices rose in the latter years of the 1930s, but production never again reached pre-Depression levels. The Picher Field did experience rejuvenation, however, in the early 1940s. New technologies were needed to mill lower-grade ores and to improve processing efficiency in the face of rising production costs and lower metal prices. Central milling was the answer. Small-scale mine-site milling gave way to larger central mills designed to process ore from numerous mine sites. With the advent of central milling, highly capitalized firms came to dominate the industry. Eagle-Picher was the largest. The company built its central mill to the southwest of Picher. In its day, it was the largest and most efficient mill of its kind in the world.[18]

In 1941, zinc production rebounded to 233,173 tons, but this number was only 60 percent of the annual production achieved in the 1920s, and the district was about to enter a period of decline from which it would not recover. In order to ensure abundant lead and zinc supplies during World War II, the federal government had paid subsidized premium prices for the metals. These subsidies were terminated in 1947, a landmark year for mine closure, and a steady decline in production occurred thereafter. Low metal prices strained profitability, but depletion of the ore deposit was a greater problem. With a diminishing resource, the mining field gave out. The last large-scale commercial mine in the Picher Field closed in 1958. Although gouging took place for several more years (the removal of the last high-grade ore deposits in the supporting pillars of mines), the field was essentially dead. As the fortune of the mining industry fell, so, too, did that of the community it had sustained. With few opportunities for alternate employment, the town's population steadily declined. By 2000, only 1,662 people remained in Picher. The economic and social woes these residents now face are substantial and their problems are compounded by living in an environment that has been devastated by half a century of metal mining.[19]

LANDSCAPE AND IDENTITY IN EARLY PICHER

The earliest written descriptions of Picher are found in regional newspapers. In October 1915, a reporter for the *Miami Record-Herald* (Miami, Oklahoma, is located to the south of the mining field) wrote, "Picher gives promise of being a famous camp." The newspaper reported that the prospecting rigs blanketing the area provided a "panorama of push and progress," and it followed the settlement's industrial development with unbridled optimism. In November 1915, a Miami reporter exclaimed: "[Picher] is here in place and permanency. . . . [I]ts prosperity is not a coincidence, nor temporary." The article was titled "Where Rainbows End Touches the Earth."[20] Later that same month the following newspaper account appeared:

> Cardin and Picher, two husky mining towns, are putting on a continuous "watch us grow" performance to an audience that is growing larger and more enthusiastic every day. . . . The restless, ceaseless activity of the people, the newness of all the houses, the maze of drills that circle each town about, the shafts that are headed "hell bent" for ore of great extent and high percentage, and the new concentrating plants being erected [are] evidence to even a tenderfoot that mining enthusiasm is rampant. . . . [T]he zinc blende twins will live to a ripe old age before the vitality of their origin is exhausted.[21]

Oklahoma City's *Daily Oklahoman* also followed Picher's rise, and like the Miami newspaper, it viewed the camp as a spectacle of industrial prosperity. In its earliest years, Picher grew rapidly and the increasing volumes of lead and zinc being produced from its mines were viewed as wondrous achievements for the nascent state of Oklahoma. So, too, was mining's transformation of the local landscape. "Busy mining towns and camps have taken the place of grazing herds, and gigantic tailings piles have taken the place of the prairie dog mounds of other days," wrote the *Miami Record-Herald* in 1915. "Instead of Indian teepees there are modern concentrating mills producing enormous quantities of zinc concentrates, and now instead of being classed as an agricultural state, Oklahoma is entitled to a place of prominence among the mining states of the American Union."[22]

The unbridled optimism of these earliest newspaper accounts was promotional in nature; sympathetic to industry interests, local newspapers were attempting to bolster Picher's image and encourage its growth. Also evident in these reports is a societal sentiment, widespread at the time, that the development of native land was an unquestionable good. Over the course of Western settlement, Indian land was widely viewed as underutilized land and native interests usually were placed behind those of Anglo industrial society. Quapaw land was no exception. In a silent newsreel produced by the Eagle-Picher Lead Company in the 1920s, panoramic scenes of mining operations are contrasted to images of "primitive" Indian settlement. Commentary accompanying these images clarifies the message: "Picher, Oklahoma, in 1915 was a prairie, earning its Indian owners fifty cents per acre a year for grazing. . . . Today, the world's greatest lead and zinc field produces almost $60,000,000 a year in ore!" The fact that the ore body underlay "restricted" Indian land was not a hindrance to mineral development. To the contrary, BIA management of Quapaw allotments was driven by a perception that their conversion to industry was a progressive transformation.[23]

Although outsiders marveled at Picher's growth in the early years, residents held a different view of the settlement. A 1939 investigation of area social conditions contains rare firsthand narratives of life in early-day Picher. *A Preliminary Report on Living, Working, and Health Conditions in the Tri-State Mining Area* (hereafter *Preliminary Report*) was produced by the Tri-State Survey Committee. Founded by the New York–based National Committee for People's Rights, the Tri-State Survey Committee was charged with documenting the area's social problems. Included in the *Preliminary Report* are interview transcripts of early residents. "You should 'a seen Picher in those days," said the wife of an original miner. "The families would come with a wagon load of furniture and keep a-drivin' over the dirt roads or through the mud till they found a clearin' where they could stay. . . . [T]hey'd unload their things right in the open fields and start a-buildin' a house around them."[24] Another resident elaborated on the challenges the first Picherites faced:

> In them days there was so much work that people rushed in here and started to git at it before they even had a roof over 'em, but the way they thought then was different than now altogether. Everybody that come here had to work hard but they didn't complain none. Watchin' the new mills go up and the new mines go down was excitin' as watchin' kids grow. Everythin' was growing over night, an' the people felt like they was part of it. . . . The mud be so deep a person couldn't hardly get through it, but I'd put on my big rubber boots an' with the bucket in one hand an' the baby in the other, off I'd go. People come in so fast then that eats was always scarce in town. . . . That's how things was here, but nobody complained 'cause it was a new thing an' they felt like part of it.[25]

Unlike outside reports, early resident accounts document the considerable hardship Picherites faced. Also revealed is the prevalence of a "make-do" attitude among the community's earliest residents. In a 1921 exposé on area living conditions, a Picher miner described his housing dilemma: "Of course I can only want a shack," he said matter-of-factly. "[I]f the mining company wants to put a shaft under my front door, or a tailing pile on the kitchen stoop, then I've got to move." Similarly, after reflecting on the want and suffering he faced growing up in Picher, longtime resident Ben Moody said, "We did not complain about these conditions, but would just make do with what we had."[26]

On the surface, such sentiment appears to support the claim that the Tri-State's Ozarkian workforce was predisposed to accept difficult living and working conditions; a self-serving assertion often used by mine operators to justify the district's substandard state. As their accounts reveal, however, Picher's first settlers were aware of their pitiable circumstance, and contrary to industry claims, their seeming acceptance of inhospitable conditions reflected their desperation. Most had moved from other Tri-State communities where mining was on the decline. For the unemployed and destitute, Picher provided hope for a better future. "When the mines opened up the people lived in boxes, any way they could," explained longtime area resident Grace Beauchamp. "All of these people needed jobs and they would work anyplace they could get the work. . . . [W]hat else could they have done?" Life in Picher, they hoped, would be better than the situation they had left behind.[27]

Also tempering residents' views of the hardships they faced was an emerging sentiment that survival through difficult times was an enriching experience. Picherites were beginning to fashion a self-identity based on their ability to endure the hardships of the mining life. Only the strong survived in Picher, and strength of character developed from this Darwinian-like struggle. Ben Moody describes this outlook in the following encounter: "I once saw a visiting Dignitary from the East looking over a group of young boys playing in Picher. They were ragged and had no shoes on, although the weather was cool. This Eastern Dignitary made the remark that all the children of Picher seemed to be strong and healthy. His host, a Picher resident, replied that he was only seeing the strong survivors and that the weak ones had not made it." Moody reflected, "[S]ome how we survived and each of us were made better men and women from the rigors we lived through in the Picher Mining Field."[28]

In comparing resident and outside accounts of early Picher, two themes relating to the town's identity emerge and these themes have proved to be long lasting. Most apparent is a disjunction of internal and external perceptions of the community. Outsiders initially ignored the hardships residents faced. Although life in Picher was extraordinarily difficult, early visitors, infatuated with the area's industrial progress, failed to recognize the community's shortcomings. The outside view of Picher would soon change, but a fundamental contrast in perception would remain as residents and outsiders continued to view the town in markedly different ways. A second notable theme is the emergence of a community identity based on residents' ability to survive and thrive in an unforgiving environment. Although conscious of life's challenges, Picherites tended to focus on the fact that they were doing their best under difficult circumstances. Residents developed pride in their ability to endure, a characteristic of local identity that would persist through the mining era and beyond.

"SORES BEYOND CURE"

Sitting atop the region's richest ore deposit, Picher quickly grew into the largest and most productive mining town in the Tri-State Mining District. Despite the town's regional prominence, however, by the mid-1920s outside opinion of Picher was changing. Interest in the area's economic progress remained, but following an initial burst of community and industry promotion, Picher began to be redefined as a mostly ramshackle and dysfunctional community. Before long, visiting journalists were focusing most of their attention on negative aspects of life in the community, and negative mining town stereotypes—elements of the mining imaginary—came to dominate outside perception.

Coverage of unlawful conditions in the town signaled the beginning of this shift in place perception. Detailed crime stories were reported in regional newspapers as journalists fixated on the seedier and often violent aspects of community life. A sensational front-page story appearing in the *Miami Record-Herald* in 1918, for example, reported the existence of a "white slave gang" operating from the Picher Hotel. This organization shipped young women out of the district "for immoral purposes." The newspaper also contained frequent accounts of underground "vice rings" engaged in gambling, bootlegging, and prostitution. Coupled with graphic descriptions of fatal mine accidents and bloody bar fights, these accounts helped Picher develop a violent reputation.[29]

Inadequate housing, transportation shortfalls, and sanitation problems also began to garner attention. In 1917 an unnamed correspondent for the *Daily Oklahoman* penned the following description of the town:

> Picher has sprung up from the prairie. It has a population of about 8,000, almost as big as Miami itself. Its growth has necessarily been of the shack character. There it sprawls on the open plain, a gangling, awkward, disheveled creature hot as an inferno under its noon sun, and treeless as a desert. Up and down its main street the traffic of the district swings ceaselessly; taxis sweating in from Miami and Joplin or returning; motor trucks creaking under their loads of machinery; ore wagons lumbering slowly past; and clouds of dust swirling forever. Sanitary conditions are of course elementary. There is no public utility service. . . . [The water supply] is pure and wholesome when delivered, but its method of storage is the primitive barrel. Mostly those barrels are covered but occasionally you see one with its top off, willingly receptive to whatever wandering germ or strolling bacillus comes its way.

The reporter went on to wonder at the wealth generated from Picher's mines, but his narrative promptly refocused on the town's atrocious living conditions. He wrote, "[I]t is impossible to get away from the water in the barrels and the utter lack of sanitary provisions." Appalled by what he saw, the writer claimed that building permanent communities in the mining region was impractical. "First," he explained, "this is Indian land . . . occupied and operated under the tenure of leases. Second, there is the potential mineral value of the town sites, which may at any time make it advisable to mine the land." The Netta Mine, which was "threatening to bite a chunk out of Picher's main street, necessitating the removal of many houses," was cited as an example. The *Daily Oklahoman* concluded that Picher's deplorable living conditions were "unavoidable" problems given the nature of lease arrangements and the priority of the mining interest. "The standards of living, manifestly, can never be brought to a normal level," the reporter surmised, voicing the hopelessness that would dominate the outside view of Picher's plight for years to come.[30]

The Depression and strike years of the 1930s hardened Picher's image as a hopelessly destitute place. The *Miami Record-Herald* paid close attention to the drop in metal prices and mine production, and it documented the economic and social impacts of industry's decline. In the early 1930s, the newspaper described how thousands of free meals were served daily to unemployed miners. It documented the charitable activities of the Picher Christian Army, the establishment of food distribution stations by the Picher Emergency Relief Association, and the shooting of rabbits in food relief hunts. Although such stories acknowledged the community's struggles, local and state newspapers tended to be unsympathetic to resident hardship. Newspaper coverage of the Tri-State Metal Workers' Strike of 1935, for example, was highly critical of the workers' cause. The *Miami-Record Herald, Daily Oklahoman,* and others were supportive of industry interests and placed blame for the area's economic woes on allegedly unreasonable worker demands for union recognition and higher wages.[31]

In the mid–1930s, a degree of optimism returned to outsider accounts of Picher. Labor tensions had abated and mine production was rebounding. In 1935, the *Tulsa Daily World* claimed that economic prosperity had returned to the mining district. In 1936, the *Daily Oklahoman* published an article titled "Happy Days in the Mines Again." Tempering this optimism, however, was an underlying theme that the region's problems were unfixable. "Although the situation is brighter . . . there is no boom in progress at Picher," the *Daily Oklahoman* reported. "Don't go rushing up to Picher looking for a job in the mines. The community still has plenty of idle workmen."[32]

Earliest accounts of Picher aside, regional newspapers were hesitant to promote the community without marked reserve, even in times of economic improvement. Surprisingly, unconditional endorsement was also absent in industry reports, some of which were generated in response to a series of scathing community exposés produced by social reformers. Representing Picher's harshest appraisals, the first of these exposés appeared in *The Survey* in 1921. Authored by labor reformer Charles Morris Mills, the article contained detailed descriptions of the Picher landscape:

> Like many other mining communities, the centers of past and present productive activity set forth a Sahara-like panorama. Mammoth tailings piles, frequently fifty to one hundred feet in height, marking the life and energy of a mining property, cover thousands of acres of formerly fertile land, which can never be reclaimed for agricultural purposes. The soil, contaminated with the overflow from the mills, becomes barren. Everything has been sacrificed in the feverish scramble to get as much ore out in the quickest time possible and nature has consequently suffered abortions from which she can seemingly never recover.

Mills was the first to document mining-related environmental problems in Picher, but the bulk of his attention focused on the mining's deplorable working conditions, such as the dangers of underground mining, the high incidence of respiratory disease in workers, and operators' exploitive wage system (Figure 4.6). He also described the lack of quality housing and the inadequacy of Picher's sanitation system, which he blamed mining companies for not addressing. "Operators in the Tri-State area, with rare exceptions, have done nothing for the welfare of their employees," Mills wrote. "[T]he whole industry stands in a Pre-Victorian period of social development." Citing familiar issues—the temporary nature of leases and the impermanency of dwellings—Mills also claimed that a "feverish unsteadiness" had "warped the social instincts and ideals" of area inhabitants. Moreover, residents had become "dwarfed and stunted by the waste and barrenness of their environment." Because of the "psychological" influence of their harsh surroundings, he claimed that Picherites "lacked the commonest incentives for decency."[33]

Although Mills was attempting to generate awareness of Picher's problems, by portraying the town as a place where nature had suffered "abortions" from which it could "never recover" and Picherites as passive inhabitants of a doomed environment, his analysis conveyed the same sense of hopelessness that was prevalent in non-reform-minded texts. Indeed, this impression was conveyed in most social reform literature produced on Picher during the mining era, the most significant of which was the Tri-State Survey Committee's aforementioned *Preliminary Report*. In its introduction, the 1939 report describes the Tri-State Mining District as a terminally ailing "death trap" where conditions "represented a denial of the basic rights of decent living."[34]

The *Preliminary Report* contains more than eighty pages of descriptive text, photographs, resident testimonials, and family histories. Much of its focus is trained on Picher, and a particularly disturbing portrait of community life is provided in

4.6 Interior of the Denver-Miami Mine, Picher Field, 1916. Fatality rates were high in the Picher Field, and underground workers faced the greatest hazards. Rockfalls were the most common cause of fatal accidents. The greatest long-term threat to worker health, however, was silicosis and related respiratory diseases. As a result of intense physical strain and exhaustion, mine shovelers were particularly susceptible to accident and disease. Paid on a piece-rate system where compensation was tied to the number of cans they could fill with ore, shovelers routinely filled 45 to 60 cans holding 1,000 pounds of ore each day. Most of these miners were physically broken down by age 30. Western History Collections, University of Oklahoma Libraries

the family histories of its residents. The eight-child family of "Mrs. R," for example, moved to Picher in 1915. After working underground for fifteen years, "Mr. R's" lungs hemorrhaged and he succumbed to silicosis. A similar fate claimed the lives of his two oldest sons. A third son contracted tuberculosis and died at age eighteen. One of several Picher families highlighted in the *Preliminary Report,* this family lost four of its members to mining, leaving behind two widows and nine fatherless children.[35]

The hazards of the Picher landscape, the landmarks of which are described as "mountainous piles of useless mining waste," are also illustrated in the *Preliminary Report*: "Chat piles loom up in the very heart of Picher. . . . [E]very wind that blows across these piles raises a miniature dust storm of pure silica." The report charged that a blanket of hazardous dust covered the community, that children were swimming in chemical-filled millponds, and that "the chance was two-to-one that any particular miner lived in a home not fit for habitation." The dwelling of a disabled Picher miner is singled out as an example of Tri-State housing at its worst: "It is a two-room shack in the outskirts of the town, reached by a rough and dusty chat road, and standing by itself on a desolate, sun-beaten plain. . . . [Its resident] has no garden or livestock. He uses about a barrel of water a day, which comes from Picher by truck without inspection. The house is half a mile from the nearest store and a quarter-mile from the school, which is built on a chat pile."[36]

The Tri-State Survey Committee's findings received national publicity, spurring Secretary of Labor Frances Perkins to sponsor a health conference on Tri-State conditions. Held in Joplin in 1940, the conference was attended by occupational health experts and representatives from organized labor and industry; testimony from all sides confirmed that serious problems existed in the region. Unfortunately, although the survey committee succeeded in publicizing conditions in the field and formed a commission to find solutions to the area's housing and health problems, no dramatic improvement occurred in the conference's wake.[37] Picher's isolation coupled with industry and government indifference to worker welfare ensured continued hardship. Perhaps most important in maintaining the status quo, however, was the ever-growing perception that Picher's problems were beyond repair. In the 1930s and 1940s, critical descriptions of the community continued to be produced, but like the earlier works of social reformers, they generated little outside compassion for the community. Malcolm Ross's *Death of a Yale Man,* a novel of the muckraking genre, illustrated Picher's industry-derived social problems. It also painted a depressing portrait of the Picher landscape. Ross, a National Labor Relations Board investigator, wrote: "[S]ome 300,000,000 tons of chat piles, high as skyscrapers, comprise the local scenery. The Oklahoma sun reflects hotly from their slopes. They add a new hardness to a physically unfavored country." Ross described how the Ozarks, "rich in hungry hillbillies," had provided an unfailing reservoir of exploitable labor, and although he sympathized with area workers, he believed that improvement in living and working conditions was hopeless: "Twenty years of silicosis, hillbilly recruiting by cow horn, and the final depression disaster," he wrote, "has galled sores beyond cure."[38]

Operators made only modest efforts to discredit this negative attention. The Tri-State Zinc and Lead Ore Producers' Association represented industry interest, and in the wake of the 1935 strike, association secretary M. D. Harbaugh responded to labor reform criticism. In an article appearing in *The Mining Congress Journal* in 1936, Harbaugh praised the independent character of district workers, claimed that a democratic relationship existed between management and labor, and lauded industry efforts to improve working conditions. Although Harbaugh defended the mining industry, he was willing to admit that unsatisfactory living conditions existed in the field, especially in Picher. He qualified this admission, however, with claims that operators were not responsible for the town's state; because no one could tell when mining operations might "require that dwellings be moved," no incentive existed for workers to construct permanent housing. Harbaugh made no apology for Picher's condition. First and foremost, Picher was a mining town where the interests of industry held precedence. Furthermore, he deflected responsibility for the community's condition onto residents, whom, he claimed, "could live elsewhere if they chose, [but] prefer to live in close proximity to their work." Citing a longstanding prejudice, he said that Picherites had low standards when it came to the quality of their environment.[39]

Other material was produced by industry, but none defended the mining industry better than Harbaugh. The most extensive industry publication to deal with Picher was a collection of articles appearing in the *Engineering and Mining Journal* in 1943. Although released at a time of improving production, the lead article was nonetheless pessimistic about the field's future, claiming that Picher could not be expected to maintain its dominant position in the nation's zinc economy. Indeed, the general tone of these articles was that of an industry on the decline. Like newspaper accounts of the day, even mining journals had a difficult time unconditionally promoting Picher. The *Engineering and Mining Journal* series also lacked discussion of the problems that existed in area living conditions, an omission that is telling of the way industry had come to view Picher's social problems. Industry felt no obligation to defend itself against the field's most commonly noted shortcomings because the negative consequences of maintaining the status quo were negligible. Despite substantial critical exposure, the state and federal governments had not demanded reforms in area living conditions. In short, the work of social reformers resulted in the generation of little public, industry, or government empathy for the community.[40]

The transformation in outside perception of Picher—from a place of industrial progress to a locale of hardship and dereliction—might have served as a stimulus for industrial reform and positive change. Sadly, however, this redefinition of place proved as insensitive to Picher's internal meaning as had earlier promotional discourse. Improvement in living and working conditions did not occur, in large part, because the works of social reformers, labor activists, and muckrakers only served to harden Picher's image as a hopelessly despoiled place. Portrayed as a community beyond help, a place sacrificed to the interests of industry, Picher seemingly held no redeeming qualities.

HARD AS THE ROCK ITSELF

Journalists and social reformers were not wrong to recognize Picher's troubles. The image they constructed, however, rarely included the views of those who called Picher home, and this omission produced a highly unsympathetic portrait of place. As local historian Velma Nieberding explained, by looking disparagingly at Picher's plight, outsiders ignored the town's function and value as a community and home. "Would you have the land as it was before the mines?" she asked. "There was only a dream then. It took strong men to shoulder that dream into railroads and highways and towns and libraries and hospitals and schools. Do not use the words waste, pain, tragedy and death. These are the words of failure. The era of King Jack [a colloquialism for zinc ore] was lusty, exciting, fearful, prodigious and cruelly strong. But it was not failure, not exploitation, not unbridled waste."[41]

Throughout the mining era, residents strove to create a more livable and lasting community, showing that they did not consider Picher a hopeless cause. Contrary to the claims of historians and others, Picher was not a company town.[42] Most of the town's infrastructure was built by individuals and was privately owned, and most municipal services were publicly managed. In light of this fact, even the community's modest accomplishments should be considered significant. The BIA land that most of Picher occupied was nontaxable, and as a result, private donations and volunteer labor made most civic improvements possible. Given the limited means of residents and the town's paltry budget, much was accomplished.

Picher was incorporated in 1918, and soon after water delivery and sewer systems were constructed. Civic organizers also canvassed for donations to build schools. Although funding was a constant burden, by the late 1920s, close to 1,900 students were enrolled in the Picher school system, an achievement residents took pride in. In 1939, resident Genevieve Stovall Craig wrote, "[A] personal visit to the schools will open up to the outsider an amazing and dramatic panorama of public education typical of the American system."[43]

Although town infrastructure generally remained substandard, resident apathy was not the cause. As Frank D. Hills, editor of Picher's *Tri-State Tribune*, explained, a determined effort was required to make improvements possible. "Picher unblushingly presents no excuse or apology for its apparent delinquencies," the newspaperman wrote. "[E]verything cannot be as one would have it and there are many things left to do to complete dreams of the future." He continued: "The improvements of the past have been made by spirited sacrifice on the part of the citizens who have labored under nearly every conceivable handicap. . . . [Picher] sprang into existence as a necessity instead of the result of a blueprinted utopia of an idealist. The vitality was here; the resources were here and the people came before preparations were made to receive them."[44]

External accounts of Picher in the mining era depict it as a place languishing under hopeless adversity. Not recognized was that Picherites were striving for, and achieving, improvement under difficult circumstances. Also ignored or discounted by claims that residents were accepting of poor living conditions was the fact that Picherites were mindful of the hardship they faced. In analyzing their own predicament, however, residents conveyed a markedly different view of the area's problems, as is evident in resident interview transcripts buried in the appendix of the Tri-State Survey Committee's *Preliminary Report*. For instance, "Mrs. C," a thirty-five-year-old Picher widow, responds to an investigator's evaluation of her home:

> The house stands on a single lot of Indian ground, the dollar-a-month rent for which has not been paid for several years. It is unpainted and has no foundation, and its yard is littered and in bad condition. It has holes in the sides, patched with tin, and holes in the roof. When asked about the latter Mrs. C replied with a laugh, "Does it leak! Look at that hole. You could throw a cat through it—and look up there; from every place you look inside you can see daylight coming through." But she regarded this as an advantage on a nice day, for it let a lot of light and air into the place.[45]

Mrs. C. had found a way to view her predicament in a positive light, and other resident commentaries in the *Preliminary Report* reflect similar sentiment. "It's a pretty unhealthy place to live," one miner remarked, "but the chemicals in the mill ponds fertilize the water and make the flowers grow." This ability to shrug off hardship, to "make-do," was common among Picherites. Iva Simpson, for example, in a community retrospective appearing in the *Tri-State Tribune*, described in a matter-of-fact way the events that led to the moving of her childhood home: "The Acme Mill chat pile had grown and spread across the length of more than a block of Ella Street; already it was knee deep in most yards. All the houses had to be moved. . . . One day the movers came, jacked our house up on timbers, and pulled it up the hill." With only a hint of resignation she said, "[O]ne phase of our life in Picher had ended." Such stoicism is also evident in Ben Moody's recollection of the Depression years. "There were so many hard times in the Picher Mining Field," he remarked, "that when the Great Depression started people only knew there was a depression because there were just a little more of hard times than usual."[46]

Resident accounts of life in the mining era lack the histrionics prevalent in external narratives. For Picherites, dilapidated housing, chemical-filled millponds, expanding chat piles, and economic hardship were parts of life one coped with. Given the effort they were making to improve conditions in the town, however, it would be wrong to claim that Picherites viewed their predicament to be beyond improvement. Acceptance of these conditions was not driven by hopeless resignation. Rather, acceptance was how Picherites coped with an extraordinarily difficult existence.

An autobiography written by revered hometown hero Mickey Mantle shows how residents were making the best of their forbidding environment. The baseball legend grew up in nearby Commerce and his father was a longtime Eagle-Picher miner. He wrote:

> One summer we claimed a spot near an abandoned mine shaft. It made a perfect baseball field, smooth and firm. One bad feature, though, was the outfield. An endless plain of alkali. You couldn't see a ditch or a fence or anything that would slow the ball down. I guess it's the main reason I became an infielder. . . . [W]henever the wind came howling in, it carried gray clouds of alkali dust, the gritty particles that swept over the field and burned into our eyes nearly blinding us. End of game. We'd cough all the way home.[47]

For Mantle and others, the mining landscape was used to advantage. Tailings ponds were converted into baseball fields, millponds became swimming holes, and chat piles served as playgrounds. As their comments show, residents were aware of many of the area's health hazards, such as dust, contaminated water, and poor living conditions. Offsetting their unease over health issues, however, was their tendency to view interaction with the mining landscape as an everyday part of life. What's more, for some, mining's physical influences even came to be appreciated. Recounting the panoramic view atop a chat pile, Picherite Marion A. Parsons described his first visit to the town in 1925. Admiration and pride, rather than disapproval, characterize his account of the mining landscape:

> I reached the top and stood in wonder—you might say awe and amazement at what I could see from this tremendously high vantage point in the sky. I could hardly believe my eyes! . . . I looked and looked; to the East, West, North and South, and then, as in a daze, slowly rotated a few degrees at a time, each time discovering new shapes, sizes, clouds of

smoke, wisps of steam, movement of trains, trucks, horses and wagons—near and far. It was a veritable land of machines, buildings, tall and short and the movements were amazing. People seemed to be everywhere.[48]

Residents adapted to the mining environment and, for the most part, they accepted mining's alterations. The mines, mills, and chat piles were a part of daily existence and were venerated, to a degree, by residents, who recognized the toil and sacrifice that had produced this mining landscape. The landscape represented determined labor in pursuit of a better life. Moreover, as noted, an important part of resident identity was rooted in their ability to survive in this difficult landscape. The term "chat rat," a nickname for Picherites, reveals the complex relationship that residents had with their town. Often used derisively by outsiders, chat rat was used as a self-identifier, too, showing that many took pride in residing amid Picher's chat piles. Indeed, residents felt little need to apologize for their lifestyle, the condition of their town, or the nature of their work. To the contrary, central to their identity was the reputation the town held as a difficult but honest place.

Onetime miner Orval "Hoppy" Ray, in an interview conducted in 1999, proudly described these attributes of the town and its people. In a matter-of-fact way, he recounted the nature of the mining occupation. "Most miners died before they was forty-five years old," he explained, "but they were hard-rock miners—hard living. My dad and brother was miners, and I was a miner. It was just living for Christ-sakes. . . . You hear a lot of people say, 'man those were the worst jobs in the world,' but Hells-bells, the temperature was the same year round, you knew who you was working with, and you knew what you had to do—you just went down and done it." For Ray, mining was an arduous yet honorable way of life, and a similar forthright spirit exists in his description of Picher, which despite its ramshackle and unruly nature was a cohesive and nurturing community:

> We had twenty-two bars here at one time, at least every third building was a bar. You could walk down Main Street, or down Second or Connell, and you'd see four, five, or six fights. Old knockdown drag-out fights. Everybody stood around and watched. . . . I'll tell you, there wasn't nothing like Picher. These old miners here, years ago, when there wasn't any hospitalization, no insurance, no nothing, if a family got down and out, they went and passed the paper. They'd go around different places, you'd sign your name and throw in a quarter. There was very few that wouldn't pitch in . . . that's the way people were around here. You didn't need to lock your doors, you didn't need to worry about anything. Oh, Picher had a rough reputation, everyone knew about Picher. We had a Hell of a reputation . . . but still, it was safe here.[49]

Longtime resident John Mott, also interviewed in 1999, expressed similar sentiment. "When I grew up, you never did hear of anybody molesting a girl or a child or anything," he said. "Kids would go to a show on Wednesday night, go downtown and walk home at ten o'clock, and this was the high days of mining. Yeah, on Saturday nights, the miners would go down to the bars and they were tough, hard-working people, and they drank and fought. Some would rather fight than eat. But the next day they would work together and never think a thing about it." He concluded, "[W]e never locked our place, didn't even have a key to our house when I grew up."[50]

County historian Velma Nieberding has described Picher as a place of "sludge ponds, tailings piles, miners' shacks, muddy streets, honky-tonk music, and bootleggers." Picher, she explained, "was a world of a reckless breed. . . . As hard as the rock itself." Clearly, Picherites have taken pride in nurturing this uncompromising yet honorable image of place and self-identity. After detailing how he managed to overcome the hardships of Picher life, for example, Ben Moody wrote, "[A]nyone who lived or worked in the Picher mining field is proud of it."[51]

It would be wrong, however, to claim that all residents were accepting of life's hardships or that an affinity for the town was universal. The desire to leave the community was strong in many, particularly in Picher women. "It's a pitiful way of living," remarked a widowed resident in the *Preliminary Report*. Before her husband died of tuberculosis, she had pleaded with him to leave the town. Unfortunately, poverty and debt bound them to place: "I always begged him to git out, but we never could put by enough money to take the risk of making a change," she said. "I never liked this mining business. . . . [F]or one thing, we couldn't ever save anything. . . . [H]e'd work a month, then the mines would shut down. . . . [W]e were in and out of debt." Another widow stated, "[E]ver since I came to Picher I wished I could leave. . . . Last year my husband died of the miners' con. Now one of my boys is away at the sanatorium tryin' to get well. Even so, I've got two boys left an' they're both well, an' now I want to git away from here more than I ever did 'cause I want to keep these last two out of the mines."[52]

For women, the mining way of life provided few rewards. Their place of toil, the miner's shack, lacked the camaraderie of the mine, and with responsibilities focused primarily on family and home, women found Picher a lonelier and more menacing place.[53] The comments of former residents Lawrence and Theo Barr, in an interview conducted in 1985, demonstrate the different way men and women viewed the community. Lawrence Barr proudly detailed the rigor of the mining occupation and he boasted of the town's boisterous nature. He said: "I got a good education in Picher. I'm not ashamed of the town and I'm not ashamed for anyone to know I'm from there." At several points in the interview, however, Theo Barr interjected with statements that tempered her husband's fond recollections. After he described how many had supplemented their income by bootlegging, she interrupted: "They never had any law and order up there. You could do anything you were big enough to do and that's the truth." Although Mr. Barr remembered fellow Picherites warmly, Mrs. Barr stated: "Those people up there were mean and tough and rough. . . . [T]hey got drunk and beat their wives and beat their kids and that's the kind of life they led. . . . [T]hat's the way the miners lived."[54]

To outsiders, Picher appeared to be a hopelessly destitute place. Residents, however, viewed the town in a more hopeful and complex way. Their attempts to improve the community reveal a concern for the quality of their lives. Picherites were making the best of a difficult situation. They recognized their hardship, but by constructing an identity centered on the mining occupation and its tough but honest life, they found meaning in their existence. To be sure, not all were happy with their lives, and resident attachments should not be overstated. For many, Picher was a cruel environment they could not escape.

Resident accounts of the mining era capture qualities of place not communicated by outsiders, most of whom were unable to portray Picher as anything other than a spectacle: briefly of wondrous industrial progress, more lastingly of shameful and unfixable destitution. But for most Picherites, the town held value as a lived-in place. Its meaning as a community and home was at odds with the views of outsiders and this disjunction in perception endured beyond the mining era and was hardened with mining's demise.

MINE CLOSURE AND COMMUNITY SURVIVAL

By the mid-1940s, most of the Picher Field's high-grade ore reserves had been extracted and operators were relying on federal mineral price subsidies to maintain profitability. When these subsidies were removed at the end of World War II, most mines shut down. "Slow-down wasn't gradual," explained Hoppy Ray. "[T]his town supplied most of the bullets for two world wars, but in 1947 the subsidy was vetoed. It was a landmark year and many people left." Indeed, Picher lost approximately one-third of its population in the 1940s and a similar percent in the 1950s. By 1960, only 2,553 residents remained, and although small quantities of lead and zinc were still being extracted through small-scale contract mining operations (gouging), all of the field's large-scale mines had ceased to operate. Picher's mining era officially ended when the company shut off the water pumps in the underground workings in 1968.[55]

Deindustrialization intensified hardship for those who stayed in Picher. Chat processing and sale, and the salvaging of industry infrastructure, provided a few jobs in Picher's dying mining economy, but no new industry stepped in to fill mining's void and unemployment levels soared. Moreover, town financing, already strained by an inadequate municipal tax base, worsened with industry's demise. Substandard community infrastructure further deteriorated and the City of Picher struggled to maintain funding for schools and other civic services.[56]

Some who left Picher found work in other hard-rock mining areas. The uranium mines of Grants, New Mexico, were a common destination. Those who stayed scrambled to find work, usually in adjacent communities like Miami where the B. F. Goodrich tire factory provided employment. According to Hoppy Ray, who left the mines in 1947 to work at the tire plant, life remained difficult for both those who left and those who remained. "There's a bunch of Picher people in Grants, New Mexico," he stated. "[Q]uite a few of the older ones came back, but most of those dudes died of cancer from the uranium mining. And that's another thing, I never realized that there were so many cancer-causing chemicals at Goodrich. I was there twenty-eight years, and the whole tube line, I'd say 50 to 60 percent of those people I worked with, died of cancer." Ray claimed that the tire factory in which many ex-miners found work was more dangerous than the mines and, in fact, legal actions were taken against Goodrich over improper use and disposal of PCBs, asbestos, and heavy metals at the factory, which closed in 1986.[57]

When asked why he remained in Picher, Ray said, "I never wanted to live anyplace else." Like many others, Ray was reluctant to sever the emotional and familial ties he had established to place. An article appearing in the *Miami News-Record* in 1986, for example, detailed the pain felt by one family, the Walkenshaws, when they were forced to leave the community. "Mining was our whole life," said Mrs. Walkenshaw, "but when the shutdown came there was nothing around here in the way of jobs." The family moved to New Mexico in 1957, but they eventually returned. Unfortunately, Picher had undergone a depressing transformation in the decades they were away. "We could hardly believe it," she lamented. "Picher's downtown had vanished. . . . In 1957, there were still crowds in Picher after work. We had clothing stores, a Safeway, a J. C. Penney, and three pharmacies." The couple, however, chose to remain despite the town's decay and Mrs. Walkenshaw explained why: "My three daughters and my son don't understand why I stay here but I came to Picher in 1920 with my parents. All my children were born here. This is my home."[58]

A booklet produced by the Picher Bicentennial Committee in 1975 provides further insight into why many remained in the community following mine closure. Local historian Genevieve Stovall Craig, in the booklet's introductory essay, cites a familiar theme of perseverance in the face of adversity: "[Residents] lived—and worked—and loved—and kept on working—and kept on loving their little slattern of a city. They would not give up!" Voicing a similar theme, resident C. Allan Mathews describes Picher's accomplishments and the outlook for its future: "We've a long way to go. On the other hand we've come a long way too!" The spirit of the town and the community's will to survive, he explains, is strong: "Picher is sixty years old. She's not the lusty lead and zinc boomtown of yester-year. She's put her roots deep. She's weathered those intangibles common to every boom camp. . . . That has been the story of her past. Perhaps that, more than anything else, is her future. By every conceivable, logical deduction, these chat piles should have been her tombstone. But there was a human factor that can't be overlooked in the miracle that is Picher. A people who wouldn't give up."[59]

Residents' will to endure was remarkable given the range of challenges they faced in the post-mining era. Amplifying the impacts of mine closure and population loss was industry's continued indifference to the community's well-being. Standing amid the ruins of an ore mill, resident John Mott described industry's lack of concern for the social and environmental problems mining had caused. Surveying the chat-strewn landscape, he said:

> When I was ten years old I started selling *Saturday Evening Posts*. . . . I had six customers on Netta Street that I delivered them to. They'd sit out on their front porch fighting to breathe. I talked to my Dad about it. He said that they had worked in the mines and their lungs were gone. They were just waiting to die. . . . I guess I'm kind of prejudiced against Eagle-Picher. I've seen so many things they done over the last forty or fifty years. My uncle worked for them all his life and never made but sixty or eighty cents an hour. They never had any insurance and when he retired he got $112 a month. That's all the retirement they did. They took so many millions of dollars out of this field and never paid anyone anything, and just look at what they left behind.[60]

Like their mining-era ancestors, Picherites continue to display an ambivalent attitude toward mining. Although proud of the town's mining heritage, residents also remain conscious of the industry's impacts. Like Mott, many have come to question whether mining's benefits have outweighed its long-term costs. This is especially true of the Quapaw. Although mineral royalties were paid to tribal members, much of the tribe's fertile agricultural land now lies buried under chat and has few productive uses. Earl Hatley, former Environmental Program Director for the tribe, explained that the Quapaw did not receive lasting benefit from mineral development. "There wasn't great wealth created for the Indians," he said. "Wealth was created, but it wasn't anything compared to what the mining companies received and the few families that did generate some wealth shared it with other tribal members. No one went hungry or without shoes or clothes. They took care of each other, they were a tribe, but that income didn't last very long. Some of those families are still better off, but are they wealthy? No."[61]

Sacrificing surface use in order to maximize exploitation of the area's mineral wealth, the mine operators wreaked havoc on the environment. Industry criticism, however, should be tempered by the fact that operators mostly comported with standard mining practices of the day: industry operated under legally acquired, BIA-negotiated leases and ore was mined using customary practices. Moreover, mine land reclamation was not a requirement at the time of the field's development. That said, mine operators showed an indifference to resident well-being throughout the mining era, which has left the industry open to criticism. Living and working conditions in the Picher Field were substandard even when compared to other hard-rock mining areas, and operators made few efforts to minimize the well-documented health and environmental impacts mining was causing.

Eagle-Picher, the area's largest operator, merits particular scrutiny in this regard, especially for amplifying resident suffering in the final years of the field's operation. A case in point was the company's decision to gouge the last high-grade ore deposits from the supporting pillars of the mines, an action that greatly hastened the town's decline. Gouging produced surface collapses throughout the community, and in the early 1950s, the threat of subsidence led to condemnation of most of Picher's downtown. This event and the ways in which residents and outsiders reacted to it reveal continued contrasts in Picher's meaning as a place.

In February 1950, Eagle-Picher officials warned of an imminent cave-in in a five-block area centered on Main Street. The mining company met with the city council and recommended that the area be closed to the public. Several businesses immediately closed but, as revealed in the *Tri-State Tribune,* there was no mass exodus. "The majority of residents affected," the Picher newspaper reported, "feel that the matter will be taken care of in the normal course of events." As many must have been aware, however, "normal course of events" meant that Eagle-Picher would force evacuation of the affected area by terminating lease agreements. True to form, the company soon issued more than 200 eviction notices, and residents and business owners were given thirty-day notice to leave.[62]

Eagle-Picher claimed that it had discovered a weakness in an underground pillar supporting the area and that it was ordering the evictions in order to protect residents, but many believed that the company had less honorable motives. Months earlier, Eagle-Picher had built a concrete support structure in the mine. The company alleged that the concrete pillar was poured to add additional roof support. According to miner Lawrence Barr and others, however, the company had built the concrete support in order to gouge an adjacent pillar of ore measuring twenty-five feet in diameter and standing forty feet tall. Barr said: "The mining companies got whorish. . . . Those pillars had ore in them, they wanted it and the only way to get it was to shoot it out. I remember they set up a drill rig in front of the bank in Picher. They drilled a hole and they were supposed to have poured a concrete pillar there to catch it [the roof of the mine]. They took out the big pillar. I never seen it but I heard it was worth a million dollars in lead. Eagle-Picher pulled it out." Although the company's true motives may never be known, allegations that Eagle-Picher was gouging beneath Picher's downtown are consistent with the way the firm had always operated in the community; maximum exploitation of the ore body was its only concern.[63]

The cave-in threat drew statewide attention. The *Daily Oklahoman* and *Tulsa World* newspapers described the spectacle of the pending collapse. They also conveyed astonishment that Picherites seemed to be going about business as usual. The *Tulsa World* claimed that everyone, except Picherites, was tremendously concerned. Resident Nona Welsh, business owner in the affected area, was quoted: "I've been around here a long time and I'm not any more worried than I was ten years ago." Another merchant said he would stay in business for as long as the company let him.[64]

Most outsiders were dumbfounded by resident reaction to the pending disaster. However, reporter John Feen of the *Daily Oklahoman* understood, in part, why Picherites weren't panicking. "Sightseers couldn't understand because they had never lived or worked in the lead and zinc mines," he observed. Picherites were accustomed to living with mining's hazards and they had learned to cope with subsidence as a part of life. The residents who refused to leave the condemnation zone were aware of the seriousness of the cave-in threat, but they were holding out only to pressure Eagle-Picher into providing financial assistance for relocation. When the company reluctantly produced a compensation package in February 1951, a full year after initially warning the community that a cave-in was imminent, all remaining leasers vacated the area.[65]

Some merchants reestablished businesses on Connell Avenue, two blocks east of the condemnation zone. Others closed their doors for good. Eagle-Picher claimed that businesses were not affected by the relocation. Long supportive of industry interests, the *Tri-State Tribune* reiterated that claim, maintaining that the town was carrying on in its usual fashion: "[Picher] shrugged her shoulder, pitched in, and emerged triumphantly." Although the newspaper accurately conveyed residents' resolve to persevere, its support for Eagle-Picher's actions was not widely shared. For most, the impacts caused by the abandonment of Picher's downtown were impossible to ignore. "There's a ghost town right in the middle of Picher," reported the *Daily Oklahoman*. "[B]locks that used to hold more than their share of the city's activity stand bleak and deserted" (Figure 4.7). Indeed, condemnation destroyed the town's commercial and social nucleus. "Eagle-Picher," stated a bitter Hoppy Ray, "ruined the whole damn town." Likewise, Genevieve Stovall Craig wrote that the leveling of Picher's downtown was a near "killing blow" to the community made all the harsher by the fact that the area did not subside. Buildings were removed and a fence was erected around the site, which stood as a painful, ever-present reminder of the community's lost vitality. Without cause, Stovall Craig grieved, the heart of the community had been transformed into a "high-fenced rubbish graveyard dense in weeds."[66]

Although subsidence never occurred in the condemnation zone, gouging did produce cave-ins elsewhere. Most notably, in July 1967 a 300-foot diameter crater engulfed three Picher houses, leaving eighteen homeless. Once again, journalists and sightseers came to witness the collapse and were stupefied by residents' seemingly indifferent attitude. Asked about the town's apparent disintegration, Mayor Harold McLain told the *Tulsa World*: "[L]ittle things like this don't shake us. It's just part of living." The mayor went on to say that he did not understand "all the fuss in the news media. . . . Now that the houses are settled thirty-five to forty feet down they will be secure," he said teasingly. "I'd kind of like to have one of those houses."[67]

Outsiders were puzzled by the local response to adversity because most remained ignorant of the coping strategies Picherites were employing. The band-

4.7 View of the condemnation zone looking south down Main Street Picher, 1996. The area, once lined with street-front businesses, boarding houses, hotels, and theaters, was condemned by the Eagle-Picher Company, and abandoned, in the early 1950s. Only a handful of Main Street commercial structures remained at the time this photograph was taken. Shown in the background, these buildings sat just outside the condemnation zone. All but one was vacant. Photograph by the author, 1996.

together and make-do attitude developed in response to the hardships of mining life was now serving the community in the post-mining years. Proving even more elusive to outside understanding, however, was recognition that Picher was retaining value as a community and home. More than other factors, emotional attachments to place were influencing residents' willingness to endure. Unfortunately, as was the case in the mining era, the external view of Picher following mine closure continued to disregard the town's internal worth. In 1972, for example, the following description of the town appeared in the *Daily Oklahoman*:

> The land surrounding Picher is gray, dingy, depressing and soiled with the spoils from the mines. Gravel covers the landscape, supporting only the hardiest brush and weeds. The earth is pockmarked with cuts and gouges, many now filled with water that has seeped up through the crushed rock. Old mill towers stand stark and lonely, their tin skin hanging in ragged, rusted shreds. Concrete foundations that resemble small monuments show where other forgotten mills once stood. Most people who have been there call it the ugliest town in Oklahoma, the armpit of the northeast.[68]

The *Daily Oklahoman* did not speak for residents when it claimed that most viewed Picher as the ugliest town in the state. And geographer John W. Morris did not consider Picherites when he listed the community in his 1978 guidebook *Ghost Towns of Oklahoma*. Remarkably, Picher was given ghost town status even though it retained a population in excess of 2,000, which shows that not only were the views of Picherites ignored in outside depictions of the community, but in some cases, their very existence was denied.[69]

Picherites were aware of these negative portrayals of their town and some were saddened about the dearth of positive accounts. "Every time a newspaper story comes out," said Mayor Bill Koontz in 1964, "it means more negative publicity for the town. Everyone writes about how our water pumps broke down or how the chief of police has to buy gasoline out of his own pocket to run the patrol car. Why doesn't someone write about some of the gains we're making?" After detailing improvements in community infrastructure, the mayor admitted that things were not perfect. But like Picher newspaper editor Frank D. Hills had explained forty years earlier residents had nothing to be ashamed of. The fact that the town was surviving was, in itself, a significant accomplishment. The mayor said, "We're just trying to keep our heads above water."[70]

THE TRAGEDY OF TAR CREEK

Picherites dealt with the trials of the post-mining era in the same way previous generations had coped with mining's hardships: they refused to be defeated and took pride in their ability to survive. Unfortunately, Picher's negative external image also was maintained. Outsiders still viewed Picher as a spectacle of degradation and their inability to recognize the town's internal value grew as the extent of the area's environmental problems emerged.

By most measures, living conditions in Picher worsened in the 1980s and 1990s. Out-migration driven by a lack of opportunity continued and by 2000 the town contained only 1,662 residents. The community had failed to diversify its economy and well-paying jobs were scarce. As a result, in 2000, Picher's median family income stood at $25,950, which was 36 percent below Oklahoma's average. Even more alarming, 21 percent of families, almost twice the state average, lived below poverty level. Because of poor economic conditions and ongoing problems with city financing—much of the townsite still occupied non-taxable BIA-leased land—town infrastructure also continued to decline. Renting or without title to land, residents were reluctant to invest in home improvements and Picher's median 2000 house value fell to a remarkably low $20,700. Given these troubles, it is not surprising that newspaper coverage continued to detail problems with community financing and services. A notable issue was the 10.5-percent city sales tax, the highest in the state, imposed to address chronic budget deficits. In addition, newspapers wrote about the low achievement of students in the Picher-Cardin schools, which came under repeated threat of losing state accreditation.[71]

Environmental issues added to the town's woes and its negative image. Picher's environmental problems received national press in the early 1980s with Superfund designation of Tar Creek. It is worth noting, however, that the area's environmental problems had been recognized before. Mining-related environmental hazards were documented as early as the 1920s; early resident accounts and reform exposés like the Tri-State Survey Committee's *Preliminary Report* described environmental decay in vivid detail. Moreover, a report appearing in the *Tri-State Tribune* in the 1940s shows that industry also had been aware of mining's environmental impacts. Authored by the Tri-State Zinc and Lead Ore Producers' Association, the document argued for the continuation of mineral price subsidies based in part on the observation that cessation of mining would cause environmental harm, because widespread acid mine drainage would occur if the mines closed. Operators noted that flooding the mines would result in the dissolution of "great quantities of soluble sulphates, metals, acids, and salts," an observation that proved prophetic.[72]

Although the region's environmental problems were acknowledged well before the 1980s, nothing was done to address them prior to this time, and this inaction had several causes. Located in the hinterland of Oklahoma, a state of marginal national status, Picher lay distant from both state and federal centers of power and its plight was easily ignored. Moreover, historically low voter turnout in northern Ottawa County compounded the problem as politicians from both parties often neglected the area because its residents were perceived as non-voters.[73]

Picher was not the only settlement of its era to be affected by mining, and its condition also reflected broader societal views on industrial progress during the period of mineral exploitation. Prior to the rise of the modern environmental movement, the impacts of industrial activities like mining were generally viewed as the acceptable costs of progress. Environmental problems, particularly in industry-dedicated settlements such as mining towns, were not paramount societal concerns. Thus, the toxicity of Picher's lead-laden chat piles was ignored. Long after lead had become a recognized toxic substance, most still considered Picher's chat piles to be recreational resources. Chat was also considered a benign construction aggregate as is evident in a 1967 newspaper article appearing in the *Tulsa World*. Titled "For Playing—a Chat Pile," the article reported:

> The mountains of gravel make excellent testing grounds for hot rods and offer good spots for motorcycle climbs. How about a wiener roast on a small plateau halfway up the side? A lover's lane? You Betcha'. Your gravel driveway has a low place? Just drive a short distance for a pickup load of replenisher. As for beauty—more than one native has been heard to say they have seen wonderful patterns—such as the face of Lincoln—as the

sun creates changing shadows. Water erosion creates unusual formations on the weather-beaten mounds. . . . To the kids they were—and are—playgrounds.[74]

Superfund legislation evolved from growing national concern over environmental issues in the late 1970s and Tar Creek's Superfund designation awakened lawmakers to mining's hazardous legacies. Sadly, however, in terms of solving the region's environmental problems, government intervention at Tar Creek has been a story of limited achievement. More than $100 million has been spent at the site, but cleanup efforts have failed to markedly improve environmental quality. To be fair, it is important to recognize that Picher's environmental problems pose an enormous challenge; few Superfund sites compare to Tar Creek in terms of the extent and complexity of environmental hazards. In spite of that fact, mistakes have been made in implementing remediation programs at Tar Creek and these errors were rooted, in part, in the area's ingrained image as a hopelessly despoiled place. Historically, this perception has dampened external resolve to intervene in Picher's quality-of-life issues and evidence suggests that this same sentiment, coupled with ignorance of the community's internal worth, has also influenced environmental decision-making.

Acid mine drainage began flowing from the Picher mines in the late 1970s. It took ten years for the mines to flood following shutdown of the underground pumps, but once filled, millions of gallons of metal-contaminated water emerged at the surface. The discharge destroyed aquatic life in Tar Creek (Figure 4.8). It also migrated downward through the corroded casings of water wells, polluting the Roubidoux Aquifer, Picher's source of drinking water. In response to resident complaints, Oklahoma governor George Nigh formed the Tar Creek Task Force in 1979 to investigate the water problem. Based on information supplied by the task force, in September 1983 the EPA placed Tar Creek on its newly created Superfund National Priorities List. At the time, the area was ranked as the nation's highest priority Superfund site. The first remediation action taken by the EPA, Tar Creek Operable Unit One (OU1), was initiated in 1984. OU1 focused on water contamination, and groundwater pollution was addressed by plugging eighty-three abandoned wells believed to be allowing mine water to migrate into the underlying Roubidoux Aquifer. Surface water problems were tackled by constructing diversion dikes designed to prevent acid mine drainage from entering Tar Creek.[75]

OU1 was completed in 1986, but as the EPA's own review of the project later showed, remediation work had largely failed. The agency determined that the Roubidoux Aquifer was meeting primary drinking-water standards. The water failed secondary standards, however, based on color, taste, and odor. The EPA claimed that these were only "aesthetic" problems, but this information was of little consolation to residents whose drinking water remained foul tasting and whose clothes still carried an indelible pink stain from being washed in the tainted

4.8 Tar Creek is contaminated by acid mine drainage flowing from underground sources and from the surface runoff of chat piles. Of note, tracks on the chat pile at left show that the mining waste remains a popular place for off-road vehicle use. Photograph by the author, 2000

water. Remediation results for Tar Creek were even worse. Mine discharge into the stream had not been appreciably reduced and water quality remained severely impacted. Indeed, the EPA later supported a state decision to downgrade Tar Creek from its original designation as a "warm water aquatic community" to an "unviable habitat," a reclassification with important ramifications. Now that the river was no longer considered to have beneficial use as a water supply, fishery, or recreation area, the EPA recommended that no further action be taken to clean up the river. Not surprisingly, many believed that the EPA and state had conspired to exclude Tar Creek from further remediation work. "That same water they were so concerned about in the mid-1980s is still there, but suddenly it's not important anymore," said Miami mayor Louis Mathia. "Why has it suddenly become invisible to the protectors of the environment?"[76]

Little activity occurred at Tar Creek in the late 1980s and early 1990s, but work was renewed after a 1994 Indian Health Service (IHS) study showed that 35 percent of area Native children had blood lead levels exceeding federal thresholds for lead contamination. Follow-up studies confirmed the seriousness of the problem; approximately 40 percent of all area children had elevated blood lead levels. The rate of juvenile lead poisoning in the Picher Field was nearly ten times the national average, a shocking revelation, but one that should not have come as a surprise to the EPA, which knew of the existence of toxic metals in Tar Creek—namely, lead, zinc, and cadmium—as early as 1981.[77] Moreover, EPA documents show that it was aware of the existence of metal contaminants in chat, later revealed to be the primary source of lead poisoning, as early as 1984. Indeed, some have claimed that the agency's delay in investigating the lead threat may have been intentional.[78] In an article titled "The Tragedy of Tar Creek," *Time* reporter Margot Roosevelt wrote, "Early on, the government confined its effort to the polluted creek, without looking at chat piles." She asked: "[W]as it a lack of knowledge of the danger, as EPA claims? Or industry influence, as environmentalists charge?" The fact that the EPA had been aware of the prevalence of lead in the Picher environment might suggest the latter; however, when the EPA came to Tar Creek in the early 1980s, lead's health impacts were still becoming known. Based on standards issued by the Centers for Disease Control (CDC), at that time the CDC's level of concern for lead in blood was three times higher than it was at the time of the IHS study. A dramatic reduction in the CDC's blood lead alert level in the early 1990s stimulated study of lead contamination in the Picher area and revealed that a problem existed.[79]

Regardless of the causes, the EPA's delay in addressing lead contamination has left it open to criticism that it was reluctant to expose industry to the financial liability of chat pile reclamation and the business costs imposed by chat regulation. Both occurred with eventual Superfund recognition of the chat-lead problem.[80] Moreover, had government felt a greater urgency to truly address the area's problems, it seems likely that action on lead contamination would have been undertaken sooner. This lack of resolve is evidence that many considered cleanup a fruitless cause in Picher's apparently hopeless environment. Dr. Robert Lynch, for example, who had conducted early blood lead studies in Picher, said, "There was an undercurrent of opinion that the place wasn't worth the money being spent to clean it up."[81]

The fact that long-term health studies have only recently been initiated to quantify lead's health impacts is also revealing. Anecdotal evidence has been compiled, showing that the Picher population has long been suffering the effects of lead poisoning. An unusually high incidence of learning disabilities and a prevalence of hypertension, kidney disease, Alzheimer's and Parkinson's diseases, and cancers have been documented in the area. For a population known to have one of the highest incidences of juvenile lead poisoning in the nation, however, the fact that it took nearly a decade for government to begin rigorously assessing lead's long-term health effects again suggests a basic lack of resolve to address the area's problems.[82]

Once lead's hazardous effects in Picher were exposed, EPA investigators quickly concluded that chat-contaminated residential soil was the leading source of lead poisoning, and in 1996 the agency initiated work on Tar Creek Operable Unit Two (OU2). Focused on residential soil remediation, OU2 also included an educational component designed to raise local awareness of the lead hazard. Under OU2, chat-contaminated soil was excavated, removed, and replaced with clean soil. High access areas, such as schoolyards, playgrounds, and other public areas, received the first attention. The EPA then focused remediation on residential yards where chat had been widely used in landscaping and road and driveway surfacing.[83]

More than 2,000 residential yards and public areas were remediated in Picher and four adjacent communities, markedly reducing rates of juvenile lead poisoning; elevated blood lead levels declined by 50 percent between 1997 and 2000. Sadly, however, blood lead levels in area children remained well above state and national averages, a sobering fact that led many to doubt the effectiveness of the EPA's soil remediation action. Furthermore, critics noted the likelihood that properties would be recontaminated by nonresidential chat sources—the hundreds of chat piles and flotation ponds, the latter containing fine mill residues—located near residential properties. It was also recognized that children were still being drawn to these toxic playgrounds. In fact, 75 million tons of lead-contaminated chat remained on the ground (Figure 4.9).[84]

Ongoing water quality problems, a questioning of the long-term efficacy of residential soil remediation, and skyrocketing cleanup costs cast doubts on whether remediation activities in Picher had been worthwhile. Although adamant that cleanup was possible if enough pressure could be placed on the government to search for effective long-term solutions, scientists—even locally invested environmental scientists like Earl Hatley, Environmental Program Director for the Quapaw Tribe—were admitting that the area was little better off than before the EPA's arrival. "OU2 may not be worth a damn in the long run if you don't get rid of the chat," Hatley said in 1999. "If all you are going to do is clean up the yards and go back to Dallas [EPA regional headquarters], then you've spent millions of dollars that will be wasted. In ten years, it will all be recontaminated." He continued:

> What we will be left with is the mine water drainage problem from OU1 that the EPA doesn't want to address, and chat piles that will still be here for decades. When they walk away from these Operable Units, will there be any visible change? No, it will all look exactly the same. Orange streams, chat piles 200 feet tall, moonscape all over the place. . . . I wouldn't be here if I didn't think there was hope, but we have to push them. If you look at the history of Superfund, the sites that get cleaned up, like Love Canal, are places that have received attention, where local citizen groups have been pushing them and giving the EPA bad press.[85]

Local environmental advocates like Hatley believed that not enough pressure had been placed on the government to force it to search for a long-term solution to the region's environmental problems. Although attention had been paid to the area both on the ground and, to a lesser extent, in the press, it was clear that Picher had not yet received the right kind of attention. Remediation activity had failed

4.9 *Chat piles surround Picher's old baseball field and chat remains pervasive in residential areas of Picher. This Little League ballpark is now closed, but it was replaced by a new sports complex built by the EPA in the late 1990s. Photograph by the author, 1996*

to improve environmental quality, and the fact that reporting of environmental issues, as had historically been the case in coverage of the town's problems, had failed to elicit serious concern was a contributing factor.

With Superfund designation of Tar Creek, Picher received a modest amount of regional and national newspaper attention. This interest, however, failed to generate lasting public concern. Part of the problem was that the media's attention focused on Superfund implementation controversies, which distracted the public from the actual environmental problems that confronted Picherites. One such well-publicized dispute over Superfund involvement at Tar Creek pitted the EPA against anti-EPA forces and mining lobbyists who argued that remediation of mine sites was a misuse of agency funds. This conflict became the focus of a House subcommittee investigation ordered by the Reagan administration.[86] Implementation issues also plagued OU2. Native replacement soils used in the remediation program had a high clay content and did not drain as well as the chat-filled soils it replaced. Clay replacement soil coupled with the fact that Picher did not have engineered street drainage—runoff from roads commonly drained onto residential properties—caused widespread flooding of reclaimed yards. The EPA and Army Corps of Engineers (the primary project contractor) initially denied responsibility for damages caused by water pooling under homes. These and other implementation controversies received more press than Tar Creek's environmental problems and their direct impacts on resident quality of life.[87]

Another problem with media coverage was that journalists failed to portray Picher as a community worth saving. A four-part special report on the Tri-State Mining District published in *The Wichita Eagle-Beacon* in 1986 was a case in point. Titled "A Legacy of Neglect," the report more than adequately documented the extent of the area's environmental problems. Like social reform exposés produced during the mining era, however, the articles portrayed the region in a highly pessimistic light. Described as "an economic and environmental wasteland," Picher was singled out as a worst-case example of the region's plight.

> [In Picher] the rituals of mourning and dying are all too familiar. . . .
> [D]eath is a way of life here. The people die at nearly twice the national
> rate from lung cancer. They are more likely to die of kidney disease, heart
> disease, stroke and accidents. . . . [But] their grief does not end there. The
> mining companies that ripped the world's richest supply of zinc out of
> the ground and then left when mining was no longer profitable poisoned
> their land, wrecked their economy and robbed them of hope. The land is
> scarred and the water is contaminated. . . . The air they breathe, the water
> they drink, the soil their children play in contain toxic metals. Their
> homes are built above abandoned mines that cave-in without warning. . . .
> The place is an environmentalist's nightmare. . . . The story of the Tri-State
> Mining District is one of neglect. A story of people who have given up.
> Who are too afraid, too poor or too uneducated to fight back. Finally, it is
> a story of a problem so large that no one knows how to solve it. Many say
> it can never be solved.[88]

In this and other reports, Picher was portrayed as a spectacle of total, seemingly irreparable, environmental decay. Moreover, another perception besetting the area since the mining days—that of resident apathy toward hardship and blight—was evident in the report. Allegedly, residents remained unconcerned about the area's health threats and paid little attention to environmental issues. "With rare exceptions," wrote one reporter, "people have accepted with little protest living in the midst of the nation's largest environmental hazard." Journalists elsewhere made similar observations. A 1981 *New York Times* article titled "No. 1 Toxic Waste Site Is Not Town's No. 1 Gripe" portrayed residents as apathetic about the area's environmental woes. "If this is the worst pollution we've got in this country," one resident is quoted, "then we're all in heaven and don't know it."[89]

Although Picher's environmental problems received media attention in the aftermath of Superfund designation, journalists failed to generate public sympathy for the community by continuing to portray the area as a spectacle of hopeless degradation and residents as apathetic bystanders to their plight. Just as in the mining era, such media coverage was detrimental to Picher's cause. Insensitive to

Picher's internal value as a community and home, these reports diminished outside resolve to find a lasting solution to the area's environmental problems. This state of affairs might have continued indefinitely had a number of factors not come together in the late 1990s to generate genuine external concern for resident well-being.

WHITHER RELOCATION?

A search for a permanent solution to Picher's environmental problems is now underway. This turning point was reached, in part, as evidence mounted that cleanup programs had failed to improve environmental quality. For more than two decades, the EPA had pursued a costly piecemeal approach to remediation, applying pollution management solutions to each emerging environmental hazard. Despite this enormous investment in time and money—federal spending at Tar Creek totaled $113 million as of January 2004—separate pollution cleanup strategies had failed to eliminate contaminants in the Tar Creek watershed. Recognition of this failure eventually produced a shift in environmental policy; rather than treating the symptoms of environmental contamination, the EPA would focus on eliminating the contaminants' sources.[90]

An awareness that the area's problems were too complex for any one agency to solve also played a role in expanding government activity at Tar Creek. Water quality impacts, lead contamination, land degradation, and mine hazards were associated problems that could only be solved by careful planning. Long-standing social and economic issues also had a bearing on cleanup objectives. Land tenure and Native American issues created legal hurdles to chat reclamation, and poverty and lack of opportunity influenced resident occupancy of the chat-covered landscape. Solving the area's woes required consideration of a broader range of issues than the EPA alone had the expertise to deal with, and once this fact was explicitly recognized, state and federal lawmakers were forced into greater involvement.[91]

Although a number of factors contributed to a reassessment of environmental policy at Tar Creek, none was more important than the effort of citizens to publicize the area's problems. As Earl Hatley had predicted, increased outside awareness of Picher's troubles was a prerequisite to action.[92] Indeed, Picher's cause received a vital boost in the late 1990s with a notable increase in media attention. For almost twenty years following Tar Creek's Superfund designation the region had received little notice. Periodic reports of EPA activity and accounts of Picher's economic struggles appeared in regional newspapers, but it was not until 1998 that the area finally began receiving exposure befitting one of the oldest Superfund sites in the country. Since 1998, Tar Creek has been featured in such notable print sources as the *New York Times, Los Angeles Times,* and *Time* magazine. National Public Radio and ABC Television's *Nightline* also have carried Picher's story, as have more than 200 Associated Press articles produced since then. State newspaper reporting also has dramatically increased. In December 1999, the *Daily Oklahoman* produced a three-part investigation of conditions in the Picher Field, the first major coverage given the region's environmental problems by Oklahoma's largest-circulating newspaper.[93]

Not only did the number of media reports increase in the late 1990s, but an important change in the nature of reporting also occurred. Increasingly, journalists began to incorporate local points of view into their stories. By directly engaging residents, Picher's woes were personalized, generating a rationale for greater outside care. A 1998 article appearing on *Tulsa World*'s front page and titled a "A Sad Place" provided a resident-focused overview of the impacts of lead contamination, as did a host of stories appearing in state newspapers, including the *Daily Oklahoman*. Yet it was the national media outlets that generated the most notable reports of this type. Stories appearing in the *New York Times* and those airing on National Public Radio and ABC Television contained impassioned, firsthand accounts of the area's troubles. Collectively, this media attention generated a more compassionate response to the area's problems. A face was placed on local suffering as internal narratives communicating hope for a better future transformed longstanding perceptions of dereliction and resident apathy.[94]

This crucial shift in outside perception was the direct result of citizen efforts to increase awareness of the area's plight. Contrary to conventional wisdom, many Picherites recognized the area's environmental threats and in the 1990s formed a number of grassroots advocacy groups whose mission focused, in whole or part, on publicizing Tar Creek's problems. No shortage of knowledgeable interviewees existed in Picher for journalists to tap for information. Likewise, Picher was filled with local guides willing to reveal the area's trouble spots. These residents included members from organizations like Tribal Efforts Against Lead (TEAL), which was a partnership of area tribes devoted to addressing childhood lead poisoning, and the Tar Creek Basin Steering Committee, a citizen advocacy group focused on property compensation issues. Members of Local Environmental Action Demanded, or LEAD Agency, also became active. Formed in 1997, the group has focused its energies on environmental education and a demand for "true" cleanup of Tar Creek. Particularly noteworthy is LEAD Agency's organization of an annual Tar Creek conference. First held in 1999, the meeting has grown into a major event attended by nationally recognized health researchers, environmental scientists, and politicians. A highlight of the 2004 gathering, held in Miami and titled "Tar Creek VI—We're Still Here," was the Tar Creek Toxic Tour. Conceived by the Cherokee Volunteer Society, a club from the Miami High School, the student-led expedition through the Picher Mining Field has become a central activity of the yearly conference.[95]

Citizen mobilization in the late 1990s and increased media coverage forced lawmakers to commit to finding a permanent solution to Picher's environmental woes. To this end, plans have progressed on several fronts. Former Oklahoma governor Frank Keating was the first to act. In January 2000, the governor created the Tar Creek Superfund Task Force, which he charged with developing a comprehensive remediation plan for the area. The ten-member panel produced a final report within ten months and its central recommendation drew considerable attention. The *Final Report* advocated the construction of a massive wetland system within the boundaries of the Superfund site and this system would include a 546-acre reservoir and more than 2,000 acres of wetlands. The area would function as a wildlife refuge and would necessitate a mandatory relocation of area residents. Estimated cost of the plan stood at $250 million, an expenditure that the task force claimed was far less than the billions of dollars needed to make the area habitable. Critics of Keating's plan argued that its cost estimates for alternative forms of remediation were grossly overestimated, especially its multibillion-dollar estimate for subsidence abatement. They also argued that the plan had been devised hastily. A number of unanswered technical and environmental issues existed, for example, regarding the construction of a reservoir atop unstable mine land. A mandatory buyout of residents also posed a number of potentially intractable problems.[96]

Because of these shortcomings, Keating's plan was shelved. It did initiate, however, a debate over how to solve Tar Creek's problems and other proposals soon followed. In October 2002, the EPA began work on a Feasibility Study for Tar Creek Operable Unit Four (OU4). A nonresidential chat cleanup program, OU4 is being designed to address threats to public health and the environment caused by the release of hazardous substances from chat piles, flotation ponds, and the transition zones of nonresidential chat areas. The U.S. Army Corps of Engineers, a contracting agent for Superfund remediation at Tar Creek, also began work on a new initiative in 2002. The aims of the Corps' Tar Creek and Lower Spring River Watershed Management Plan are to develop a long-term solution to chronic flooding problems in the mining field and to improve local ecosystems. Both the EPA and the Army Corps of Engineers are focusing on remediation solutions that cover the entire Tar Creek watershed. As of April 2006, however, the specific strategies these plans will pursue have yet to be determined.[97]

While the EPA and Army Corps of Engineers continued to assess the area's problems, work progressed at a faster pace elsewhere. U.S. senator Jim Inhofe (R-OK) backed an initiative known as the Oklahoma Plan for Tar Creek. Oklahoma Plan team members also include the Oklahoma Department of Environmental Quality, the Quapaw Tribe, and the University of Oklahoma. In brief, the Oklahoma Plan has four objectives: to improve surface-water quality through construction of passive treatment systems (small-scale wetlands); to reduce exposure to lead by increasing chat utilization in asphalt mixes, paving chat-surfaced roads, and revegetating chat piles; to attenuate mine hazards by filling vertical mineshafts with chat; and to reclaim unproductive land through chat removal and revegetation. Work began on several of these projects in 2004. The estimated cost of the Oklahoma Plan is $45 million. With Inhofe's support, funding was obtained from a variety of federal agencies.[98]

The Oklahoma Plan is more limited in scope than Keating's plan or the EPA and Army Corps of Engineers' still-evolving initiatives; the Oklahoma Plan's remediation activities are being undertaken primarily in peripheral areas of the mining field. By limiting remediation to privately owned lands in sparsely settled areas of the Superfund site, the Oklahoma Plan is sidestepping legal obstacles resulting from restrictions the BIA has placed on chat use.[99] It also is avoiding the controversial issue of resident relocation. By steering clear of these issues, the Oklahoma Plan allowed remediation work to be rapidly initiated. Indeed, the plan's team members see their efforts as the first tangible steps in developing a comprehensive solution to problems that plague the entire field.[100]

The Oklahoma Plan is testing long-overdue chat remediation strategies and, in this regard, its work is vital. Nevertheless, many believe that more drastic measures must be taken to address the area's health threats. Two general approaches exist to addressing lead contamination: eliminating lead sources and removing lead receptors. To date, most efforts have focused on eliminating the lead sources. Increasingly, however, demands to remove the lead receptors—Tar Creek's residents—have gained momentum. Oklahoma governor Brad Henry (D), former Congressperson Brad Carson (D-OK), and the Tar Creek Basin Steering Committee were the leading proponents of a community buyout focusing on the town of Picher but also including residents living elsewhere in the Superfund site. Arguing that lead poisoning represented an urgent public health crisis, they demanded that lawmakers recognize their obligation to immediately remove residents from the polluted area.

The relocation issue represents the greatest challenge Picher has faced in its tumultuous ninety-year history. The community's continued existence is now in question and, not surprisingly, the issue has polarized politicians and residents into opposing camps. Although Governor Henry and Congressman Carson supported remediation activity undertaken under the Oklahoma Plan, they also believed that government has a moral obligation to address the immediate health concerns of residents and both have supported use of government funds for a voluntary buyout. Senator Inhofe has stood on the other side of the relocation debate. As chairman of the U.S. Senate Environment and Public Works Committee, whose jurisdiction extends over the EPA and Army Corps of Engineers, Inhofe has held commanding influence over legislation affecting Tar Creek and he has steered federal involvement clear of the buyout option. Inhofe has stood firm in his belief that the Oklahoma Plan addresses the area's long-term environmental problems and that it is more economically feasible than a buyout.[101]

In June 2003, Inhofe announced that federal buyouts were officially off the table in further discussions of Tar Creek's future. His attempt to quell the issue, however, only strengthened the convictions of his opponents who moved on their own to finance resident relocation. In May 2003, Carson introduced the Tar Creek Restoration Act to Congress. The bill directed the EPA to provide relocation assistance to residents of the Tar Creek Superfund site but it languished in subcommittee review and never became law. At the state level, however, Governor Henry introduced the Oklahoma Child Lead Poisoning Prevention Act, which was passed into law in June 2003. The act funded the relocation of families to areas outside the region of lead contamination. Targeting those most vulnerable to lead poisoning—only families with children aged six and under qualified for relocation—the voluntary buyout was accepted by fifty-two families in 2005, 186 people in total. The state purchased their homes for an amount equal to the average cost of comparable housing in unaffected regions of Ottawa County. The state spent approximately $3 million for this purpose and most of the purchased properties were demolished.[102]

Calls for relocation assistance to be provided to all residents living in the Tar Creek Superfund site have increased since passage of the Oklahoma Child Lead Poisoning Prevention Act, and now that the urgency of the health threat has been formally recognized in law, such demands are commanding attention. A community-wide voluntary buyout is gaining momentum and even Senator Inhofe has begun to soften his position on the issue. Although he remained opposed to the use of government funds for relocation, Inhofe endorsed a private sector alternative in 2004 that would allow brownfield redevelopment companies to purchase properties within the Tar Creek Superfund site.[103]

Thus, it appears that the first steps have been taken toward Picher's dissolution, which, many contend, the government should have facilitated long ago. In fact, community relocation was considered by the EPA during early planning for the Tar Creek Superfund site, but it was rejected because the agency believed it had a feasible and cost-effective plan to remediate the area. In retrospect, the EPA clearly underestimated the costs and technical challenges involved in addressing the area's problems. Moreover, an early community buyout would have prevented lead poisoning in many area children. In "Whither Relocation?" an editorial appearing in *The Tulsa World* in 2003, a powerful argument in support of relocation was crafted from these issues. The editorial also presented a list of environment-related buyout sites conducted elsewhere in the country to show that precedence existed for relocating Tar Creek's communities. Unfortunately, the article did not explore the drawbacks of buyout programs, which, experience shows, rarely provide a panacea to complex environmental problems.[104]

Community buyouts on a scale as large as Tar Creek have never been attempted by the EPA and questions surround their economic feasibility.[105] The U.S Army Corps of Engineers has estimated that an extensive property acquisition and relocation program for the approximately 2,000 residents living in the Superfund site would cost $118 million, a total approximating the amount the

EPA already has spent on remediation at the site.[106] Because substantial federal resources have already been committed to further cleanup activities and any change of course would be tantamount to admitting that more than twenty years of costly remediation work had been a waste of federal dollars, it is possible that the State of Oklahoma will be left to finance buyouts on its own. It is doubtful, however, that the resources exist at the state level to finance large-scale community relocation. Should the state's desire for relocation remain strong, Oklahoma lawmakers may continue over time to fund small-scale buyouts. Unfortunately, this approach might generate unrest among those anxious to leave. Moreover, a troublesome set of issues surround resident willingness to relocate.

Despite substantial threats to public health, unanimous support for community buyouts is rare and sizeable portions of affected populations often refuse to abandon their homes. Mandatory buyouts are the most problematic as they come into conflict with private property rights. Remediation programs that require depopulation, like Keating's shelved plan, can generate serious conflict even when small numbers of residents refuse to leave. Although voluntary buyouts face fewer legal hurdles, they create social inequities that can negatively impact quality of life for those who choose to stay on. As a community's population dwindles, those unwilling to leave face potential school closures, the loss of public and private services, higher utility costs, increased taxes, and depreciated property values. In addition, they often shoulder the emotional burden of living amid the ruins of dismantled and stigmatized communities.[107] Many of these issues have already emerged in Picher.

The exact number of Picherites opposed to community relocation is difficult to determine. An unscientific resident survey conducted in 2002 by the Tar Creek Basin Steering Committee, a vocal advocate for relocation, suggests that most are in favor of moving. When asked if consideration of a buyout proposal was in their best interest, 448 of 556 polled residents, approximately 80 percent, responded in the affirmative. Although questions surround the survey's precision, it does appear to have captured majority opinion; most are in favor of considering a buyout. As the survey showed, however, a substantial number of residents are opposed to relocation, and this group has been outspoken in their opposition to the issue. Assuming that approximately 20 percent are determined to stay and projecting that figure across the approximately 2,000 residents living in Picher and adjacent areas of the Tar Creek Superfund site, there are an estimated 400 potential holdouts.[108]

In the ongoing debate over community relocation, the possibility that several hundred residents might turn down buyout offers has yet to receive careful consideration. To date, discussion has focused mostly on the economic costs of relocation and the rights of those wishing to leave. Without question, an adequately funded buyout would attend to the demands of those wanting to remove their families from an environment that poses an immediate threat to public health. On that fact alone, it is reasonable for lawmakers to table buyout options. It would be a mistake, however, to assume that relocation will solve the region's problems or address the needs of all Picherites, many of whom will refuse to abandon their homes.

THE "TOWN THAT JACK BUILT"

Throughout Picher's history, an undercurrent of opinion existed that Picherites were ignorant of the region's blight and environmental decay, a myth that dampened outside resolve to address the town's problems. As researchers, journalists, and politicians began to pay greater attention to Tar Creek in the late 1990s, however, this misperception was finally discarded. It now is generally accepted that Picherites are aware of the hazards they face, so it is initially difficult to grasp why a substantial portion of the town's population is opposed to relocation. Indeed, it would be relatively easy to avoid a holdout problem if it was simply the result of ignorance because increased emphasis on lead-hazard education would likely convince the vast majority to leave. But Picherites are not ignorant of their town's environmental hazards.

It is true that some old-timers, having lived long and apparently healthy lives amid Picher's chat piles, downplay the region's environmental problems. Many opposing a buyout come from this elderly cohort. When Tar Creek first was listed as a Superfund site, a reporter from the *New York Times* was treated dismissively when she questioned residents about the area's environmental woes. "I don't pay no more attention to that than nothing," remarked longtime resident Adelia Hanna. "It's just our way of life here by the mines." Ex-miner and lifelong Picher resident Hoppy Ray expressed similar sentiment. When asked about the dangers of chat, he said, "I've been here since 1925 and I've never had any problems. I don't understand what the big scoop is on all that crap. These chat piles are supposed to be toxic, but for crying-out-loud, I played on those things all my life!" Ray recognized that the chat piles were a source of lead poisoning, but he believed that if individuals looked after themselves and their children—washing regularly and keeping clothes and homes clean—they had little to worry about. "It's all about how you take care of yourself," he said.[109]

Ray, a buyout opponent, is not ignorant of the lead hazard. His comments do reflect, however, a desensitization to the area's problems that is the result of life-long interaction with the mining landscape. Environmental degradation remains, for some, a fact of life. This observation was confirmed by Kent Curtis, an environmental official for the Cherokee Nation, who wrote: "For almost twenty years, people in the Tar Creek area have been painfully aware of the harmful legacy that mine wastes have brought to their lives. Although these problems are serious, people have shown a remarkable ability, or perhaps resignation, to live with them. People have lived with these problems for so long that they have become accustomed to them and may simply accept them as a part of life."[110]

Picher's elderly may be more willing to accept environmental degradation, but this tendency should not be overstated. John Mott has long been cognizant of the area's health problems and has been active in raising awareness of environmental quality issues in Picher. Mott said: "Some people don't fully understand the lead problem. They've been here all their life and don't understand what it's all about. But my grade school was built on a chat pile. The kids played in it everyday and I went to school with kids that just couldn't learn. Even then, we knew something was wrong. They just passed them on, from the third grade on, to get them out of school. They were going to be adults in the third grade! We didn't understand it, but we knew something was wrong." Hoppy Ray's grandson, Steven Ray, confirmed that a high level of environmental awareness exists across age groups in Picher. "After being presented with the facts, most have come to believe that the chat needs to be cleaned up," the younger Ray said. "Sure, there are still a few who say 'I've been here forty or fifty years and I don't see a problem,' but that would be maybe 1 percent of the population." Ray stated emphatically, "People in Picher understand heavy-metal poisoning."[111]

If they are aware of the area's environmental hazards, why are so many Picherites reluctant to leave? Part of the answer lies in resident distrust of government. Picherites are skeptical of the government's ability to address their problems. In an environmental awareness survey conducted by the TEAL organization in 1997, for example, residents were asked to list the major obstacles to preventing lead poisoning. Various concerns were listed, including doubts over continued government funding of remediation projects and criticism of its handling of cleanup efforts. "The government is not willing to go the extra mile to clean it up," wrote one respondent. Others wrote, "[T]he EPA is not keeping their promises," and, "[T]he EPA should have addressed this twenty years ago." Such sentiment stems mostly from past remediation failures. Rebecca Jim, executive director of LEAD Agency, has written: "The people in the local communities trusted the officials, both the state and federal, to find ways to solve the environmental problems that surround the area they call home. . . . [But] it has now been nearly twenty years since the first orange, rust-stained water appeared . . . and no one has stopped its seasonal return."[112]

Government distrust is also the result of past management controversies at Tar Creek, particularly the EPA's and Army Corps of Engineers' shifting positions on chat cleanup and their failure to establish good community relations. Steven Ray explained that the EPA initially was viewed as a "savior" in Picher, but no longer: "At first, the EPA said that the chat piles were not a problem and that to remediate them would cost approximately $500 million. They said they could not possibly come up with the funds for that. They said, and I quote, '[T]he people of Oklahoma and of the country will not pay that much money for the people of Picher.' Then they said that the chat piles contained toxic materials. . . . It's always been back and forth, they contradict themselves regularly. . . . It depends on who you talk to whether or not the chat piles are viewed as the biggest enemy in the town, or if they're nothing to worry about." Ray also described how the EPA's soil remediation program, work coordinated by the Army Corps of Engineers, has created problems that have left many residents angry:

> [The EPA and Army Corps of Engineers] talked about all the various things they were going to do. It was wonderful. They were going to remove the lead and return the yards to the way they were with no problems. . . . But they took out the topsoil and they put clay back in. This created an impermeable barrier to water. The water ran across this clay barrier and collected under the houses. There is a mold and mildew problem with almost every one of these houses and you have homes where floors rotted through. . . . A lot of people were strong-armed into the remediation work and there was a lot of resentment. Those who complained were labeled "chronic complainers."[113]

Soil remediation created severe drainage problems in many residents' homes, including Ray's, and the EPA's initial denial of responsibility—it took several years for residents to be compensated for the damages remediation had caused—created tensions that worsened government standing in the community. As this controversy played out, Ray remained a cleanup advocate. He appreciated that soil remediation had reduced the incidence of juvenile lead poisoning. Like most, however, Ray had become wary of government involvement at Tar Creek. Now nearly all Picherites are skeptical of government claims regarding new initiatives designed to solve the area's problems.[114]

For most, government distrust has strengthened their resolve to leave Picher. "I grew up with lead and now I've got great-grandkids who are growing up here with the same lead problems I faced," exclaimed Mott. "I'm sick and tired of some SOB telling me to wait for another study." John Sparkman holds similar opinions. Spokesperson for the Tar Creek Basin Steering Committee and the area's fiercest buyout advocate, Sparkman stated on ABC Television's *Nightline,* "The federal government has two choices, they can either spend the billions of dollars it's going to take to make this safe and livable for 1,600 people or they can get us the hell out of here." In a newspaper interview, Sparkman said: "If John F. Kennedy had tasked these people who were in charge of Tar Creek to go to the moon, we never would have made it. This place is never going to be fixed."[115]

For a smaller group of residents, however, government resentment has intensified their resistance to buyout proposals. As historians have noted, Picherites have long held an independent mind-set. Attitudes of self-determination remain strong, and for some, buyouts represent unwanted government meddling in their lives. Also furthering relocation opposition are fears that buyouts may not be fairly implemented. Property compensation issues are a legitimate concern, particularly in light of the EPA's failure to provide timely and adequate compensation for past soil remediation damages. House values in Picher remain well below regional averages, and because many houses occupy BIA leases, property values often exclude the price of land. If fair market property value is used as a compensation formula in these cases, residents choosing to relocate may find that their meager reimbursements do not provide enough capital to reestablish homes elsewhere.

Concern that the community will be unable to function once residents and businesses begin to leave is also an issue for those determined to stay. Many believe that a community-wide voluntary buyout will guarantee Picher's downfall. Although all would have the option to leave, voluntary buyouts have no acceptable outcome for those who choose to remain behind and must experience the community's post-relocation demise. Mayor Sam Freeman has predicted that Picher would not immediately die following a large-scale buyout, but the buyout would mean the end of the town "over a very short period of time thereafter." He explained: "The city income would be such that we can't furnish a police department and a fire department and . . . water and sewer, can't maintain the streets. . . . [T]here wouldn't be any money to do any of that for those people that stayed" (Figure 4.10). The fact that many BIA leases would be terminated by a buyout is also a concern, because buyouts would deprive the Quapaw of lease revenues.[116]

Given the prevalence of government distrust and the existence of buyout implementation concerns, it should come as no surprise that many oppose community relocation. The root cause of this resistance, however, stems from sentiment that is less immediately apparent—namely, Picher's internal value as a place. As described, Picherites have exhibited a history of persistence in the face of adversity, and despite the chronic economic and environmental problems that exist in the area, attachments to community remain strong. Unfortunately, as in the past, these aspects of the town's identity are continuing to elude public attention.

Picher remains a paradoxical place. Picherites are aware of the town's problems, but as in the mining era, many retain an emotional bond to place. When asked in 1999 to comment on the town's future, Steven Ray expressed considerable ambivalence. He described environmental hazards, high taxes, land ownership problems, and the town's negative reputation as posing serious obstacles to the town's viability. Nonetheless, Ray explained that the community retained favorable qualities: "Most people look down on Picher as an unacceptable place and economically it is very depressed. Its negative reputation also comes from the miners' rough reputation. The miners were tough but honest and that social legacy remains. . . . Sure, it's a different way of life here, not the social norm, but people stand up for each other, and for what they believe in. Aesthetically the town is really bad, but as far as the people, I grew up here, and the people are really good." Ray also provided a frank assessment of Picher's persistence. "What's keeping people here," he said, "are memories and economics. . . . [I]t's a very cheap place to live. You have those who are locked in because they can't afford to live anywhere

4.10 *Many of those opposing voluntary community buyouts fear that a further decline of Picher's municipal tax base and the loss of civic services and remaining businesses, like those pictured on Connell Avenue above, will effectively destroy the community. Photograph by the author, 2000*

else, or who don't know how to seek out an education and have been told, 'You're just a chat rat, you can't go to college.' Unfortunately, some of them believe it. . . . Myself, I moved away but came back because of family and memories of good things. My family did the same thing. A lot of people don't move away because of family ties."[117]

As Ray observed, some have remained in Picher because of poverty and lack of opportunity. Their situation is comparable to mining-era families trapped by similar circumstances, and if provided adequate compensation, these residents will be the first to leave. Buyouts, however, have far less appeal for those who have willingly remained in Picher, those who, as Ray described them, retain fond memories of place and attachments to community and home. When asked why he had painted the message "NO BUY OUT" on his garage door, Picher mail carrier Nick Koronis said: "I just want to show that not everybody is for this buy out relocation idea. I'm not convinced this is the best thing for the community and I really don't believe it's the best thing for my family. . . . I'm angry. . . . I might be forced out of my home." Bill Lake holds similar views. A lifelong Picher resident with two small children, Lake vehemently opposes a buyout. "My goal is to make Picher a safe place to live," he told the *New York Times*. "I don't want people coming to tell me to sell my house when my house is not for sale." Lake believes that Picher can, and should, be saved, and he explained why on *Nightline*. While scanning old photographs of miners displayed in one of the town's mining museums, he said: "We have a heritage here. We have a legacy. . . . My great-grandpa was killed in a mining accident, and my second grandpa. . . . Those people and what they did are just as important today as they were when they did it, and I am their descendant and so are a lot of other folks. . . . [T]o just simply throw that away . . . [to pretend] Picher never existed . . . wiped off the face of the earth. I can't do that, because these people existed, their lives were real, and we're here because they were here."[118]

When Picher's mines closed in the 1960s, many left the community. The town survived, however, because a substantial number of residents were unwilling to give up. Conscious of the sacrifices made by a generation of miners before them, Picherites endured the hardships of deindustrialization. Today, Bill Lake and others feel similarly obliged to see Picher overcome the environmental problems that now threaten its existence. A spirit of endurance remains strong in Picher. Rooted in the mining past, this perseverance remains central to the community's character. It also lingers as an important facet of personal identity.

Confounding the fact that mining's social and environmental legacies are the cause of Picher's problems is that the community maintains an identity based on its mining culture. As the local landscape bears evidence, residents remain attentive to their mining heritage. Welcome signs reading "TOWN THAT JACK BUILT, WELCOME TO PICHER" receive visitors to the community. The term *Jack* is a colloquialism for zinc ore, and as the signs make obvious, the community continues to tie its existence to mining. This fact is also reinforced elsewhere in the built landscape: Picher has two mining museums housing collections of mining-era memorabilia and artifacts; ore cans, once used to haul rock and men in and out of the mines, decorate the sidewalks of Connell Avenue; and in a nearby park the supporting structure for the children's slide has been fashioned to resemble a mine derrick, the hoisting structures that once stood atop area mine shafts.

An array of public murals also adorns Picher. Some portray lively scenes of mining life: miners seated around the dining table at Ma's Boarding House; the Follies at the Mystic Theater; or children tobogganing down snowy chat piles. Testimony to the harsher realities of the mining past, other murals display disquieting images. Depictions of the mining environment are bleak and gray; they accurately capture the desolation of Picher's chat-dominated landscape. One mural depicts the aftermath of a mine accident. Two men carry a miner's lifeless body from a shaft, while his grieving wife is consoled nearby. The mural captures the tragedy of the mining way of life and it is significant that the town's public artworks bear unsettling qualities. In this regard, the town's most interesting mural is its most abstract. Painted on a Connell Avenue commercial building is the image of an ore can that is filled to the rim with glinting ore. Two faces are superimposed on the sides of the can. Shown in profile, the faces are those of two

4.11 As displayed in this public mural, the mining past produces ambivalent emotions in Picherites. The mural is located on a Connell Avenue commercial building. Photograph by the author, 2000

miners: one is laughing, the other crying (Figure 4.11). Painted by Picher High School students, the mural represents the simultaneous joys and hardships of Picher's existence. It is a powerful expression of the complex meaning the town has, and continues to hold, as a lived-in place.[119]

Mining remains important to the community's identity, which is evident during Picher's Annual Miners' Reunion. First held in 1979, the reunion draws thousands of visitors to the town, including many former residents. With parades, amusement rides, concerts, and cookouts, the reunion returns a mining-era energy to Picher's streets. It also stimulates an outpouring of historical reminiscing. Special editions of the *Tri-State Tribune* with resident-submitted essays are produced for the reunions. Like the town's murals, the essays convey both positive and negative aspects of the mining past. Picherites remember that living and working conditions were extraordinarily hard, but they also recall that life in Picher had its rewards. Positive assessments of the social legacies of mining—community cohesiveness, a sense of mutual caring, and a belief in the benefits of hard work and persistence—are conveyed.

Resident recollections also include commentary on mining's physical legacies, which Picherites continue to imbue with redeeming qualities. In a poem written by resident Jimmie Etheridge, the area's chat piles are depicted as monuments to those who died in the Picher Field. Appearing in a reunion edition of the *Tri-State Tribune,* the poem contains the following verses: "Remaining are the memories and remnants of what was there before. / Mountains of chat reaching toward the sky, / Picher's monument to the ones that died." Elsewhere in the *Tri-State Tribune,* the mines, mills, and chat piles are remembered with a degree of fondness. "Who can forget," wrote one resident, "the willow trees and silver maples around the sludge ponds and damp sand piles . . . sledding down snowy chat piles . . . the smell of ore on damp overalls?" In another essay, Frank D. Woods proudly delivers a roll call of Picher's chat piles, which are identified by the mines that created them. Such local knowledge lends a sense of familiarity to the mining landscape, which for some is a powerful symbol of home. "When I go away," explained Bill Lake, "the first thing I see [coming back] are the chat piles. You can see them ten miles away. . . . [T]he chat piles are a sign that you're home."[120]

Picherites have a relationship with the mining landscape that is difficult for outsiders to comprehend. Visitors see a chaotic assemblage of hazardous mining waste when they look at the Picher landscape. Residents, however, have a more complex and personal view. Although they are aware of the land's plight, the mining landscape also holds historical and sentimental value. In fact, the coexistence of these opposing perceptions is fundamental to the town's meaning. Like their mining-era ancestors, Picherites recognize the positive and negative legacies of mining because both are essential to their identity; for residents, this difficult, unpretentious, and unyielding landscape reflects their lives. Resident Dean Sims provides proof of the lasting nature of this sentiment. In an essay that appeared in the *Tri-State Tribune* in 1999, Sims explained that Picher was both the "kindest" and "meanest" town in the Tri-State Mining District, and he described both these facets with equal pride, stating, "I am pleased to recall the good with the bad, [for] the bad was just normal for the people who had to be as hard as the hard rock they mined."[121]

The harshness of the Picher environment and residents' ability to persist in this rugged setting remain central to the community's character. Unfortunately, although mining's physical legacies hold powerful sentimental meaning, they are also the primary source of the community's problems, which creates a dilemma for Picherites. If the mining landscape is reclaimed, a necessity if the town is to be made safe for continued habitation, an important part of the community's character will be lost. In fact, some have already lamented alterations to the mining landscape caused by decades of chat sale and mine site salvaging. Gone, for example, are the Eagle-Picher Central Mill and chat pile, the area's largest milling complex, and many regret its disappearance. "You saw chat piles in other places but none were as big as those in Picher," said area resident Grace Beauchamp. "The Central Mill pile was huge, the biggest one, but they're all down now compared to what they used to be. The chat piles looked like mountains before, but now they just look like piles. We were so used to seeing them, someday they will all

4.12 *Steven Ray surveys the toppled remains of the Wesah Mine derrick, the last hoisting structure standing in the Picher Field. Photograph by the author, 2000*

be gone." Also remembered with sadness is the loss of the Wesah Mine derrick. Destroyed in a windstorm in the mid-1990s, it was the last derrick standing in the Picher Field (Figure 4.12).[122]

When asked about the future of Picher's chat piles, Hoppy Ray expressed a desire to see the landmarks preserved. "Most of the chat is already gone," he said. "I'd like to see a few of them stay. . . . [T]hey're a part of the community." In the interest of protecting public health, however, it will be necessary for residents like Ray to forgo their attachments to the chat piles as their removal is likely to be a central part of any potential future remediation plan. Fortunately, such an alteration of the industrial landscape is unlikely to destroy public memory of mining. Reminders of the mining past endure in public artwork, museums, miners' reunions, community histories, and the stories Picherites pass down from one generation to the next. Moreover, mining's social legacies—the community's cohesiveness and its honest, unpretentious, and unyielding nature—are qualities of place not necessarily dependent on the mining landscape for their continuance. Reclamation may eventually eliminate many of mining's physical reminders, but given that residents are committed to maintaining Picher's identity, the community will likely remain, at least in spirit, a mining town.[123]

In the last decade, lawmakers have developed a greater awareness of the problems confronting Picherites and a commitment to address the area's problems has emerged. In the midst of this progress, however, Picher's value as a lived-in place has remained largely unrecognized. As a result, mistakes of the past threaten to be repeated as community buyouts move forward. Most relocation advocates believe that the region's environmental problems are irreparable. In this respect, Picher still is viewed as a hopeless cause. A sentiment that discouraged outside intervention in quality-of-life issues for most of its history, this perception is now driving calls for the community's abandonment. Yet, should lawmakers remain unaware of the pivotal motivation underlying residents' opposition to relocation—their sentimental attachment to place—buyouts will leave behind a burdened populace. A community will continue to exist, albeit one in diminished state, long after voluntary buyouts have been completed. Those who remain will face even greater social and economic challenges. They will also continue to suffer the area's environmental hazards. Although Picher has always been home to a population burdened by such troubles, it would be a tragedy if the plight of those most committed to Picher was overlooked at a time when there exists a resolve to finally address the town's problems.

Like residents before them, many remain willing to endure the hardships of life in Picher. Although Picher's holdouts are aware of the area's problems, their ability to overcome adversity is part of a cherished identity that no amount of environmental education will alter. And these residents will not be enticed into relocation by promises of adequate property compensation. The ties they hold to community and home—attachments rooted in an arduous yet rewarding mining past and strengthened through decades of determined survival—are not so easily broken. Lawmakers would be foolish to ignore the likelihood that a significant number of Picherites will refuse to abandon the community, and these holdouts will pose an obstacle to the practical implementation of reclamation programs. Thus, whatever strategies emerge for addressing the area's environmental problems must continue to include efforts to make the area a safer place to live, as not all Picherites are willing to sever their emotional ties to place.

NOTES

1. For additional information on the Tar Creek Superfund Site's National Priorities List (NPL) ranking, see Hearing of the Committee on Energy and Commerce, *Tar Creek: Implementation of Superfund*, Serial No. 97–155, 97th Cong., 2nd Sess., Washington, DC, 1982, 7, 16. In 2001, Tar Creek was identified as one of 112 Superfund "megasites," the most expensive sites on the NPL. See Katherine N. Probst and David M. Konisky, *Superfund's Future: What Will It Cost?* (Washington, DC: Resources for the Future, 2001), 175–177.

2. Arrell M. Gibson, *Wilderness Bonanza: The Tri-State District of Missouri, Kansas, and Oklahoma* (Norman: University of Oklahoma Press, 1972), 3; Samuel Weidman, *The Miami-Picher Zinc-Lead District, Oklahoma* (Norman: Oklahoma Geological Survey Bulletin No. 56, 1932), 1.

3. Kenneth V. Luza, *Stability Problems Associated with Abandoned Underground Mines in the Picher Field, Northeastern Oklahoma* (Norman: Oklahoma Geological Survey, Circular 88, 1986), 1, 16; U.S. EPA, "EPA Announces Release of Five Year Review," Tar Creek Superfund Site Fact Sheet, April 15, 1994, 1–3.

4. Lorraine Halinka Malcoe, Community Health Action and Monitoring Program (CHAMP), Final Report, July 1996–June 1997, draft; U.S. EPA, "Tar Creek Superfund Site," Tar Creek Superfund Site Fact Sheet, April 1999, 3–7.

5. Richard Thoman, "The Changing Occupance Pattern of the Tri-State Area: Missouri, Kansas, and Oklahoma" (Ph.D. dissertation, University of Chicago, 1953); Arrell M. Gibson, *Wilderness Bonanza,* 68; George G. Suggs, *Union Busting in the Tri-State: The Oklahoma, Kansas, and Missouri Metal Workers' Strike of 1935* (Norman: University of Oklahoma Press, 1986), 18–21.

6. Charles Morris Mills, "Industrial Conditions in the World's Greatest Zinc Center," *The Survey* 45 (1921): 657–664; Suggs, *Union Busting,* 15–16.

7. Suggs, *Union Busting,* 7–10, 20–22; M. D. Harbaugh, "Labor Relations in the Tri-State Mining District," *The Mining Congress Journal* 22 (June 1936): 19–24; Gibson, *Wilderness Bonanza,* 205.

8. Gibson, *Wilderness Bonanza,* 127, 249; W. David Baird, *The Quapaws* (New York: Chelsea House, 1989); Arrell Gibson, "Leasing of Quapaw Mineral Lands," *Chronicles of Oklahoma* 35 (Autumn 1957): 338–347.

9. Gibson, *Wilderness Bonanza,* 39–40.

10. Ibid., 254.

11. "Zinc Blende Twins Are Growing Fast," *Miami Record-Herald,* November 5, 1915, 1; "Picher's Progress in 1918 to Reach Highest Mark Despite Unusual Conditions Confronting Citizens," *Miami Record-Herald,* January 4, 1918, 6.

12. U.S. Bureau of the Census, *Fourteenth Census of the United States, 1920, Oklahoma,* Washington, DC; Frank D. Hills, "A Historical Sketch of Picher, Oklahoma, and the Area," *Tri-State Tribune,* June 10, 1999, 1, 5; "A Different Picher Last Week; Still Different Next," *Miami Record-Herald,* November 19, 1915, 8.

13. "Deposits of Miami Area Pronounced Richest in World," *Daily Oklahoman,* August 12, 1917, 2B; Luza, *Stability Problems,* 11; Suggs, *Union Busting,* 22–24, 29–31; Gibson, *Wilderness Bonanza,* 82, 179–195; Gerald Markowitz and David Rosner, "'The Streets of Walking Death': Silicosis, Health, and Labor in the Tri-State Region, 1900–1950," *The Journal of American History* 77:2 (September 1990): 525–552.

14. Edwin T. McKnight and Richard P. Fischer, *Geology and Ore Deposits of the Picher Field, Oklahoma and Kansas* (Washington, DC: Geological Survey Professional Paper, No. 588, 1970), 89, 90–101; James H. Jolly, *U.S. Zinc Industry* (Baltimore: American Literary Press, 1997), 69–70.

15. Sanborn-Perris Map Company, New York, fire insurance maps for Picher, 1920 and 1928; John Mott, interview with author, Picher, Oklahoma, December 15, 1999.

16. Suggs, *Union Busting,* 10–11.

17. Ibid.; Thoman, "The Changing Occupance Pattern," 70.

18. McKnight and Fischer, *Geology and Ore Deposits,* 99–101.

19. Ibid.; U.S. Bureau of the Census, *Census of the United States, 2000, Oklahoma,* Washington, DC.

20. "Picher Gives Promise Being Famous Camp," *Miami Record-Herald,* October 1, 1915, 1; "Where Rainbows End Touches the Earth," *Miami Record-Herald,* November 19, 1915, 1. See also "Picher, Panorama of Push and Progress," *Miami Record-Herald,* October 8, 1915, 2; "It's a Pretty Picher Is this Growing Town," *Miami Record-Herald,* June 16, 1916, 1.

21. "Zinc Blende Twins," *Miami Record-Herald,* November 5, 1915, 1.

22. "$3,000,000 Worth of Lead and Zinc Ores Being Mined," *Daily Oklahoman,* November 14, 1915, 1, 3; "Ore Piles Succeed Prairie Dog Mounds," *Miami Record-Herald,* November 12, 1915, 2.

23. *Pigs of Lead,* News Reel, Prod. Rothacker Industrial Films, Chicago, Illinois, n.d.; Baird, *The Quapaws,* 83–93; Gibson, *Wilderness Bonanza,* 154–159. See also Gertrude Bonnin, Charles H. Fabens, and Matthew K. Sniffen, *Oklahoma's Poor Rich Indians* (Philadelphia: Office of the Indian Rights Association, 1924).

24. Tri-State Survey Committee, *A Preliminary Report on Living, Working, and Health Conditions in the Tri-State Mining Area* (New York, photoprinted by the committee, 1939), 14–15.

25. Ibid., appendix B: 15–16.

26. Mills, "Industrial Conditions," 662; Ben Moody, "Yester-Year in the Picher Mining Field," *Tri-State Tribune,* August 11, 1994, 4.

27. Grace Beauchamp, interview with author, Miami, Oklahoma, December 14, 1999.

28. Moody, "Yester-Year," 4.

29. See "Picher's Progress," 6; "White Slave Gang Operating in the Mining District," *Miami Record-Herald,* January 18, 1918, 1; "Uncover Big Spy Plot at Picher," *Miami Record-Herald,* May 10, 1918, n.p.

30. "Deposits of Miami Area," 1–2B.

31. See *Miami Record-Herald:* "Mining Costs in September," November 29, 1931, 1; "Netta and Short Horn Plants Close Down," November 29, 1931, 15; "Calls for Free Food Increase in Picher," January 6, 1931, 2; "Legionnaires Bag 50 Rabbits in Relief Hunt," November 22, 1931, 15; Suggs, *Union Busting,* 29–50.

32. H. B. Hutchison, "Prosperity Plays Encore in Mining District," *Tulsa World,* November 3, 1935, 12; "Happy Days in the Mines Again," *Daily Oklahoman,* May 31, 1936, D1.

33. Mills, "Industrial Conditions," 657–658, 664.

34. Tri-State Survey Committee, *Preliminary Report,* n.p.

35. Ibid., 16, appendix: 24.

36. Ibid., appendix: 26.

37. For additional information, see "Silicosis Program in States Scored," *New York Times,* November 27, 1939, 19; "Silicosis: Tri-State Dust Storm," *Business Week* (December 9, 1939): 51–52; "Zinc Stink," *Time* (December 4, 1939): 63; and Gerald Markowitz and David Rosner, "The Streets of Walking Death," 525–552.

38. Malcolm Ross, *Death of a Yale Man* (New York: Farrar & Rinehart, 1939), 184–185, 204. Also of the muckraking genre is Lallah Davidson's *South of Joplin: Story of a Tri-State Diggin's* (New York: W. W. Norton & Company, 1939).

39. Harbaugh, "Labor Relations," 19–24.

40. Various articles, *Engineering and Mining Journal* 144:11 (1943): 68–122. See also Karl L. Koelker, "Has the Miami-Picher District Passed Its Zenith?" *Engineering and Mining*

Journal 117:4 (1924): 168–170; and Evan Just, "Living and Working Conditions in the Tri-State Mining District," *Mining Congress Journal* 25 (1939): 44–45. Safety reforms and silicosis prevention in the work place was legislated in the wake of the Tri-State Survey Committee's *A Preliminary Report*; however, the effectiveness of these reforms has been questioned. See Markowitz and Rosner, "The Streets of Walking Death," 525–552.

41. Velma Nieberding, *The History of Ottawa County* (Marceline, MO: Walsworth, 1983), 82.

42. See, for example, Gibson, *Wilderness Bonanza,* 255; and Hills, "A Historical Sketch," 5.

43. Genevieve Stovall Craig, "The Story of Picher Schools," *Tri-State Tribune,* June 10, 1999, 5.

44. Hills, "A Historical Sketch," 1.

45. Tri-State Survey Committee, *A Preliminary Report,* appendix: 34.

46. Ibid., appendix: 29; Iva Simpson, "Ben Osborne, Entrepreneur," *Tri-State Tribune,* August 11, 1994, 15-B; Moody, "Yester-Year," 4.

47. Mickey Mantle and Herb Gluck, *The Mick* (Garden City, NY: Doubleday & Company, 1985), 3, 9.

48. Marion A. Parsons, "I Got Lost in Picher," *Tri-State Tribune,* August 11, 1983, 2.

49. Orval "Hoppy" Ray, interview with author, Picher, Oklahoma, December 14, 1999.

50. Mott, interview.

51. Nieberding, *The History of Ottawa County,* 74–75; Moody, "Yester-Year," 4.

52. Tri-State Survey Committee, *A Preliminary Report,* Appendix, 25, 34.

53. It should be noted that women also were engaged in economic activities outside of the home. For information on the role women played in the Picher Mining Field, see Nieberding, *The History of Ottawa County,* 91–93; and "A Tribute to the Wives of Miners," *Tri-State Tribune,* August 12, 1993, 18.

54. Lawrence and Theo Barr, interview by Joel L. Todd, Videotape, Tulsa, 1985, Oklahoma Historical Society, Archives and Manuscript Division, Oral History Program, Oklahoma City.

55. Hoppy Ray, interview; U.S. Bureau of the Census, *Sixteenth Census of the United States, 1940, Oklahoma,* Washington, DC; U.S. Bureau of the Census, *Seventeenth Census of the United States, 1950, Oklahoma,* Washington, DC; U.S. Bureau of the Census, *Eighteenth Census of the United States, 1960, Oklahoma,* Washington, DC; Ralph Marler, "Picher Mine Field Destined to Die," *Tulsa World,* July 28, 1968, 1.

56. See, for example, "Picher Penniless; Fire Chief Washes Cars to Buy Equipment," *Daily Oklahoman,* November 10, 1963, 16.

57. Hoppy Ray, interview.

58. Pam Keyes, "Picherite Recalls Mine Closing Exodus," *Miami News-Record,* March 9, 1986, 1.

59. Genevieve Stovall Craig, "Picher, Oklahoma: The Lead and Zinc Boom Town That Would Not Die," in *Picher, Oklahoma* (Picher: Picher Bicentennial Boosters Committee, 1975), n.p.; C. Allan Mathews, "What's in the Future?" in *Picher, Oklahoma* (Picher: Picher Bicentennial Boosters Committee, 1975), n.p.

60. Mott, interview.

61. Harlan Snow, "Final Tally on Cost of Mining Still Out," *Joplin Globe,* January 5, 1986, 22; Earl Hatley, interview with author, Quapaw, Oklahoma, December 16, 1999.

62. "Eagle-Picher Claims Five Block Square Is Dangerous," *Tri-State Tribune,* February 9, 1950, 1; "Picher Carries on in Usual Manner," *Tri-State Tribune,* February 16, 1950, 1.

63. Barr, interview.

64. "It's Business As Usual Over Picher Pits," *Daily Oklahoman,* March 12, 1950, 15; Gilbert Asher, "Picher Calm Despite Mine Cavein Threat," *Tulsa World,* February 9, 1950, 1.

65. John Feen, "Here's What Holds Picher From a Disastrous Cave-In," *Daily Oklahoman,* February 12, 1950, 1.

66. "Picher Business Firms Re-Locating Still Here As Time Marches On," *Tri-State Tribune,* April 12, 1951, 1; Paul Hood, "Picher Finally Has Abandoned Its Doomed Business Center," *Daily Oklahoman,* February 11, 1951, 2; Hoppy Ray, interview; Stovall Craig, "Picher, Oklahoma," n.p.

67. Charlotte Cox, "18 Homeless, But None Badly Hurt in Cave-in," *Tulsa World,* July 23, 1967, 1; "Thousands Flock to Cavein," *Tulsa World,* July 24, 1967, 1–2.

68. Phil Frey, "Picher Rebounding from Played Out Past," *Orbit Magazine, Daily Oklahoman,* December 27, 1972, 6–7.

69. John W. Morris, *Ghost Towns of Oklahoma* (Norman: University of Oklahoma Press, 1978), 147–149.

70. Francis Thetford, "Things Are Looking Lots Brighter in Picher," *Daily Oklahoman,* February 26, 1964, 5.

71. U.S. Bureau of the Census, *2000 Census of Population, Oklahoma,* Washington, DC; Manny Gamallo, "Small Town Has Big Tax," *Tulsa World,* March 31, 1996, A1; Jim Killackey, "Picher-Cardin Academic Audit Sought," *Daily Oklahoman,* December 16, 1994, 25; "Six State Schools Placed on At-Risk List," *Daily Oklahoman,* July 28, 1995, 1.

72. "Three-State Waste Site Called Nation's Worst," *New York Times,* November 14, 1981, 8; Tri-State Survey Committee, *A Preliminary Report*; Tri-State Zinc and Lead Ore Producers' Association, "Why Conservation of Marginal Lead and Zinc Ores Means So Much to Our National Economy and Security," *Tri-State Tribune,* 1947(?), n.p.

73. Bill Honker, letter to author, December 1, 2004.

74. Wayne Mason, "For Playing—a Chat Pile," *Your World Magazine, Tulsa World,* July 23, 1967, 10–11. See also "Big Dipper for Bike Riders," *Orbit Magazine, Daily Oklahoman,* January 26, 1964, 12–13.

75. "Three-State Waste Site," 8; U.S. EPA, *Superfund Record of Decision: Tar Creek Site, Oklahoma* (Washington, DC: The Agency,1984); Richard E. Meyer, "Acid Water Drowns Tar Creek As Clean Up Delayed," *Daily Oklahoman,* February 6, 1983, n.p.; U.S. EPA, "Tar Creek Superfund Site," Tar Creek Superfund Site Fact Sheet, April 1999, 1–2.

76. U.S. EPA, *Five Year Review: Tar Creek Superfund Site Ottawa County, Oklahoma* (Washington, DC: The Agency, 1994); Gary Garton, "EPA Gives Up on Tar Creek Clean Up," *Joplin Globe,* March 1, 1997, n.p.

77. Pamela A. Meyer et al., "Surveillance for Elevated Blood Lead Levels Among Children," United States, 1997–2001, *Morbidity and Mortality Weekly Report* 52 (2003):1–21; U.S. EPA, "NPL Site Narrative for Tar Creek (Ottawa County)," Federal Register Notice, September 8, 1983.

78. U.S. EPA, *Superfund Record of Decision: Tar Creek Site, Oklahoma* (Washington, DC: The Agency, 1984), 6.

79. Margot Roosevelt, "The Tragedy of Tar Creek," *Time* (April 26, 2004): 44.

80. Historically an important industry in Picher, chat processing and sale has declined since 1999, the year the EPA designated chat a "hazardous substance." See F. W. Netzeband, "Profit from Mineral Waste: Tri-State Tailings Yield Commercial Products," *Engineering and Mining Journal* 138:5 (1937): 251–254; and U.S. EPA, "Mining Waste," Tar Creek Superfund Site Fact Sheet, November 1999.

81. Robert Lynch, interview with author, Oklahoma City, Oklahoma, October 26, 1998.

82. Tar Creek Superfund Task Force, *Health Effects Subcommittee Final Report* (Oklahoma City: Office of the Secretary of the Environment, 2000).

83. U.S. EPA, *Superfund Record of Decision: Tar Creek (Ottawa County), OU 2* (Washington, DC: The Agency, 1997).

84. U.S. EPA, "Tar Creek Superfund Site," Tar Creek Superfund Site Fact Sheet, April 1999, 1–3; Renee Ruble, "Task Force Votes to Continue Soil Remediation," *Tulsa World,* March 30, 2000; Joe Robertson, "Piling Up: Rules Barring Sale of Indian Chat Create Hardship," *Tulsa World,* May 23, 1999, 3.

85. Hatley, interview.

86. Leading an unsuccessful effort to block Superfund action at Tar Creek was Eagle-Picher, one of eighteen responsible parties targeted by the EPA to pay for cleanup costs. See U.S. Congress House Committee on Energy and Commerce, Subcommittee on Commerce, Transportation, and Tourism, *Tar Creek: Implementation of Superfund: Hearing Before the Subcommittee on Commerce, Transportation, and Tourism of the Committee on Energy and Commerce,* 97th Cong., 2nd Sess., June 14, 1982; Jean Hays, "Eagle-Picher Dominated Fight to Block Clean Up," *The Wichita Eagle-Beacon,* April 30, 1986, 1, 14; Angelia Herrin, "Why Superfund Hasn't Worked: Uncertain Funding, Internal Problems Shift Focus," *Wichita Eagle-Beacon,* April 28, 1986, n.p.

87. Steven Ray, interview with author, Picher, Oklahoma, December 14, 1999; Mott, interview; Hatley, interview. See also Steven Ray, "EPA Says the Problems Are Already There," *Tri-State Tribune,* August 12, 1999, 1; Steven Ray, "Area Plagued with Flooding," *Tri-State Tribune,* May 6, 1999, 1; and Tom Lindley, "EPA Site Due Scrutiny," *Daily Oklahoman,* January 6, 2000, n.p.

88. "A Legacy of Neglect," *Wichita Eagle-Beacon*, special report, 27 April, 1986, H1.

89. Ramona Jones, "Residents Handle Dangers with Stoic Acceptance," *Wichita Eagle-Beacon,* April 30, 1986, A14; Judith Cummings, "No. 1 Toxic Waste Site Is Not Town's No. 1 Gripe," *New York Times,* December 9, 1981, A16.

90. Shaun Schafer, "Tar Creek: Cleanup, Buyout Costs Compared," *Tulsa World,* January 6, 2004, n.p.

91. Recognizing that no single authority has the ability to resolve the area's problems, the federal agencies involved at Tar Creek in 2003 signed a Memorandum of Understanding that requires them to work in a coordinated fashion with all stakeholders to develop and implement a comprehensive solution. See U.S. EPA, *Memorandum of Understanding for the Tar Creek Superfund Site,* May 1, 2003.

92. The relationship between media coverage and Superfund cleanup activities has been well documented. See Allan Mazur, *A Hazardous Inquiry: The Rashomon Effect at Love Canal* (Cambridge, MA: Harvard University Press, 1998).

93. See, for example, Ross Milloy, "Waste From Old Mines Leaves Piles of Problems," *New York Times,* July 21, 2000, A10 (reprinted in the *Los Angeles Times* on-line edition, http://www.latimes.com [accessed July 21, 2000], July 20, 2000); Roosevelt, "The Tragedy of Tar Creek," 44; Robert Siegal, Melissa Block, and Greg Allen, "Failed cleanup efforts of Tar Creek in Oklahoma," *All Things Considered,* National Public Radio, July 16, 2003; John Donovan, "Our Town: Welcome to Picher," *Nightline,* ABC Television, March 2, 2001; and Tom Lindley, "Who Will Save the Children of Ottawa County?" *Daily Oklahoman,* December 9, 1999, 1; "Scars of Lead Poisoning," December 10, 1999, 1; and "Another Broken Promise," December 11, 1999.

94. Joe Robertson, "A Sad Place," *Tulsa World,* August 6, 1998.

95. Rebecca Jim, interview with author, Miami, Oklahoma, December 13, 1999.

96. Governor Frank Keating's Tar Creek Superfund Task Force, *Final Report* (Oklahoma City: Office of the Secretary of Environment, 2000), 2, 9, 18–23; Robert Nairn, telephone interview with author, August 19, 2004.

97. Tar Creek Operable Unit Three (OU3), completed in 2000, involved emergency removal of chemical drums at the Eagle-Picher laboratory in Cardin, Oklahoma. See U.S. EPA, "Tar Creek Superfund Site," Tar Creek Superfund Site Fact Sheet, April 1999, 1–4. U.S. EPA, Administrative Order on Consent for RI/FS for OU4, Tar Creek Superfund Site, 14; U.S. Army Corps of Engineers, Tulsa Division, Draft Reconnaissance Phase, Tar Creek and Lower Spring River Watershed Management Plan, 2004, http://www.swt.usace.army.mil/ (accessed April 2, 2006).

98. *Oklahoma Plan for Tar Creek,* http://www.deq.state.ok.us/LPDnew/Tarcreek/index.html (accessed April 2, 2006), 6–8.

99. For many years, the BIA viewed chat as an income-generating resource for the tribe. In fact, during the mining era, the BIA prohibited mining companies from filling abandoned workings with the waste, a common practice in other areas of the Tri-State Mining District. Instead, the BIA required that chat be left on the surface. Hence, the legacy of the chat piles is, in part, the BIA's own creation. In 1997, however, the BIA placed a moratorium on chat sale from Indian land. The agency was concerned that it might be held liable for chat-related lead contamination problems. Chat sale, however, continued on private land; thus, the moratorium in effect only eliminated the most economically productive use of Quapaw mining lands. Although the BIA's chat moratorium was lifted in 2001, the agency has continued to place roadblocks to chat utilization. Approximately 70 percent of area chat sits on land owned by Quapaw tribal members. See Robertson, "Piling-up," 1, 3.

100. *Oklahoma Plan,* 1–8; Nairn, telephone interview.

101. Governor Brad Henry, Homepage, http://www.governor.state.ok.us/issues.php (accessed September 2004); U.S. Representative Brad Carson, Homepage, http://carson.house.gov (accessed September 2004); "Inhofe Still Firm on Tar Creek," *Tulsa World,* July 9, 2003, n.p.

102. "Move Chat, Not Towns, Inhofe Says," *Tulsa World,* June 28, 2003, A1; Jim Myers, "Tar Creek Buy Out Off Table, Inhofe Says," *Tulsa World,* June 17, 2003, A1; "Carson Bill Seeks Buy Out," *Tulsa World,* May 16, 2003, A1; Tar Creek Restoration Act, 108th Cong., 1st Sess., H.R. 2116; "Henry Signs Tar Creek Buy Out Bill," *Tulsa World,* June 3, 2004, A1; "Tar Creek: Buy Outs to Start Soon," *Tulsa World,* June 12, 2004, A1; Oklahoma Child Lead Poisoning Prevention Act, 49th Legislature, 2nd Sess., Senate

Bill 1490; Omer Gillham, "Buyouts in Picher Urged at Meeting," *Tulsa World,* January 6, 2006, n.p.

103. "Private Sector Group Moves Forward in Tar Creek Purchase Process," Press Release, Senator James M. Inhofe, January 25, 2004, http://inhofe.senate.gov (accessed April 2004).

104. Ed Curran, EPA Region 6, correspondence to U.S. Representative Tom Coburn, September 3, 1997, unpublished document; U.S. EPA, *Superfund Record of Decision: Tar Creek (Ottawa County), OU 2* (Washington, DC: The Agency, 1997), 51, 55, 89; Janet Pearson, "Wither Relocation?" *Tulsa World,* June 29, 2003, G1.

105. According to the 2000 census, the towns of Picher and Cardin contained 683 occupied residences. Adding additional housing, businesses, churches, schools, and other structures elsewhere in the Tar Creek Superfund site, the total number of properties qualifying for a buyout exceed 800. To date, the largest relocation conducted under Superfund occurred in 1985 at Times Beach, Missouri, where dioxin contamination necessitated a buyout of 600–700 residences at an estimated cost of $33 million. The majority of the EPA's Superfund relocations have involved fewer than 50 residences. See U.S. EPA, Superfund Permanent Relocations, http://www.epa.gov (accessed January 2005); Pearson, "Whither Relocation?" G1.

106. Schafer, "Tar Creek," A1.

107. The best example of a forced buyout occurred in Centralia, Pennsylvania, where underground mine fires necessitated a congressionally mandated community buyout in 1984. More than 500 residences and businesses were acquired and the majority of residents moved, but many refused to leave. In 1992, condemnation procedures were initiated on more than 50 remaining properties, whose residents became squatters in their own homes. See David DeKok, *Unseen Danger: A Tragedy of People, Government, and the Centralia Mine Fire* (Philadelphia: University of Pennsylvania Press, 1986).

108. Rod Walton, "Tar Creek Residents Favoring a Buyout," *Tulsa World,* June 8, 2002, n.p.

109. Cummings, "No. 1 Toxic Waste Site," n.p.; Hoppy Ray, interview.

110. Kent Curtis, "The Legacy" in *Tar Creek Anthology* (Tahlequah, Oklahoma: Talequah Daily Press: 1999), ix-x.

111. Mott, interview; Steven Ray, interview.

112. TEAL Project, "Community Leader Survey: Ottawa County Area," 1997, unpublished document; Rebecca Jim, "Introduction," in *Tar Creek Anthology* (Tahlequah, OK: Talequah Daily Press, 1999), iv.

113. Steven Ray, interview.

114. "Some Tar Creek Residents Unhappy with EPA Settlements," *Tulsa World,* April 21, 2004, n.p.; Steven Ray, interview.

115. Gary Garton, "Picher Residents React with Skepticism of plan," *Joplin Globe,* December 10, 2003, n.p.; Donovan, "Our Town"; Shaun Schafer, "Superfund: Damage Control," *Tulsa World,* December 14, 2003, A1.

116. Siegal, Block, and Allen, "Failed Cleanup Efforts."

117. Steven Ray, interview.

118. Donovan, "Our Town."

119. "Mural Depicts History of Mining Field," *Tri-State Tribune,* August 11, 1994, 1.

120. *Tri-State Tribune,* Special Edition, Miners' Reunion #20, June 10, 1999 (see articles: Jimmie Etheridge, "Wearers of the Old Hard Hat," B11; Beverly B. Walker De Santo, "Memories to Last a Lifetime," A8). Frank D. Woods, "I Remember Picher," *Tri-State Tribune,* August 10, 1989, A2; Donovan, "Our Town."

121. Dean Sims, "Remembering the Trials of Life in the Mining District and Other Mining Areas," *Tri-State Tribune,* Special Edition, Miners' Reunion #20, June 10, 1999, 11.

122. Beauchamp, interview; Steven Ray, interview; Gerald Breedson, "Wesah Derrick Stands Alone," *Miami News-Record,* 1982(?), 3.

123. Hoppy Ray, interview.

CHAPTER FIVE

Conclusion

I N THE ANTHRACITE COAL MINING TOWNS OF PENNSYLVANIA, BEN MARSH OB-
served: "[T]HERE is a paradox to these valleys. . . . The land means much, but
gives little." Marsh explained this contradiction by showing that a broad concept of place includes consideration of the physical support a landscape provides,
or its *means,* as well as its less tangible *meanings.* His research is revisited in order to
highlight its salience to the case studies presented in this book. Residents of the
mining communities herein also have maintained attachments to landscapes that
have provided, or continue to provide, limited material reward. Indeed, Marsh
was correct in suggesting that this phenomenon stems from a common set of
experiences in historic mining areas. "The same history that so degraded this
countryside," he wrote of the anthracite coal region, "has solidified this society."[1]
The same holds true for Toluca, Cokedale, and Picher.

In fact, these commonalities in place experience are especially notable given
the diversity of the case studies. All are turn-of-the-twentieth-century rural mining communities, but each occupies a different physical and cultural region of the
central United States. Each was settled by people of different ethnic and national

backgrounds, and mining's operational lifespans and the mineral commodities produced also varied. So, too, have mining's economic and physical impacts. Deindustrialization has produced varied economic outcomes and each community now confronts different planning challenges and different degrees of environmental problems. Regardless of these differences, however, there exists in each community a shared attachment to place that is rooted in the mining past. In each case study, the mining landscape draws residents toward that past, reflecting and reinforcing central aspects of identity.

At the broadest level, the case studies show that place value is not necessarily wedded to aesthetic attributes or to the physical and economic support a place provides for survival. As shown, there is a dichotomy to place experience in historic mining regions. Historically, outsiders have viewed these places as derelict locales, whereas residents have tended to emphasize their positive experiential values. In general, the mining life has created emotional bonds to place that the industry's physical legacies assist in maintaining, but it would be wrong to suggest that variations in place meaning do not exist. At a more focused level, the case studies show that historic mining regions, like all symbolic landscapes, are perceptually complex. Thus, it would be counterproductive to oversimplify the relationship residents and outsiders have to these places as they are already burdened by abstractions—popular generalizations and myths of the mining imaginary. Although occupation of mining landscapes is not necessarily dehumanizing, it must be noted that life in these places is not inevitably rewarding and rarely is it trouble free. In fact, attachments to place produce a difficult future for the residents of historic mining towns who are reluctant to abandon communities and environments that are detrimental to quality of life from a socioeconomic or environmental standpoint.

The mining past remains central to the production and maintenance of a local sense of place. Although mine closure eliminated these communities' economic ties to the mining industry, it did not sever emotional ties to the mining way of life. Residents continue to associate mining with their communities' reason for being and this is one of the most obvious ways in which the industrial past contributes to place meaning. Mining provides a context for existence. Moreover, in many ways, the mining-era represents a time of clearer purpose, especially in Cokedale and Picher where no new industries have filled mining's economic void and where the present function of community is unclear. Even in Toluca, however, which began life as an agricultural trade center and has now returned to its farming origins, mining is at the fore in historical reminiscences of place. In all of the case studies, mining is ingrained in local history. In all three towns, residents turn to their mining heritage to validate their communities' existence.

For the residents of Toluca, Cokedale, and Picher, mining provides an answer to the question, why are we here? In addition, it plays a vital role in defining personal and social-group identity. It is in the mining past that residents find answers to the question of who they are. Identity is rooted in and reinforced by memories of the mining way of life.

It is not surprising that mining remains an essential part of self-identity for onetime miners. They do not forget their mining experiences, especially those who worked underground, and rarely do they hesitate to share these experiences with pride. Although aware that they were poorly compensated and toiled in a dangerous occupation, they nonetheless remember mining as a noble and even rewarding profession. Mining was honest work that provided advantages not found in other jobs, including freedom to work at one's own pace, freedom from super-vision, and worker camaraderie. Also observed, particularly in Toluca and Picher, is the existence of a kind of "rambunctious fraternity," where miners hold collec-tive pride in the rough-and-tumble nature of their existence.[2] Viewed in this way, the dangerous and the raucous life of miners added a sense of excitement to the mining years. This sentiment remains particularly strong among elderly miners. For them, the tough but honorable nature of the work and the combination of skill, strength, and stamina that mining required are sources of self-esteem. Min-ing, as the adage goes, is in their blood and they draw satisfaction from the belief that they are as hard as the rock they mined.

Akin to the regard that is afforded veterans of war, respected status is given to those who worked in the mines and survived to tell their stories, especially as their numbers dwindle. Direct connections to the mining past are lost as old-timers die, but the industry's influence on local identity does not disappear. Residents remain aware that they follow in the footsteps of those who endured the ordeals of a mining existence. They are conscious that generations before them overcame con-siderable hardship to build their communities and to create meaningful lives in these places. Residents remember this fact when dealing with the challenges of the post-mining era. They take pride in knowing that they are responding to the challenges of mine closure with the same resolve their predecessors showed in their daily descent into the mines. Self-respect is derived from the realization that they are survivors. Like those before them, residents consider themselves to be strong, hardworking members of enduring communities. An ability to directly confront hardship and show strength in the face of adversity is a key aspect of individual and community identity, both past and present.

As a result of common hardships faced in the mining era, working-class resi-dents learned to turn to each other for support; indeed, the case studies confirm that mining towns are "marked by a strong sense of communal identity based upon the hazards of work and a history of common fate in the face of adversity."[3] Meager pay, dangerous occupations, and conflict with the management class drew workers and their families and communities together; prevalent in all of the study areas are local accounts of community solidarity and altruistic behavior. Consid-erable pride is taken in the fact that doors were kept open for neighbors; that hats were passed for needy families; that each looked out for the safety of children; and that workers stood together to defend their interests. True, acrimony existed between classes, particularly during periods of labor unrest. As well, incivility within the working class was relatively common in the saloon and clubhouse. During times of labor peace and away from alcohol, however, an atmosphere of cohesion existed that originated in the mines but remains with these communities today.

Ethnic group interactions also strengthened community cohesiveness, particularly in Toluca and Cokedale. Sharing a common cultural background and a marginalized social status, Italians, Eastern Europeans, Hispanos, and others banded together. In both towns, the members of ethnic groups occupied distinct neighborhoods, worked at similar occupations, and generally interacted within bounded social networks. In this way, ethnicity served to strengthen a sense of belonging to place. Unfortunately, ethnicity also functioned as a dividing force. As with class divisions, tensions existed between ethnic groups and some of this animosity has persisted into the post-mining era. On the whole, however, class and ethnic group affiliations ensured that almost everyone had a nurturing sub-community to which they could turn, and in all of the study sites there remains a feeling of unity within these groups. Cokedale's closely knit Hispanic population and Toluca's Italian community are excellent examples.

Ethnic and class cohesion not only assisted residents in coping with the problems of mining, but it also helped them address the problems of mine closure.[4] This book confirms that community persistence is a plausible outcome of deindustrialization in historic mining towns. Mining settlements are established to serve a well-defined utilitarian function: to extract and process minerals. Often, however, they develop other, longer lasting roles as they come to serve as valued communities and homes. Although a range of factors contributed to their survival, attachment to place played an important role in each case study. Indeed, testimony to the strength of place attachments is that many elected to stay despite the fact that mine closure initially amplified life's hardships.

With its productive agricultural setting, Toluca probably would have survived mine closure even had residents not developed bonds to place. Would it have emerged with as large a population or as productive an economy, and would it be as vibrant had fewer mining-era residents decided to endure? The likely answer is no—Toluca would be a lesser place. The same holds true, perhaps more so, for Cokedale and Picher where miners and laborers had fewer opportunities to find alternate work. At best, both would have experienced greater depopulation had residents not developed a connection to place. At worst, these communities might have disappeared. Instead they struggled on. As they had always done, residents made sacrifices, banded together, and found the means, however meager, to survive. Staying on was considered a better option than leaving those places they called home.

Toluca, Cokedale, and Picher show that place attachments can facilitate community persistence, but they do not guarantee it. A variety of factors contribute to the survival of a mining town and many vanish. Onetime mining settlements that have experienced this fate neighbor Cokedale and Picher. Some were company towns whose operators evicted residents and demolished town infrastructure following mine closure. Others had locational disadvantages, such as inadequate resource bases or isolation that inhibited economic restructuring. In contrast, residents living in the towns studied here were provided with the opportunity to remain in their homes and had a basic means to support themselves. Residents in Toluca turned to agriculture and then to manufacturing. Those in Picher and Cokedale commuted to nearby communities for work. It also must be noted that not all residents were willing to make the sacrifices required to stay in their community. For every inhabitant that resisted the pressure to migrate, an equal or greater number left following mine closure. For those who left, attachments to place were weak or were considered secondary to the practical need to provide for one's self or family. For many, the mining town was foremost a place of work; mining was the only occupation they knew and it was time to move on when the mines closed. Having moved from mining towns before, many miners considered relocation a part of the mining way of life.

Nonetheless, place attachments played a significant role in maintaining these towns in the post-mining years. A bond to place was referenced by virtually every resident who remained after mine closure, and this bond also underlies instances of return-migration, usually by retirees. Perhaps most significantly, however, by weeding out those for whom the bonds to place were weak, mine closure served to strengthen community cohesiveness and a sense of collective place value. Deindustrialization created post-mining communities that were weaker from an economic standpoint but internally stronger with regard to community.

The fact that many were willing to leave following mine closure shows that attachments to place are not universal in historic mining towns. Moreover, even those loyal to place recognize their community's blemishes; residents tend to be realists when it comes to evaluating their communities and their lives within them. Although they look to the mining past to cultivate a sense of place and identity, residents do not ignore the hardships that the past has created. The coexistence of opposing feelings, an ambivalence in place meaning, exists in all of the study sites. In this sense, the historic mining town is a paradox bearing qualities that both attract and repel.

Women are more likely to express this ambivalence. Mining communities are gendered spaces. In the mining era, few women worked outside of their homes and even fewer were employed in mining. Their labor, however, played an important role in the economy. Solely responsible for maintaining the home and caring for children, many women also procured their own food, cultivating vegetable gardens and raising livestock. Commonly, they also managed room-and-board facilities in their homes. As a result, working life for women above ground was often as exhaustive as that experienced by men underground, but with fewer rewards. As described in the case studies, women's place of toil lacked the camaraderie of the mine. They were excluded from membership in the miners' "rambunctious fraternity" but were forced to deal with its negative consequences on the home front: domestic abuse and little money, particularly when pay was squandered on alcohol. Most tragic of all, women were frequently left to cope with the near impossible task of raising their families after their husbands were killed or disabled by mining's occupational hazards. With responsibilities focused primarily on family and home, women's lives were often lonelier and more menacing, which tends to temper their views of the mining past. It also moderates their attachment to place. Men, especially the elderly, remember the mining era fondly, whereas women's recollections are inclined to alternate between admiration and scorn. Likewise, men tend to embrace the miner's identity, but that of the miner's wife has a weaker hold on women.

Degrees of hardship and the passage of time also affect place perception. Accordingly, Picherites display the strongest ambivalence toward place because generally they experienced a more difficult existence than the other study sites. Place perception is rooted in both positive and negative aspects of the mining past, and the problems the industry has wrought are commonly conveyed by Picherites. True, more than Toluca and Cokedale, Picher has suffered greatly from mining's impacts, particularly its environmental effects on the environment. Indeed, these negative legacies of mining are impossible to ignore, but Picherites also acknowledge them because they have become central to local identity. Picher's residents have come to believe that this tough, unpretentious, unyielding landscape reflects who they are. Confounding the fact that mining's social, economic, and environmental legacies are the cause of Picher's problems is that the community maintains an identity based on the totality of its mining heritage.

In Cokedale, place meaning and local identity are also entangled with positive and negative opinions of mining's influences. Longtime residents recognize that although life was difficult in Cokedale and company control was oppressive, the community worked hard, banded together, and persevered. As in all of the case studies, the residents of Cokedale are proud of this achievement, but they have had a more difficult time expressing these contesting sentiments. The utopian mythology has inhibited their ability to project an identity based on the full range of mining-era experiences like Picherites have done. Less ambivalence exists in place meaning in Toluca. Most Tolucans today recognize that those who established the community and endured the mining life faced significant hardship. Few remain, however, to communicate this fact, and the length of time that now separates the mining past from the present has facilitated its romanticization. In addition, economic recovery in Toluca also has contributed to the construction of a more favorable view of mining's influences.

Indeed, when the study sites are compared, degrees of ambivalence in place meaning appear to be related to the length of time that has passed since mine closure and to the outcomes of deindustrialization. In this regard, Toluca and Picher lie at opposite extremes. In Picher, where many can remember firsthand the hardships of mining and where life remains negatively affected by the industry, ambivalence in place meaning is strong. This contradiction is best explained using Marsh's conceptualization of place: in historic mining towns like Picher, the enriching *meanings* of place are locked in an emotional tug-of-war with the land's limiting *means*. In Toluca, by contrast, place meaning is less contested by memories of hardship or by mining's negative impacts; thus, residents embrace their mining identity with fewer reservations. Conceptually, Cokedale occupies a complex middle ground.

Generational differences also affect place perception. The elderly display a deeper commitment to place and a willingness to remain than do younger residents. In fact, all of the study sites have experienced a graying of their populations as younger residents have migrated elsewhere to pursue education and employment opportunities. Of course, this situation is common in rural communities; there is nothing particularly remarkable about this aging phenomenon. What is somewhat unexpected, however, is the degree to which the mining identity has been passed on to younger generations, many of whom claim a personal connection to the mining past. The affiliation is not as strong as in the elderly, but many of the young reference their mining heritage when talking about their community's identity. This identification with the past was directly observed in both Toluca and Picher, both of which maintain a significant school-aged demographic.

Mining has a lasting hold on local identity. Community folklore and recounted memories of the mining life facilitate passage of the mining heritage from one generation to the next. No pathway is more important, however, than that of the mining landscape. All cultural landscapes have the capacity to reflect and constitute individual and social-group identities.[5] In this regard, mining landscapes are particularly powerful. Industrial ruins like crumbling coke ovens, mill foundations, and collapsed mine derricks provide tangible reminders of the mining past. So do occupied structures dating from the mining era, such as miners' houses, commercial structures, and public buildings. As shown in the case studies, even the wastes of mine production—piles of gob, tailings, and chat—can stand as valued elements of the local landscape. It often does not matter that these features threaten public health and the environment, like Picher's chat piles and to a lesser extent Cokedale's tailings pile, or that they have been sanitized of much their mining-era authenticity, like Toluca's reclaimed Jumbo, because these features stand as reminders of an industry that was vital to the development of community. The public display of mining-related artifacts, icons, and artwork also serve this purpose. Even community welcoming signs communicate the same message in each case study: namely, that these are mining towns.

To outsiders, the mining landscape appears blighting. For residents, however, ruined industrial structures and waste piles represent the labor of ancestors, the men who worked beneath the earth, sweltered in mills, or toiled aside smoking coke ovens so as to provide for their families. Moreover, the industrial landscape stands as a memorial to those who perished pursuing that life. Functioning as nearly sacred ground, Toluca's Jumbo is most notable in this regard. And residents often look past the decay and obsolescence that appear to dominate mining-era infrastructure. To residents of these towns, working-class neighborhoods and miners' housing represent the homes of old families and friends, and their continued occupation, like that of the town itself, is viewed as a sign of endurance. In commercial areas and public spaces, mining-era structures that have been adapted to new uses are emphasized rather than those that have fallen into disuse and dereliction. Residents evaluate the landscape in their own terms. Living in communities that have always found a way to get by, residents draw solace from the landscape, which reflects this quality. The land mirrors their fortitude, and in its tough and obdurate appearance, residents observe qualities that assist in defining who they are.

Mining's physical and social legacies sustain place meaning in Toluca, Cokedale, and Picher. Unfortunately, negative outside perceptions of the mining landscape and the social, economic, and environmental problems mining has caused have distracted outsiders from valuing these communities as lived-in places. Initially, each town was portrayed as a symbol of industrial progress. Promoters used this imagery to encourage development as mining provided the economic impetus for growth. After this initial boom, images of decay and dereliction, hallmarks of the mining imaginary, took hold. Through this cycle of boom and bust, outsiders rarely considered internal place experiences. Only the mining town's industrial function was recognized; that it also served as a community and home was not.

Of all of the study sites, Picher was the most difficult one for outsiders to understand as a lived-in place. The era of promotion was short-lived in Picher, and before long images of dereliction and unavoidable hardship became solidified in the outside imagination. Deindustrialization only served to harden these perceptions. Outsiders showed concern for the plight of Picherites, but the stories they recounted of residents' anguish lacked recognition of the community's worth and were dominated by such a sense of hopelessness that they generated little resolve to address the town's problems. Cokedale had greater success projecting a favorable image. In fact, Cokedale's utopian mythology lies in opposition to the mining imaginary. This counterintuitive depiction, however, ignores the internal meaning of place and, in the precision of its opposition to mining town stereotypes, reveals its connection to them. Acceptance of Cokedale's utopian myth relies on the belief that mining towns are necessarily derelict and dehumanizing environments. In Cokedale, as in all of the study sites, outside observers have failed to come to terms with the fact that despite hardship, the town was serving as a valued home.

A significant transformation occurred in outside perceptions of Toluca following mine closure. Like Picher, Toluca was represented as a quintessentially rough and disheveled mining town, a settlement built for a single purpose: to mine a mineral commodity. Outside attention also focused on the seedier aspects of community life. Toluca was represented as a boisterous and unlawful place, and this sensational portrait only began to change following mine closure. Toluca eventually emerged from deindustrialization as a more likeable community. Time and economic recovery facilitated this reconceptualization of place. Negative perceptions of Toluca faded as mining town associations became less apparent. Ironically, outsiders who had been critical of mining's influences began to revere the industry's vanishing remnants. Nostalgia set in and the Jumbos came to represent curious relics of a lost, but valued, mining era.

External views of place show variation in the case studies, but the mining imaginary, particularly the notion of dereliction and its debasing social influence, has prejudiced outside opinion of each. As noted, insiders and outsiders view historic mining towns in different ways. Whereas residents' views of place emphasize landscape meaning, the external focus lies on the more tangible means the historic mining town affords for survival. To be more precise, outsiders tend to see only the mining landscape's aesthetic drawbacks and its social, economic, and environmental problems. Lacking intimate experience with place and expecting to find dereliction and decay, outsiders are apt to uncover precisely that. But these external views should not be ignored for they communicate a sobering reality: historic mining towns are often troubled locales and the problems caused by mining present significant challenges. Outsiders must understand, however, that residents of these places may value these apparent relics of decay as symbols of a cherished past.

The government bodies that are charged with addressing problems in historic mining towns properly hold resident health, economic well-being, and environmental quality as their primary concerns. From their perspective, the landscape's experiential qualities may seem inconsequential, but they are not. If all remnants of its mining history are removed, the landscape is robbed of one of its most important life-supporting traits: a capacity to reinforce and maintain a local sense of place. An indispensable aspect of the human experience, sense of place should be managed and protected alongside more tangible quality-of-life issues. This has occurred in Toluca and, to a lesser extent, in Cokedale.

In Toluca, infrastructure development and environmental quality concerns posed threats to mining's most important and meaningful physical legacies, the Jumbos. First construction activity and later abandoned mine land reclamation came into direct conflict with local desires to maintain the Jumbos' landscape impress. Residents, however, fought to protect the piles of mining waste, and the state eventually incorporated their demands into reclamation planning. An innovative reclamation design was devised that satisfied both internal and external concerns. Reclamation succeeded in meeting the goals of environmental protection *and* community desires to see the Jumbos preserved.

Cokedale also provides insight into preservation planning in mining landscapes. Holding National Register designation, the value of Cokedale's mining heritage and its uniqueness as a place have been formerly acknowledged. Preservation efforts, however, have proven to be contentious and have failed to protect or interpret key aspects of the town's mining identity. Moreover, many longtime residents have resisted preservation activities, which they view as being driven by outside interests. Although not opposed to preservation per se, Cokedale's old guard did not consider it necessary to maintain the landscape's integrity or meaning because the town held value in its decayed condition. Indeed, in many ways, the settlement reflected a more genuine sense of its mining-era character prior to receiving Historic District designation, which was based largely on its alleged uniqueness as a model company town. Cokedale's utopian mythology provided a rationale for preservation, but the initiatives it stimulated, like the myth itself, have failed to communicate the toil and hardship of the mining life. No significant attempt has yet been made, for example, to preserve industrial features such as Cokedale's decaying coke ovens. Having produced the town's namesake commodity, they symbolize the community's reason for being more than any other landscape feature. And the heritage landscape does not include evidence of the crowded tenements that once stood in the settlement or interpretation of the authoritarian company rule under which residents lived.

Picher's case is in many ways more challenging than the other two. There is no simple way to resolve the fact that many in Picher remain attached to a landscape that is harmful to their health. Sadly, as those attachments remain mostly unrecognized by outsiders, additional hardship likely will be forthcoming for those intent on maintaining their community. As in all of the study sites, residents of Picher express a desire to preserve their mining heritage. If their community is to become a healthier place to live, however, Picherites have no choice but to support environmental remediation activities that, in effect, obliterate many of mining's physical legacies. For those focused on preserving the mining landscape's most important element, the town itself, this compromise ultimately should be acceptable. It is not yet known whether Picher will survive voluntary government buyouts. Given the attachments many have to place and their ability to endure adversity, however, it seems likely that many Picherites will resist abandoning their community. To date, politicians have mostly ignored this likelihood and overlooked the additional hardship that relocation will create for those unwilling to sever their connection to place. Ignoring this fate also has perils for government, as it seems likely that any environmental remediation plan that requires evacuation of the Picher Mining Field is destined to run into problems with resident holdouts.

In various ways, the mining landscape is sustaining place meaning in Toluca, Cokedale, and Picher, and an important lesson emerges from the case studies relating to natural and cultural resource management and planning in historic mining areas. It is necessary to abandon the spectator stance when evaluating the worth of these places. Notions of dereliction that devalue a community's value as a lived-in place must not be allowed to override awareness that mining's physical and social legacies can be of significant experiential value. Understanding the inherent value of these landscapes is a prerequisite to effective management of mining environments and one that can be achieved by incorporating meaningful community participation into the decision-making processes that shape the future of these and other places shouldering similar burdens. Indeed, as resource depletion and deindustrialization continue to occur and as the processes of globalization and urbanization reshape the economic landscape, communities of all types will fall into decline. Despite the problems that will exist in these locales, however, many of their residents will likely choose to remain in place. The production of economically defunct, but internally valued communities is a phenomenon that will not abate and to assume, as has occurred with historic mining towns, that these are necessarily derelict and dehumanizing environments will only serve to hinder effective management of the problems their residents face.

Mining has caused much hardship in Toluca, Cokedale, and Picher, but it is this mining past and the landscape mining has created that provide residents a context for existence. Similarly, the boom and bust nature of the mining economy has posed a threat to the survival of these settlements, but it has also created cohesive communities. Weak and forsaken in many respects, these towns are strong in others. The historic mining town is an enduring place where resident attachments produce challenges that are difficult but important to overcome, as in other seemingly derelict locales where residents are attempting to hold on to meaningful, albeit hard ways of life.

NOTES

1. Ben Marsh, "Continuity and Decline in the Anthracite Towns of Pennsylvania," *Annals of the Association of American Geographers* 77:3 (1987): 337–352.

2. Kent C. Ryden, *Mapping the Invisible Landscape: Folklore, Writing, and the Sense of Place* (Iowa City: University of Iowa Press, 1993), 181.

3. John Agnew, "Devaluing Place: 'People Prosperity Versus Place Prosperity' and Regional Planning," *Environment and Planning D: Society and Space* 1 (1984): 36.

4. Marsh, "Continuity and Decline," 339.

5. Richard H. Schein, "The Place of Landscape: A Conceptual Framework for Interpreting an American Scene," *Annals of the Association of American Geographers* 87:4 (1997): 660.

Bibliography

MANUSCRIPTS

Eric Margolis Collection, Archives, University of Colorado at Boulder Libraries, Boulder, Colorado.

Oklahoma Historical Society, Archives and Manuscript Division, Oral History Program, Oklahoma City.

UMWA documents, Edward Lawrence Doyle Collection, Western History Department, Denver Public Library, Denver, Colorado.

University of Colorado, Institute of Behavioral Science, Coal Project, Norlin Library, Western Historical Collections, Boulder, Colorado.

INTERVIEWS AND PERSONAL CORRESPONDENCE

Aimone, Pete. Interview with Anna Mae Johnson Terrell, Toluca, Illinois, n.d.

Arguello, Bette. Interview with author, Cokedale, Colorado, June 15, 1999.

Barr, Lawrence and Theo. Interview by Joel L. Todd, Videotape, Tulsa, 1985, Oklahoma Historical Society, Archives and Manuscript Division, Oral History Program, Oklahoma City.

Beauchamp, Grace. Interview with author, Miami, Oklahoma, December 14, 1999.

Bell, Richard. Interview with author, Cokedale, Colorado, July 13, 1999.

Brandt, Marion. Interview with author, Toluca, Illinois, February 12, 1998.

DeRubeis, Barney. Interview with author, Toluca, Illinois, February 12, 1998.

———. Interview with author, Toluca, Illinois, June 3, 2001.

Ferraro, Emilio and Gertrude. Interview transcript, May 22, 1978, Cokedale, Colorado, Eric Margolis Collection, 9-8, Archives, University of Colorado at Boulder Libraries.

Flynn, Gilbert. Interview with author, Toluca, Illinois, February 9, 1998.

Gerardo, Jack. Interview with author, Toluca, Illinois, February 9, 1998.

Gregg, Jim. Telephone interview with author, Norman, Oklahoma, February 18, 1999.

———. Interview with author, Toluca, Illinois, June 25, 2001.

Harber, Larry. Interview with author, Toluca, Illinois, February 12, 1998.

Hatley, Earl. Interview with author, Quapaw, Oklahoma, December 16, 1999.

Holdread, Doug. Interview with author, Cokedale, Colorado, July 15, 1999.

Honker, Bill. Letter to author, December 1, 2004.

Huhn, Pat. Interview with author, Cokedale, Colorado, July 14, 1999.

Hurtado, Horace. Interview transcript, May 24, 1978, Eric Margolis Collection, 14-3, Archives, University of Colorado at Boulder Libraries.

Jim, Rebecca. Interview with author, Miami, Oklahoma, December 13, 1999.

Johnson, John. Interview with author, Cokedale, Colorado, July 26, 1999.

Johnson Terrell, Anna Mae. Letters to author, May 7, 1999, and September 2000.

Lynch, Robert. Interview with author, Oklahoma City, Oklahoma, October 26, 1998.

McCall, William. Interview with author, Toluca, Illinois, February 9, 1998.

Mott, John. Interview with author, Picher, Oklahoma, December 15, 1999.

Nairn, Robert. Telephone interview with author, August 19, 2004.

Pearson, Elton. Interview with author, Toluca, Illinois, February 11, 1998.

———. Letters to author, January 27, 1998, and October 20, 2000.

Ray, Orval "Hoppy." Interview with author, Picher, Oklahoma, December 14, 1999.

Ray, Steven. Interview with author, Picher, Oklahoma, December 14, 1999.

Scamehorn, H. Lee. Letter to author, June 27, 1999.

Schorr, Pat. Interview with author, Cokedale, Colorado, July 14, 1999.

Vallino, Joe. Interview with Anna Mae Johnson Terrell, Toluca, n.d.

Venturi, Pete. Interview with author, Toluca, Illinois, February 9, 1998.

Williams, Vernon L. Interview with author, December 8, 1999.

NEWSPAPERS

Bloomington Pantagraph. 1996, 1999.

Chicago Daily News. 1962.

Chicago Tribune. 1996.

Daily Oklahoman. 1915, 1917, 1936, 1950–1951, 1963–1964, 1972, 1983, 1994–1995, 1999–2000.

Denver Post. 1980.

Henry (Illinois) *News Republican.* 1924.

Joplin (Missouri) *Globe.* 1986, 1997, 2003.

Lacon (Illinois) *Home Journal.* 1923–1926, 1999.
Miami (Oklahoma) *News-Record.* 1982, 1986.
Miami (Oklahoma) *Record-Herald.* 1915–1916, 1918, 1931.
New York Times. 1939, 1981, 2000.
Peoria Journal-Star. 1975, 1996, 2001.
Pueblo Chieftain. 1976.
Streator (Illinois) *Times-Press.* 2000.
Toluca (Illinois) *Star.* 1893, 1895, 1938, 1985–1986, 1996–1997, 2001.
Trinidad (Colorado) *Chronicle News.* 1907, 1911, 1913, 1947, 1976.
Tri-State (Oklahoma) *Tribune.* 1947, 1950–1951, 1983, 1989, 1993–1994, 1999.
Tulsa World. 1935, 1950, 1967–1968, 1996, 1998–2000, 2002–2004.
Wall Street Journal. 1985.
The Wichita Eagle-Beacon. 1986.

GOVERNMENT DOCUMENTS

Abbott, Grace. *The Immigrant and Coal Mining Communities of Illinois.* Springfield: Illinois Department of Registration and Education, Immigrants Commission, 1920.

Andros, S. O. *Mining Practice in District I (Longwall).* Illinois Coal Mine Investigations Cooperative Agreement Bulletin, No. 5. Urbana: University of Illinois, 1914.

———. *Coal Mining in Illinois.* Illinois Coal Mining Investigations Cooperative Agreement Bulletin, No. 13. Urbana: University of Illinois, 1915.

Bradford, Susan Carol. "Mining Methods, Geology, and Sampling Procedures Used to Study Colliery Waste from the Historic Longwall Mining District, North-Central Illinois." In *Geologic Study of Longwall Mine Sites in Northern Illinois,* by Illinois State Geological Survey. Springfield: Abandoned Mine Lands Reclamation Council, 1983.

———, et al. *Characteristics and Potential Uses of Waste from the Historic Longwall Coal Mining District in North-Central Illinois.* Environmental Geology Notes 118. Champaign: Illinois State Geological Survey, 1987.

Cady, Gilbert H. *Coal Resources of District I (Longwall).* Urbana: State Geological Survey, University of Illinois, 1915.

Campbell, Marius R. "The Trinidad Coal Field, Colorado." In *Contributions to Economic Geology,* United States Geological Survey Bulletin 381. Washington, DC: GPO, 1910.

Carson, U.S. Rep. Brad. Homepage. http://carson.house.gov (accessed September 2004).

Colorado, Department of Natural Resources. "Close-Out Report: Cokedale Project." Denver, n.d.

———. "Colorado Inactive Mine Inventory Problem Area Date Forms: Cokedale Problem Areas." Denver, 1980.

———, Inactive Mine Program. *Their Silent Profile: Inactive Coal and Metal Mines of Colorado.* Denver: The Program, 1982.

Colorado State Inspector of Coal Mines. *Fourth Annual Report of the State Inspector of Coal Mines, 1916.* Denver: Smith-Brooks Printing, State Printers, 1917.

———. *Biennial* and *Annual Reports of the State Inspector of Coal Mines.* Denver: Smith-Brooks Printing, State Printers, 1911–1929.

Curran, Ed. Correspondence to U.S. Rep. Tom Coburn. September 3, 1997, unpublished document.

Henry, Gov. Brad. Homepage. http://www.governor.state.ok.us/issues.php (accessed September 2004).

Keating, Gov. Frank. Tar Creek Superfund Task Force. *Final Report*. Oklahoma City: Office of the Secretary of Environment, 2000.

Illinois Bureau of Labor Statistics. *Annual Coal Report of the Illinois Bureau of Labor Statistics*. Springfield: The Bureau, 1894–1910.

———. *Annual Report of the State Bureau of Labor Statistics, Coal in Illinois*. Springfield: The Bureau, 1894–1898.

Illinois Department of Energy and Natural Resources. *Directory of Coal Mines in Illinois*. Champaign: Illinois State Geological Survey, 1996.

Illinois Department of Mines and Minerals. *Annual Coal Report of Illinois*. Springfield: The Department, 1917–1924.

Illinois Department of Natural Resources. "Abandoned Mined Lands Inventory and Assessment." File document PU-094. Springfield, 1981.

Illinois State Mining Board. *Annual Coal Report of Illinois*. Springfield: The Board, 1911–1916.

Inhofe, James M. "Private Sector Group Moves Forward in Tar Creek Purchase Process." Press Release, January 25, 2004. http://inhofe.senate.gov (accessed April 2004).

Johnson, Ross B. *Coal Resources of the Trinidad Coal Field in Huerfano and Las Animas Counties, Colorado*. United States Geological Survey Bulletin 1112-E. Washington, DC: GPO, 1961.

Krapac, I. G., and C. A. Smyth. "Geochemical Evaluation of Colliery Waste from the Historic Longwall Mining District, North-Central Illinois." In *Geologic Study of Longwall Mine Sites in Northern Illinois,* by Illinois State Geological Survey. Springfield: Abandoned Mine Lands Reclamation Council, 1983.

Lloyd, W. B. "The Cokedale Mine." In *Thirteenth Biennial Report of the State Coal Mine Inspector*. Denver: The Inspector, 1909.

Luza, Kenneth V. *Stability Problems Associated with Abandoned Underground Mines in the Picher Field, Northeastern Oklahoma*. Norman: Oklahoma Geological Survey, Circular 88, 1986.

McKnight, Edwin T., and Richard P. Fischer. *Geology and Ore Deposits of the Picher Field, Oklahoma and Kansas*. Washington, DC: Geological Survey Professional Paper, No. 588, 1970.

National Park Service. National Register of Historic Places Inventory Nomination Form: Cokedale Historic District. Washington, DC, 1985.

Oklahoma Child Lead Poisoning Prevention Act. 49th Cong., 2nd Sess. Senate Bill 1490.

Oklahoma Plan for Tar Creek. http://www.deq.state.ok.us/LPDnew./Tarcreek/index.html (accessed April 2, 2006).

Spude, Robert L.S., David A. Poirier, and Ronald, M. Greenberg, eds. *America's Mining Heritage*. Washington, DC: National Parks Service, 1998.

Tar Creek Superfund Task Force. *Health Effects Subcommittee Final Report*. Oklahoma City: Office of the Secretary of the Environment, 2000.

U.S. Army Corps of Engineers, Tulsa Division. Draft Reconnaissance Phase, Tar Creek and Lower Spring River Watershed Management Plan, 2004. http://www.swt.usace.army.mil/ (accessed April 2, 2006).

U.S. Bureau of the Census. *Census of the United States* (for Colorado, Illinois, and Oklahoma). Washington, DC: GPO, various years.

U.S. Commission on Industrial Relations. *Final Report and Testimony.* Senate Doc. 415, 64th Cong., 2d Sess. Washington, DC: GPO, 1916.

U.S. Congress, House Subcommittee on Mines and Mining. *Conditions in the Coal Mines of Colorado.* Pursuant to H.R. 387, 63rd Cong., 2d Sess. Washington, DC: GPO, 1914.

———. Hearing of the Committee on Energy and Commerce. *Tar Creek: Implementation of Superfund.* Serial No. 97-155, 97th Cong., 2nd Sess. Washington, DC: GPO, 1982.

———. Tar Creek Restoration Act. 108th Cong., 1st Sess., H.R. 2116. Washington, DC, 2003.

U.S. Department of the Interior. *Surface Mining and Our Environment.* Washington, DC: GPO, 1962.

———. Public Law 95-87, *Surface Mining Control and Reclamation Act of 1977,* Title IV. Washington, DC: GPO, n.d.

———. Problem Area Summary, Toluca Coal Company. Abandoned Mine Land Inventory System (AMLIS), Office of Surface Mining Reclamation and Enforcement, Washington, DC, n.d.

U.S. Environmental Protection Agency. "NPL Site Narrative for Tar Creek (Ottawa County)." Federal Register Notice, September 8, 1983.

———. *Superfund Record of Decision: Tar Creek Site, Oklahoma.* Washington, DC: The Agency, 1984.

———. *Five Year Review: Tar Creek Superfund Site Ottawa County, Oklahoma.* Washington, DC: The Agency, 1994.

———. Creek Superfund Site Fact Sheet. April 15, 1994.

———. *Superfund Record of Decision: Tar Creek (Ottawa County), OU 2.* Washington, DC: The Agency, 1997.

———. Tar Creek Superfund Site Fact Sheet. November 1999.

———. Tar Creek Superfund Site Fact Sheet. April 1999.

———. *Memorandum of Understanding for the Tar Creek Superfund Site.* Washington, DC: The Agency, May 1, 2003.

———. Superfund Permanent Relocations. http://www.epa.gov (accessed January 2005).

Weidman, Samuel. *The Miami-Picher Zinc-Lead District, Oklahoma.* Norman: Oklahoma Geological Survey Bulletin No. 56, 1932.

BOOKS

Alanen, Arnold R. "Considering the Ordinary: Vernacular Landscapes in Small Towns and Rural Areas." In *Preserving Cultural Landscapes in America,* ed. A. R. Alanen and R. Z. Melnick, 112–142. Baltimore: Johns Hopkins University Press, 2000.

Allen, James B. *The Company Town in the American West*. Norman: University of Oklahoma Press, 1966.

Baird, W. David. *The Quapaws*. New York: Chelsea House, 1989.

Barton, Holly. *Cokedale 1907–1947: Anatomy of a Model Mining Community*. Privately published, 1976.

Basso, Keith H. "Wisdom Sits in Places." In *Senses of Place,* ed. S. Feld and K. H. Basso, 53–90. Santa Fe: School of American Research Press, 1996.

Beck, Leslie K., and Mike Kirchereds. *Down Home in Bon Carbo: Memories of a Dream*. Trinidad: Paperworks, 1988.

Bement, Alburto. *Shipping Mines and Coal Railroads of Illinois and Indiana*. Chicago: Peabody Coal Company, 1903.

Bonnin, Gertrude, Charles H. Fabens, and Matthew K. Sniffen. *Oklahoma's Poor Rich Indians*. Philadelphia: Office of the Indian Rights Association, 1924.

Bowles, Roy Tyler. *Little Communities and Big Industries*. Toronto: Butterworths, 1982.

Buck, F. P. *The Cherry Mine Disaster*. Chicago: M. A. Donohue and Company, 1910.

Burt, John Spencer, and William Edward Hawthorne. *Past and Present of Marshall and Putnam Counties, Illinois*. Chicago: Pioneer, 1907.

Caudill, Harry M. *Night Comes to the Cumberlands: A Biography of a Depressed Area*. Boston: Little Brown and Company, 1962.

Clements, Eric L. *After the Boom in Tombstone and Jerome, Arizona: Decline in Western Resource Towns*. Reno: University of Nevada Press, 2003.

Clyne, Rick J. *Coal People: Life in Southern Colorado's Company Towns, 1890–1930*. Denver: Colorado Historical Society, 1999.

Craig, Genevieve Stovall. "Picher, Oklahoma: The Lead and Zinc Boom Town That Would Not Die." In *Picher, Oklahoma*. Picher Bicentennial Boosters Committee, 1975.

Curtis, Kent. Foreword, "The Legacy." In *Tar Creek Anthology,* vii–viii. Tahlequah, OK: Talequah Daily Press, 1999.

Davidson, Lallah. *South of Joplin: Story of a Tri-State Diggin's*. New York: W. W. Norton & Company, 1939.

DeKok, David. *Unseen Danger: A Tragedy of People, Government, and the Centralia Mine Fire*. Philadelphia: University of Pennsylvania Press, 1986.

Deutsch, Sarah. *No Separate Refuge: Culture, Class, and Gender on an Anglo-Hispanic Frontier in the American Southwest, 1880–1940*. New York: Oxford University Press, 1987.

Donachy, Patrick. *Coal the Kingdom Below*. Trinidad: Inkwell, 1983.

Doss, Erika L. *Spirit Poles and Flying Pigs: Public Art and Democracy in American Communities*. Washington, DC: Smithsonian Institution Press, 1995.

Dublin, Thomas. *When the Mines Closed: Stories of Struggles in Hard Times*. Ithaca: Cornell University Press, 1998.

Duncan, James. "Place." In *The Dictionary of Human Geography,* ed. R. J. Johnston, D. Gregory, and D. M. Smith, 442–443. Oxford: Blackwell, 1994.

Eavenson, Howard N. *The First Century and a Quarter of American Coal Industry*. Pittsburgh: Blatimore Weekly Press, 1942.

Emmons, David. *The Butte Irish: Class and Ethnicity in an American Mining Town, 1875–1925*. Urbana: University of Illinois Press, 1989.

Francaviglia, Richard V. *Hard Places: Reading the Landscape of America's Historic Mining Districts*. Iowa City: University of Iowa Press, 1991.

Gallaher, Art, and Harland Padfield, eds. *The Dying Community*. Albuquerque: University of New Mexico Press, 1980.

Garner, John S. *The Model Company Town: Urban Design through Private Enterprise in Nineteenth-Century New England*. Amherst: University of Massachusetts Press, 1984.

———. *The Company Town: Architecture and Society in the Early Industrial Age*. New York: Oxford University Press, 1992.

Gibson, Arrell M. *Wilderness Bonanza: The Tri-State District of Missouri, Kansas, and Oklahoma*. Norman: University of Oklahoma Press, 1972.

Gitelman, Howard M. *Legacy of the Ludlow Massacre: A Chapter in American Industrial Relations*. Philadelphia: University of Pennsylvania Press, 1988.

Glacken, Clarence. *Traces on the Rhodian Shore: Nature and Culture in Western Thought from Ancient Times to the End of the Eighteenth Century*. Berkeley: University of California Press, 1967.

Goin, Peter, and C. Elizabeth Raymond. *Changing Mines in America*. Santa Fe: The Center for American Places, 2004.

Greever, William. *Bonanza West: The Story of the Western Mining Rushes, 1848–1880*. Norman: University of Oklahoma Press, 1963.

Hoffmann, John. *A Guide to the History of Illinois*. Westport, CT: Greenwood, 1991.

Illinois Sesquicentennial Commission. *Illinois Guide and Gazetteer*. Chicago: Rand McNally & Company, 1969.

Jakle, John, and David Wilson. *Derelict Landscapes: The Wasting of America's Built Environment*. Savage, MD: Rowman & Littlefield, 1992.

Jenson, Vernon H. *Heritage of Conflict: Labor Relations in the Non-Ferrous Metals Industry up to 1930*. Ithaca: Cornell University Press, 1950.

Jim, Rebecca. "Introduction." In *Tar Creek Anthology*. Tahlequah, OK: Talequah Daily Press, 1999.

Johnson, Susan L. *Roaring Camp: The Social World of the California Gold Rush*. New York: W. W. Norton, 2000.

Jolly, James H. *U.S. Zinc Industry*. Baltimore: American Literary Press, 1997.

Laslett, John H.M. "Scottish-Americans and the Beginnings of the Modern Class Struggle: Immigrant Coal Miners in Northern Illinois, 1865–1889." In *Labor Divided: Race and Ethnicity in United States Labor Struggles, 1835–1960*, ed. Robert Asher and Charles Stephenson, 178–188. Albany: State University of New York Press, 1990.

Lingenfelter, Richard E. *Hard Rock Miners: A History of the Mining Labor Movement in the American West*. Berkeley: University of California Press, 1974.

———. *The Mining West: A Bibliography and Guide to the History and Literature of Mining in the American and Canadian West*. Lanham, MD: Scarecrow Press, 2003.

Llewellyn, Richard. *How Green Was My Valley*. New York: Macmillan, 1940.

Long, Priscilla. *Where the Sun Never Shines: A History of America's Bloody Coal Industry*. New York: Paragon House, 1989.

Loof, David H. "Growing Up in a Dying Community." In *The Dying Community*, ed. A. Gallaher and H. Padfield, 207–236. Albuquerque: University of New Mexico Press, 1980.

Lowenthal, David. "Not Every Prospect Pleases." In *Changing Rural Landscapes*, ed. E. H. Zube and M. J. Zube, 129–139. Amherst: University of Massachusetts Press, 1977.

————. "The Beholding Eye: Ten Versions of the Same Scene." In *The Interpretation of Ordinary Landscapes,* ed. D. W. Meinig, 33–48. New York: Oxford University Press, 1979.

Lynch, Kevin. *Managing the Sense of a Region.* Cambridge: MIT Press, 1976.

Mantle, Mickey, and Herb Gluck. *The Mick.* Garden City, NY: Doubleday & Company, 1985.

Marshall County Historical Society. *History of Marshall County, Illinois.* Dallas: Taylor, 1983.

Mathews, C. Allan. "What's in the Future?" In *Picher, Oklahoma,* ed. Picher Bicentennial Boosters Committee. Picher: The Committee, 1975.

Mazur, Allan. *A Hazardous Inquiry: The Rashoman Effect at Love Canal.* Cambridge: Harvard University Press, 1998.

McGill, Douglas C. *Michael Heizer's Effigy Tumuli: The Reemergence of Ancient Mound Building.* New York: Harry N. Abrams, 1990.

McGovern, George S., and Leonard F. Guttridge. *The Great Coalfield War.* Boston: Houghton Mifflin, 1972.

Meinig, D. W. "Symbolic Landscapes: Some Idealizations of American Communities." In *The Interpretation of Ordinary Landscapes,* ed. D. W. Meinig, 164–192. New York: Oxford University Press, 1979.

Morris, John W. *Ghost Towns of Oklahoma.* Norman: University of Oklahoma Press, 1978.

Muhly, James D. "Foreword." In *Social Approaches to an Industrial Past: The Archaeology and Anthropology of Mining,* ed. A. Bernard Knapp, Vincent C. Pigott, and Eugenia W. Herbert, xv–xvi. New York: Routledge, 1998.

Mumford, Lewis. *Technics and Civilization.* New York: Harcourt, Brace & World, 1962.

Neil, Cecily, Markku Tykklainen, and John Bradbury, eds. *Coping with Closure: An International Comparison of Mine Town Experiences.* New York: Routledge, 1992.

Nieberding, Velma. *The History of Ottawa County.* Marceline, MO: Walsworth, 1983.

Northern Illinois Coal Operators. *Statement of Northern Illinois Coal Operators with Particular Reference to the Mining Machine Differential and Household Coal for Employees.* Chicago, 1923.

O'Connor, Harvey. *The Guggenheims: The Making of an American Dynasty.* New York: Covici Friede, 1937.

Paulsen, Judy. *Toluca—100 Years: 1893–1993.* Toluca: privately published, 1993.

Porteous, Douglas. *Planned to Death: The Annihilation of a Place Called Howdendyke.* Toronto: University of Toronto Press, 1989.

Probst, Katherine N., and David M. Konisky. *Superfund's Future: What Will It Cost?* Washington, DC: Resources for the Future, 2001.

Ripley, Earl A., Robert E. Redmann, and Adele A. Crowder. *Environmental Effects of Mining.* Delray Beach, FL: St. Lucie Press, 1996.

Robertson, Leslie A. *Imagining Difference: Legend, Curse, and Spectacle in a Canadian Mining Town.* Vancouver: University of British Columbia Press, 2005.

Ross, Malcolm. *Death of a Yale Man.* New York: Farrar & Rinehart, 1939.

Rowse, Alfred Leslie. *The Cousin Jacks: The Cornish in America.* New York: Scribner, 1969.

Ryden, Kent C. *Mapping the Invisible Landscape: Folklore, Writing, and the Sense of Place.* Iowa City: University of Iowa Press, 1993.

Scamehorn, H. Lee. *Mill & Mine: The CF&I in the Twentieth Century.* Lincoln: University of Nebraska Press, 1992.

Schafer, Rollie. *The Schafers of Cokedale, A Century in America.* Trinidad, CO: privately published, 1993.

Seamon, David. "Phenomenology and Environment-Behavior Research." In *Advances in Environment, Behavior, and Design,* ed. G. T. Moore and E. Zube, 3–27. New York: Plenum, 1987.

Sinclair, Upton. *King Coal.* New York: Macmillan, 1917.

———. *The Coal War.* Boulder: Colorado Associated University Press, 1976.

Smith, Duane A. *Rocky Mountain Mining Camps: The Urban Frontier.* Lincoln: University of Nebraska Press, 1967.

———. *Mining America: The Industry and the Environment, 1800–1980.* Lawrence: University Press of Kansas, 1987.

Smith, John M., Andrew Light, and David Roberts. "Introduction: Philosophies and Geographies of Place." In *Philosophies of Place,* ed. A. Light and J. M. Smith. New York: Rowman & Littlefield, 1998.

Spence, Clark. *Mining Engineers and the American West: The Lace-Boot Brigade, 1849–1933.* New Haven: Yale University Press, 1970.

Stewart, Kathleen. "An Occupied Place." In *Senses of Place,* ed. S. Feld and K. H. Basso, 137–166. Santa Fe: School of American Research Press, 1996.

———. *A Space on the Side of the Road: Cultural Poetics in an "Other" America.* Princeton: Princeton University Press, 1996.

Suggs, George G. *Union Busting in the Tri-State: The Oklahoma, Kansas, and Missouri Metal Workers' Strike of 1935.* Norman: University of Oklahoma Press, 1986.

Tri-State Survey Committee. *A Preliminary Report on Living, Working, and Health Conditions in the Tri-State Mining Area.* New York: photoprinted by the committee, 1939.

Tuan, Yi-Fu. *Space and Place: The Perspective of Experience.* Minneapolis: University of Minnesota Press, 1977.

Wabel, Lewis. *Charles J. Devlin: Coal Mines & Railroads, His Empire.* Henry, IL: privately published, 1991.

Wallwork, Kenneth L. *Derelict Land: Origins and Prospects of a Land-Use Problem.* London: David & Charles, 1974.

Wyman, Mark. *Hard Rock Epic: Western Miners and the Industrial Revolution.* Berkeley: University of California Press, 1979.

Young, Otis E., and Robert Lenon. *Western Mining; An Informal Account of Precious-Metals Prospecting, Placering, Lode Mining, and Milling on the American Frontier, from Spanish Times to 1893.* Norman: University of Oklahoma Press, 1970.

Zola, Emile. *Germinal.* New York: A. A. Knopf, 1937.

ARTICLES

Agnew, John A. "Devaluing Place: 'People Prosperity Versus Place Prosperity' and Regional Planning." *Environment and Planning D: Society and Space* 1 (1984): 35–45.

Aschmann, Homer. "The Natural History of a Mine." *Economic Geography* 46:2 (1970): 171–190.

Bridge, Gavin. "Contested Terrain: Mining and the Environment." *Annual Review of Environment and Resources* 29 (2004): 205–259.

Bussell, Eleanor. "A Sunday Tour in Summer." In *County Chaff*. Lacon, IL: privately published, 1960.

Cheng, Antony S., Linda E. Kruger, and Steven E. Daniels. "'Place' As an Integrating Concept in Natural Resource Politics: Propositions for a Social Science Research Agenda." *Society and Natural Resources* 16 (2003): 87–104.

Davies, Christopher S. "Wales: Industrial Fallibility and Spirit of Place." *Journal of Cultural Geography* 4:1 (1983): 72–86.

de Wit, Cary W. "Field Methods for Investigating Sense of Place." *North American Geographer* 5:1–2 (2003), 5–30.

Engineering and Mining Journal 144:11 (1943).

Gibson, Arrell. "Leasing of Quapaw Mineral Lands." *Chronicles of Oklahoma* 35 (Autumn 1957): 338–347.

Godoy, Ricardo. "Mining: Anthropological Perspectives." *Annual Review of Anthropology* 14 (1985): 199–217.

Gottlieb, Amy Zahl. "British Coal Miners: A Demographic Study of Braidwood and Streator, Illinois." *Journal of the Illinois State Historical Society* 72 (1979): 179–192.

Guiterman, Kenneth S. "Mining Coal in Southern Colorado." *The Engineering and Mining Journal* 87:21 (1909): 1009–1015.

Gutman, Herbert G. "The Braidwood Lockout of 1874." *Journal of the Illinois State Historical Society* 53 (1960): 5–28.

Harbaugh, M. D. "Labor Relations in the Tri-State Mining District." *The Mining Congress Journal* 22 (June 1936): 19–24.

Jackson, John Brinckerhoff. "Goodbye to Evolution." *Landscape* 13:1 (1963): 2.

Just, Evan. "Living and Working Conditions in the Tri-State Mining District." *Mining Congress Journal* 25 (1939): 44–45.

Keane, John L. "The Towns That Coal Built: The Evolution of Landscapes and Communities in Southern Colorado." *Yearbook of the Association of Pacific Coast Geographers* 62 (2000): 70–94.

Koelker, Karl L. "Has the Miami-Picher District Passed Its Zenith?" *Engineering and Mining Journal* 117:4 (1924): 168–170.

Lewis, Peirce. "Defining a Sense of Place." *The Southern Quarterly* 17:3 (1979): 29.

Magnusson, Leifur. "Company Housing in the Bituminous Coal Fields." *Monthly Labor Review* 10:4 (1920): 215–222.

Markowitz, Gerald, and David Rosner. "'The Streets of Walking Death': Silicosis, Health, and Labor in the Tri-State Region, 1900–1950." *The Journal of American History* 77:2 (September 1990): 525–552.

Marsh, Ben. "Continuity and Decline in the Anthracite Towns of Pennsylvania." *Annals of the Association of American Geographers* 77:3 (1987): 337–352.

Marshall County Historical Society, "From Coal Mining to Salad Dressing." *Marshall County Historical Society Newsletter*. January 19, 1956.

———. "Toluca Built on Devlin's Coal." *Heritage Sampler No. 2*. Lacon: Henry News Republican, 1965.

Meyer, Pamela A. "Surveillance for Elevated Blood Lead Levels Among Children, United States, 1997–2001." In *Morbidity and Mortality Weekly Report* 52 (2003): 1–21.

Mills, Charles Morris. "Industrial Conditions in the World's Greatest Zinc Center." *The Survey* 45 (1921): 657–664.

Mosher, Anne E. "'Something Better than the Best': Industrial Restructuring, George McMurtry and the Creation of the Model Industrial Town of Vandergrift, Pennsylvania, 1883–1901." *Annals of the Association of American Geographers* 85:1 (1995): 84–107.

Netzeband, F. W. "Profit from Mineral Waste: Tri-State Tailings Yield Commercial Products." *Engineering and Mining Journal* 138:5 (1937): 251–254.

Reese, Joan. "4 Rooms and a Path." *Rocky Mountain Empire Magazine* (May 23, 1948): 4–5.

Robertson, David. "'Heaps of History': Toluca and the Historic Longwall Mining District," *Journal of Illinois History* 3:3 (2000): 162–184.

Rohe, Randall. "The Geography and Material Culture of the Western Mining Town." *Material Culture* 16 (1984): 115.

Roosevelt, Margot. "The Tragedy of Tar Creek," *Time* 163:17 (April 26, 2004): 42–47.

Schein, Richard H. "The Place of Landscape: A Conceptual Framework for Interpreting an American Scene." *Annals of the Association of American Geographers* 87:4 (1997): 660.

Shortridge, James R. "The Concept of the Place-Defining Novel in American Popular Culture." *Professional Geographer* 43:3 (1991): 280–291.

Shotter, John. "'Duality of Structure' and 'Intentionality' in an Ecological Psychology." *Journal for the Theory of Social Behavior* 13 (1983): 19–43.

"Silicosis: Tri-State Dust Storm." *Business Week* (December 9, 1939): 51–52.

Simpson, John W. "The Emotional Landscape and Public Law 95-87." *Landscape Architecture* 75:3 (1985): 60–63, 108–109, 112–113.

Wyckoff, William. "Postindustrial Butte." *The Geographical Review* 85:4 (1995): 478–496.

"Zinc Stink." *Time* 34:23 (December 4, 1939): 63.

UNPUBLISHED THESES, DISSERTATIONS, AND PAPERS

"Big Jumbo Dedication." Program Brochure, privately printed, Toluca, Illinois, 2001.

Cokedale Tourism Committee. "Cokedale: A Historic Coal Mining Camp," walking tour brochure, privately published, n.d.

Dixon, Harry M. "The Illinois Coal Mining Industry." Ph.D. thesis, University of Illinois, 1951.

Halinka Malcoe, Lorraine. Community Health Action and Monitoring Program (CHAMP), Final Report, July 1996–June 1997.

Holdread, Joyce. "The Town That Wouldn't Be a Ghost Town," unpublished essay, n.d.

Jones, Michael S. "Dedication at the Jumbos Invocation," speech transcript, Toluca, Illinois, June 3, 2001.

Joyce, Richard Patrick. "Miners of the Prairie: Life and Labor in the Wilmington, Illinois, Coal Field, 1866–1897." M.A. thesis, Illinois State University, 1980.

Lindsey, Gary L. "Creating Presence: The Early Twentieth Century Company Store in Three Coal Mining Towns in Southern Colorado." M.A. thesis, Abilene Christian University, 1998.

Lutgens, Nancy. "I Just Came to Look-A: Italian Immigration to Toluca, Illinois, 1894–1918," paper presented at the Illinois History Symposium, Springfield, 1995.

Robertson, David. "Enduring Places: Landscape Meaning, Community Persistence, and Preservation in the Historic Mining Town." Ph.D. thesis, University of Oklahoma, 2001.

TEAL Project. "Community Leader Survey: Ottawa County Area," 1997, unpublished document.

Thoman, Richard. "The Changing Occupance Pattern of the Tri-State Area: Missouri, Kansas, and Oklahoma." Ph.D. dissertation, University of Chicago, 1953.

Toluca Coal Mine Preservation and Development Committee. "Development Survey Response." Toluca: unpublished document, 1998.

Trinidad Abstract & Title Company. Index to property deeds, Cokedale, 1947–1983, Trinidad, Colorado.

MISCELLANEOUS

CNN Today, January 6, 1997.

Donovan, John. "Our Town: Welcome to Picher." *Nightline,* ABC Television, March 2, 2001.

Leonetti, Doc. "Cokedale Holds History for Massarotti." *Trinidad Plus Hometown Spotlight.* http://www.trinidadco.com/plus/spotlight99/massarti.html (accessed May 17, 2001).

Pigs of Lead. News Reel, Prod. Rothacker Industrial Films, Chicago, Illinois, n.d.

Polk's Trinidad City Directory, 1935, vol. 17. R. L. Polk Directory, 1935.

Sanborn-Perris Map Company. Fire Insurance Maps for Toluca. New York, 1910.

Siegal, Robert, Melissa Block, and Gregg Allen. "Failed Cleanup Efforts of Tar Creek in Oklahoma." *All Things Considered,* National Public Radio, July 16, 2003.

Trinidad City Directory. Colorado Springs: Rocky Mountain Directory, 1948 & 1952.

Index

Page numbers in italics indicate illustrations.